GEORGE WASHINGTON
Republican Aristocrat

GEORGE WASHINGTON
Painted in 1775 or 1776 by Samuel King

BERNARD FAŸ

GEORGE WASHINGTON

REPUBLICAN ARISTOCRAT

BOSTON AND NEW YORK
HOUGHTON MIFFLIN COMPANY
The Riverside Press Cambridge
1931

The Riverside Press

CAMBRIDGE · MASSACHUSETTS

PRINTED IN THE U.S.A.

PREFACE

I HAVE many people to thank for the help they gave me when I was preparing and writing this book. Dr. Jameson, of the Library of Congress, should be the first one, then M. de la Roncière, Conservateur des Imprimés à la Bibliothèque Nationale, and M. Girodie, Conservateur du Musée Américain de Blérancourt, who showed me manuscripts, pamphlets, books, and prints.

Miss Yorke, Mr. Imbs, and several other kind friends have been generous enough to think my English worthy of their attention. The mistakes are still mine. The rest is largely theirs.

All the friends who guided and helped me when I was studying Franklin had their share in making suggestions or giving advice for this 'Washington.' Please see the list in the Preface of my 'Franklin.'

Without them I should never have ventured to speak of so great a man. Now I have done so, I hope they will not regret it.

B. F.

PARIS, *July*, 1931

CONTENTS

ILLUSTRATIONS AND MAPS

INTRODUCTION

In the eighteenth century, so overcrowded with great men, George Washington stands alone, a unique figure. Because of his stature, he towers above others; because of his silence, he is distinguished from the ordinary run of heroes; because of his attitude, he makes these heroes seem mere actors and contemptible stage-players, while he, himself, is like a statue for all eternity to contemplate.

Voltaire and Frederick are fawned on for their genius and Rousseau for his incomparable soulfulness. Before Washington we stand motionless, because we feel something of the divine. Is it not a curious fact that this epoch — perhaps the most frivolous and scoffing that mankind has ever witnessed — should have felt no scruples in kneeling before a heavily booted gentleman of the New World, who bore neither title nor decoration?

To his contemporaries he gave the impression of being superhuman; even those who were most on the defensive against their imagination and their sentiment were won over to him. The Comte de Chastellux, a member of the French Academy and General of the Armies of the King of France, was a man of poise; nevertheless he wrote these words: 'The most characteristic feature of this respected man is the perfect harmony existing between the physical and moral attributes of which he is made up. Given one characteristic, it would be easy to gauge the others. If you should examine medallions of Cæsar, of Trajan, or of Alexander, upon seeing their features you might ask what was their height and the shape of their bodies; but if, amongst the ruins you discover the head or some marble fragment of an ancient Apollo, you would not trouble about the other pieces, but would be confident that all the rest belonged to a god.' [1]

Voltaire, Frederick, Rousseau, Pitt are great men whom their contemporaries observed with curiosity and loudly applauded. But their absurdities and their meannesses made as great an impression as their greatness; and it was necessary that they die that they should accomplish their destiny and that the silence which haloes the dead should give time for the legends of them to grow. These men were too real, too human, too individual to be transformed into holy idols immediately. Washington, on the contrary, without having either to die or to wait for long years to pass, stepped with firm tread into immortality. It would seem that the legends of other great men slowly take shape round about their memory; in the case of Washington it formed itself out of the man himself and in his lifetime. He created his own silence whilst the others were obliged to wait for the hand of Time. The Vicomte de Chateaubriand, while never inclined to admire others too much, said of him in the beginning of the nineteenth century: 'Washington's actions are surrounded by a certain quietude; he acts slowly. One might say he feels himself burdened with the liberty of the future and that he fears exposing it to danger. It is not his own fate which this new sort of hero upholds, but that of his country. Washington represented the needs, the ideas, the enlightenment, the opinions of his day; instead of impeding the development of modern ideas, he promoted them; he desired that which he should desire, the very thing for which he felt a calling; therefore the consistency and the continuity of his achievements. This man, who is not conspicuous because he possessed a just sense of proportion, threw in his lot with that of his country. His glory is the patrimony of civilization; his fame is ever-increasing, like one of those public sanctuaries flowing with an abundant and never-failing spring.' [2]

Others are born eloquent; he was born legendary.

Of all the legends of the eighteenth century, his is the most fruitful and the most original.

The eighteenth century had arranged its stage sumptuously for all kinds of heroes: great captains, writers, legislators, scholars, philosophers, celebrated kings. But, above all, it looked forward with joy to the arrival of the 'enlightened Despot.'

At this time, when everyone was weary of the monarchy and saw no possibility of birth of any other form of government, hopes were all centred upon this 'enlightened despot,' whom we should today call a 'dictator'; because each political system in its decline (once it was monarchy, now it is democracy) looks to dictatorship as a means of prolonging its span, at the same time that it loses faith in its principles.

They dreamed of an 'enlightened despot'; they hoped nothing from the people, but everything for the people; that is, if there could be given to the people all that an enlightened intelligence and an iron rule would give them. They wanted a great sovereign leader with precepts borrowed from the philosophers and who would apply their ideas regardless of the opposition or foibles of the common herd. This desire haunted Voltaire, Turgot, and even Franklin, as his first letters mentioning George III prove. In turn, they looked to the Grand Duke of Tuscany, to Frederick II, to Gustave III, to Joseph II for the incarnation of this ideal, which they were to meet at last in Napoleon.

Washington arrived at the very moment when these ideas obtruded themselves upon all minds, when any possibility of a republic seemed an empty dream, since Rome and Greece were the only model republics with republican heroes who were neither bandits nor tradesmen. So all eyes were turned with curiosity upon him to find out what new variation of the 'enlightened despot' he would turn out to be: the easygoing, the severe, the compliant, the lofty ...

But Washington proved to be the republican hero.

He was a gentleman. He was rich. He was a soldier. There was nothing of the revolutionary about him. And, for the first time in more than fifteen centuries, he exemplified the type of hero who declined supreme power and wished to command only to serve.

The world did not expect this; and it surprised the upper classes more than any other attitude would have done. And throughout the entire world the conservative classes, the middle classes, the enlightened nobility, and the people who, even though most cautious, were desirous of change, beheld the serene, great man with an astonishment which soon turned to enthusiasm. Washington accomplished, by the legend which so immediately surrounded him, more than anyone else had done. By his personality he prepared the extremists and the traditionalists to accept democratic ideas.

Born and brought up amongst the landed aristocracy, General George Washington, at the critical moment of the century, not only stood for republican precepts of government, but he allied himself with a party which was to transform democracy, until then merely an abstract, historical ideal. Silently, unhesitatingly, he succeeded in a thing which the most intrepid reformers of his day had not dared to attempt, a thing which the most emancipated philosophers — Rousseau, Voltaire, even — still looked upon as chimerical. In this way he became one of the spiritual leaders of his country and of the world. He has come to be the prototype whom millions of human beings have tried to imitate since his time.

Crowds of writers have tried to depict him, bands of historians to interpret him. Some have written worthy books, others books which have sold well. They have published every possible detail they could discover about him, regarding his actions, his gestures, his family, his friends, his enemies; all those who knew him or who did not know him have discussed him. They are even preparing an edition containing every word he ever penned as well as those written by his secretaries. At the hands of his very worshippers as well as by his pitiless biographers, this genuinely great man has been subjected to a mass of detail which, instead of elucidating his character, has obscured its presentation.

I should not like to add a further discordant note to this clamour, but, on the contrary, to restore to him a little of the silence which is his due. Since all sources have been explored, since investigation has been carried as far as possible, the time has come to proffer a balance-sheet. In Paris, London, Philadelphia, and Washington, I, too, have discovered documents hitherto unused, but I shall only make use of them where they can throw a new and brilliant light upon this august countenance, or, as out of an anecdote, there can come an idea.

I do not wish, moreover, to pay tribute to Washington as the hero of a group, but as one of the leaders of mankind.... I should like to depict here all those things which, as a new type of character, he gave to the world during that great period of struggle and creation — the eighteenth century.

I wish to present him encompassed by his silence and by the Universe.

GEORGE WASHINGTON
Republican Aristocrat

GEORGE WASHINGTON

.·.

CHAPTER I

GEORGE WASHINGTON, GENTLEMAN

GEORGE WASHINGTON was an aristocrat, a feudal lord. His birth and upbringing inevitably made him such. It was not his choice, it was his destiny which determined this; it was not a pose but quite his manner of being. He came by his aristocratic characteristics so naturally that it surprises no one that the founder of the American Republic should have been an aristocrat and the son of an aristocrat. Indeed, many people have entirely overlooked the fact.

But that air of authority, of greatness and of detachment with which he was endowed (qualities useful to him throughout his career), really the very qualities by which history describes him, are the essential marks of an aristocrat. All who approached him, whether gentlemen, writers, preachers, tradesmen, or poets, all felt immediately that they were in the presence of a born leader. The election to the presidency merely ratified and consecrated this title; it did not bestow it.

In truth he was born into and grew up in one of the most aristocratic, one of the most genuinely feudal societies the world has ever known.

Feudalism in Virginia[1]

In the rest of the world aristocracy was writhing in its death agony.

Having lost their rights as well as their halo of feudalism, the nobles were in process of becoming government officials. The position of the French monarchy had been strengthened during the days of Richelieu and of Louis XIV. The monarchical system of the Bourbons of Spain was patterned after that of the Bourbons of France; the Habsburgs were led into imitating them through having had to fight them, and the Hohenzollerns and the Romanoffs aped them, so that everywhere the monarchy would tolerate no other political or sovereign power but its own. Thereafter, no class was to exist between the king and the people.

The aristocracy was no longer the nobility, but had become 'the upper classes.' These were merely decorative. In case of necessity the aristocracy could be called upon for war, for diplomatic service, or for court life; but for all really important matters, such as finance, commerce, or administrative duties, the more practical, pliable middle class was preferred. The nobility retained the more obvious of its privileges, but the middle classes acquired riches and authority. Colbert, the greatest of France's ministers between 1650 and 1789, was the son of a draper.

But such was not the case in England. The aristocracy had put up a better fight for its rights. Attaching themselves to the people's cause, they expelled the Stuarts, who would have liked to imitate the example of the Bourbons. The rich, noble families held the

Hanoverian dynasty in check by manipulating public opinion. With the power furnished them by the House of Lords in which they sat by right of heredity, and by the House of Commons in which they bought seats, thanks to their great wealth, they formed a ruling class whose power became firmer as the century advanced.

The part they played in Parliament gave them as much importance in England as prestige in the outside world. At that grandiloquent period, when the aristocracies of the other countries were forced to keep silence or confine their discussions to the salon, the English nobility, by its outspoken and pompous parliamentary discussions, drew the attention of the whole world unto itself. Thanks to his genius and the piquancy of his style, M. de Montesquieu succeeded in making it fashionable all over the world.

A new conception of liberty, formed by a happy combination of the examples given in London and in Rome, became the ideal of Europe, particularly the ideal of the upper classes. From all parts of the old continent, noble families sent their children to London to admire the majestic spectacle of an independent aristocracy — an aristocracy retaining all its privileges, which privileges, in order to be on good terms with the middle classes whose assistance it found indispensable, it politely called 'liberty.'

The colonists of Virginia, in their far-away exile, were also fascinated by this magnificent spectacle. They sprang from the nobility, or from classes closely related to it (besides, does not every voluntary exile feel himself ennobled by the fact that he has risked his fortune?), and they set out to follow the example before them.

Conditions were not the same as in the mother country. There was no rival middle class to be taken into consideration, and the virgin soil had proved generous indeed in its gifts, so that the copy of the New World went beyond the limits of the original.

In spite of her name, Virginia was not a land dedicated to virtue and piety, as was New England. She was opened to colonization by a company of speculators whose aim was to make money. She was colonized by men who were unable to find it in Europe. That burning desire for the possession of land which had created and developed feudalism during the Middle Ages likewise created the feudalism of Virginia. At the outset, Virginia was a mirage of wealth, happiness, and feudal power. In order to attract the emigrant to the New World, did they not say that if he went to Virginia, he would find soil so fertile that in one day he would be able to clear enough space, plough enough land, and plant enough corn to feed himself for a year? In 1650, an author writing about Virginia described it as a land of rock crystal which the Indians employed for their arrow-heads, of cliffs and even hills of silver which might afford great pleasure to white colonists and, finally, he said that in the interior, 'on the banks of a river whose source sprang from the mountain,' [2] there was a red sand apparently containing copper and, perhaps, GOLD.

All this they dangled before the eyes of the miserable people of Europe who had been harassed by national wars, by civil strifes, by religious persecutions, and by all manner of epidemics. Most of all, these people had need of hope and they were given it by the bushelful. Thus, from the beginning, the colonization of Virginia was a success and greedy crowds hastened to her glittering shores. From 1550 to 1594, and again during the middle of the seventeenth century, France was a prey to both civil and religious wars; from 1618 to 1648, one of the most horrible wars ever witnessed by Europe took place in Germany. England was no better off, for after the ferocious religious struggles of the sixteenth century she fell into a period of revolution which lasted from 1637 to 1660. First she expelled the Puritans and then the Cavaliers; so it was that New England and Virginia were populated. In truth, it was far less the shine of gold than the hope of finding vast, rich lands which drew the English colonists to Virginia.

Unlike the Puritans, these colonists were not middleclass tradesmen who had acquired culture by travel. Neither were they endowed with the wild imagination of the Spanish conquistadors. The mountains of pearls and precious stones said much less to them than the prospects of a solid, stone dwelling overlooking extensive fields, or of servants toiling with bent backs. These, to them, were the symbols of wealth and respectability. After being driven from England and their estates, they were eager not only to discover a newer world, but to reëstablish, for their future benefit, a world older than that they had left. They still retained their feudal instincts and they went to America to gratify them.

Virginia was suited to their purposes. It was a completely new feudalism which was established on the banks of the Potomac and the James Rivers, but the system was identical with the old one in its importance and strength, its disadvantages and merits.

Looking back upon it, we are only too prone to regard the thing merely as a sordid performance — an unbridled, instinctive desire for gain, as it were, invading a virgin country only to sully it. This is untrue. The feudalism in Virginia was born of peril and struggle, as was the greatest European feudal movement of the Middle Ages: it deserves the same consideration.

The beginning of this adventure was attended with nothing but dangers. There was the Atlantic to be crossed in ships so feeble that the hurricanes tossed and threatened to destroy them, or else they stood motionless for weeks at a time, in a dead calm, while the humans on board were huddled together like herrings in a cask, exposed to all the sufferings of a too close proximity and to the risks of epidemics.[3] In the eighteenth century it was the rule never to allow on board a troop-ship more than one soldier to every two tons of shipping, but in the transporting of emigrants in the seventeenth century two persons were allowed for every ton of shipping. On one of these barks of one hundred and fifty, one hundred and twenty, or one hundred tons, more than two hundred passengers were collected, together with their luggage, the ship's stores, letters and parcels, the victuals for the colony, and the cannon for defence against pirates and freebooters. Anything of all this could be cast into the sea when the weather became wild.

In addition, all sorts of epidemics raged on board the English and French sailing-ships in the seventeenth century. Filth, exhaustion, and seasickness were the causes of scurvy, yellow fever, London plague, smallpox, and scarlet fever, which oppressed the homeless and disheartened emigrants. At times, as many as one hundred and thirty died out of the one hundred and eighty passengers on a single voyage, and if the half of a shipload reached port, it was considered a good proportion. Nevertheless, such was the greed of the contractors for the transport and the cupidity of the captains, that there was no possibility of any amelioration of these awful conditions during the whole of the seventeenth and eighteenth centuries. Only the strong and the courageous survived, and of these were the members of an aristocracy which had already been tried by a long ordeal of suffering.

Once arrived, these Englishmen, both rustics and gentlemen, found themselves in that tropical climate of Virginia, where the winter is damp and warm, the summer torrid, the spring sudden, and the autumn alternating with cold and heat. Along the coast bordered by marshlands, they were the prey of mosquitoes, and more than one died of fever and of misery. Food, moreover, was scarce. Corn when the Indians had not burnt their fields, the birds of the air when these could be procured, the wild animals in the woods when they dared to enter the forests without fear of being scalped, furnished coarse but sufficient nourishment. But these English, used as they were to their cabbage and their beef, were not always able to endure this strange and monotonous diet.

But worst of all were the Indians. Seen from distant Europe, they were charming; they seemed most attractive and picturesque, their heads decorated with feathers, their hairy bodies covered with dresses of leaves, such as we still see represented on the doorways of Renaissance houses in France and England, crowned with the Latin inscription 'AMERICANUS.' Near at hand, the Indians were worse than savage beasts, for they were craftier and harder to understand. They roamed, almost invisible, on the outskirts of the woods or in the brush about the European encampments. Their animosity towards the invaders was implacable: whenever they saw a chance, they would attack the white man, burn his house and his fields, shoot him in the back with arrows, scalp his wife and his children. If they were numerous enough or if they were drunk, they would even go so far as to attack villages.

Certain white colonists, mostly those of French origin, managed to come to terms with the Indians by living amongst them and learning their language. But most of the Virginians had neither enough curiosity nor adaptability to mix with this hostile people. It became a continuous, brutal struggle in which the whites left many sanguinary relics.

In 1622, the Indians massacred three hundred and fifty whites in a single encounter and, several years later, they began anew. During the entire seventeenth century, and three quarters of the eighteenth century, the farms on the frontiers were exposed to their attacks. The practical-minded Virginian, with his sense of order, would never allow himself to think of the Indian as anything other than a savage. And the Indian paid him back in his own coin.

So, in Virginia, the people had always to be in readiness. In the beginning the colony was a small, military dictatorship where the Governor, in the name of the King, exercised sovereign power over the land-owners or the Company. He instructed his administrators in the art of war and was careful to keep them in training, nor did he hesitate to rid himself of those who lacked either courage or discipline. The first governors, and especially Berkeley, ruled with iron hand, but they were successful and the colony lived.

Many colonists, however, died. In 1622, out of more than five thousand emigrants who had left the shores of England for those of Virginia, there remained but eleven hundred. From the middle of the seventeenth century, fifteen thousand servants were landed in Virginia from Europe every year, and only twelve thousand of their total number were alive in 1683.[4]

The others did not all die, it must be admitted. Many of them managed to emigrate from this cruel land. The large proportion of those who arrived in Virginia in the seventeenth century were drawn from the riffraff of England which sent, without discrimination, criminals, beggars, vagabonds, young men far too improvident and wenches far too gay, to her colony. There were also a good number of stupid and miserable peasants who made the voyage at the expense of the Company or of the ship's captain. On arrival, these were sold to the highest bidder. These

unfortunate people were known as 'indentured servants,' or servants bound by contract. They were
forced to serve for five, six, or even ten years without
wages. The law — always so far-seeing and just —
even specified that, if the husband died during the
voyage after half of the passage had been completed,
the wife must serve double time to compensate the
captain for his loss.

This slavery had but one extenuating feature: it was
temporary, and, once over, its victims became free
again — at least in theory. But they were as naked
as they were free, without a penny in a land where
distances were boundless, where there were no towns,
or no modest corners where humble folk might meet
their fellows over a glass of rum, such as could be
found in all the ports of New England. The sort of
democracy which springs from a mingling of weak
creatures who put shoulder to shoulder and incite
each other to action could not come into being in this
exclusively rural land and sparsely populated region.

A discharged servant, to earn his living, was obliged
to return to his former master or some neighbour, or
risk his chances along the frontier or in a near-by
colony. In Europe the aristocracy was uprooted and
dying, and the people growing stronger and stronger,
established itself easily everywhere, while in Virginia
a stolid and powerful aristocracy was fast gaining
control and a weak and dying proletariat was being
wiped out.

Like the feudal system of the Middle Ages, Virginia
was made up of three classes: the serfs, the freedmen,
and the nobility.

To establish a dynasty in the colony one had to arrive with money and references, to be a soldier and a friend of the Governor, to be able to acquire land, to marry well.

The Governor was not to be disregarded. He was placed at the head of the colony, first, as a sort of absolute despot and, later, as a monarch with a council chosen by himself to assist him. People who wanted to have any authority had to keep on good terms with him and, similarly, if they desired to make money. If they looked for large concessions, they had to depend on the Governor. On the other hand, if he was tactful, he closed his eyes at the propitious moment, which he did not fail to do if he felt that a man was worth the trouble.

With his aid, it was easy for a wealthy family to hold its piece of territory. In this new and sparsely settled colony the only centres were the plantations of the big landowners and the parishes. Thus the rich man had the main body of electors directly in his power and had no difficulty in getting a place in the House of Burgesses. Backed by his clergyman, who was wholly supported by him, he could easily become vestryman * and so control the local government.

Since the entire activity of Virginia was agricultural, the small landholders were unable to stand up for their rights and the Assemblies in the villages or towns, which so soon acquired importance in New England, could not exist there.

Virginia weakened the weak and strengthened the

* The vestryman of Virginia had functions analogous to those of our municipal councillors.

strong, '... for he that hath, to him shall be given: and he that hath not, from him shall be taken even that which he hath.'

A gentleman arriving with money could immediately obtain lands. And if, subsequently, he bought slaves, he likewise was entitled to more land in proportion.

His fortune increased itself like a rolling snow-ball. It varied according to the current prices of tobacco, the principal commodity of Virginia.

From 1627 Virginia (founded in 1607) sent five hundred thousand pounds' worth of tobacco to London and soon the whole of Europe was supplied by America. But the tobacco crops quickly exhausted the soil and only those could go on producing whose land and capital were practically unlimited. The farmer with a small holding dared not thus exhaust his soil and so he lived along poorly doing a little scratch-farming. Inevitably the larger landowners soon occupied the entire territory.

Debts were the thorns in the flesh of the Virginian aristocrats. The tobacco was marketed in London, where each important planter had an agent, or merchant, commissioned to sell it at the highest price and also to do his buying for him. Because of slow transportation and the commercial customs of the times, one or even two years might elapse before the planter could know what his harvest had brought in, or what he had spent. During this period he bought everything that he required in England. Usually, therefore, he was deeply in his English agent's debt and saw very little, if any, of his large gains.

The only remedy lay in marriage. The most successful families in Virginia were not those who possessed the most glorious ancestral line, nor the greatest geniuses, nor the boldest captains, nor those with the most culture and piety, nor even with an excess of commercial skill, but those families in which the young people of each generation had married the most advantageously, always supplying the plantation with ready capital. In this and in other respects, the system was feudal, for the families of Virginia preferred to leave the family estate to the eldest sons, while the daughters received a small portion of land and money. A good marriage enabled a young man to have a good set of tools as well as credit. Widowhood was a blessing from Heaven. The largest fortune in Virginia, that of the Byrds, was established in this way.[5]

Woe to bachelors and to colonists without credit! Between 1700 and 1715, the population lived through cruel years. The War of the Spanish Succession ruined commerce, shipping was precarious, and credit nowhere given. Only the most solidly established and the best-married could put up a fight. The middle classes, established by the fruitful years at the end of the seventeenth century (1678-1700), were seriously affected. For them, the fatal blow was the increasing importation of blacks. In 1619, the Dutch began to introduce negro slaves into America and made enormous sums out of this traffic. The planters preferred the blacks, who were slaves for life, to the whites, who were only temporary slaves. The exceedingly rough and difficult work of cultivating tobacco was better done by these savages than by the sons of European artisans or peasants, and it was easier to force them to do it. Undoubtedly they were but cattle and were more accustomed to the climate; also, they were cheap; a black could be bought for six pounds. Naturally, the best were more costly, but there was always a slave to suit every purse. For a white servant, the ship passage alone represented from eight to ten pounds, while his purchase price was as much as twenty to thirty pounds.

The introduction of black labour drove the whites from the large plantations and almost wiped out the small planters, who were forced to resort to the most costly manual labour and could not afford to own enough blacks to organize their plantations on the model of their well-to-do neighbours. Of course, slavery was illegal and would never have been tolerated had not the King been concerned in the traffic. Since he had speculated in the black slave trade, the colony had no trouble in passing laws for the control of this traffic and in obtaining their ratification.

About 1730, the suppression of the small holders was general, and certain favourable laws were voted in England which helped the big planters to enjoy for the next two years a period of great prosperity.

The great lords of Virginia were not evil men. Like all the young and strong, they were cruel, not because it gave them pleasure but because it was customary and profitable. They were rich. Some of them owned as many as 60,000 acres.[6] William Byrd II at his death left 170,000 acres and Lord Fairfax was master of a huge property of 6,000,000 acres. In 1783, in the

County of Gloucester, a single planter owned 93 negro slaves; another, 138; a third, 162. Mr. Daingerfield had 91 and Mann Page 157. Under such conditions it was not astonishing that the number of slaves increased from 3,000 in 1689 to 23,000 in 1715, and to 120,000 in 1765.

The present was theirs completely, the future also, as this aristocracy had laid hands on all productive land. By 1730 they considered that they held in their possession all land, good and bad, in the East and all the land in the West that would have any value, which they were holding without cultivating it, probably as a heritage for their children.

Children were numerous, six, eight, and sometimes ten to a family. It was necessary to find 'places' for them; because the conditions there were not similar to those in New England, where, owing to the rapid development of social life, varied employments and posts were open to the young. There were no respected and well-paid lawyers, none of those urban professions — book-selling, scrivening, trading — to support the middle classes in the towns. Schoolmasters were rare.

Religion did not offer a living. The clergy were few in number and but little considered. Life in a small, isolated parsonage, with your nearest neighbour ten miles away, was not gay, especially as you had to rely on the few rich planters of the parish for your maintenance and with perhaps only a twentieth part of the population communicating. It would have been necessary to be a saint, and the Church of England could not boast many of these! In 1661, four fifths of the parishes in Virginia were without clergymen, and among the remaining fifth provided with clergy, many would have been better off without, since the kind of ecclesiastic sent to them was often drawn from the scum of England.

It was the ground alone which could always be depended upon to provide. To own it and be a planter on a large scale was the only certain thing, otherwise one had to become a soldier to conquer and defend it or a land-surveyor to explore and exploit it — the only two other professions in Virginia which gave one social standing.

His plantation always on the shore of a bay or the edge of a river, so that the English ships might fetch his tobacco and bring him supplies from overseas, the rich planter lived in the midst of a real settlement and surrounded by his white servants and his black slaves. His clergyman, probably some miles distant, would receive his visit from time to time on a Sunday and he would solemnly take part in the Church of England services to set a good example and to gossip with his neighbours. Once a year, he would go to the capital, Jamestown or Williamsburg, a village embellished with a few official buildings. There, he would dance at the house of the Governor, drink at the inn, play at cards or billiards, discuss the overseas news or the price of land and slaves. There he would plan his speculations.

Or else he would indulge in a few little gallantries — but very mildly, for life was patriarchal, the family the principal institution and the fountain-head of the colony. And it was indeed respected. The rather rude and simple customs allowed of a certain promiscuity and old-time comradeship, but rendered complicated intrigues and licentiousness out of the question. In the manors where abundant hospitality was proffered, in the inns where everybody crowded together merrily in some little room, men and women jostled each other boldly, but amongst the restricted, shut-in aristocracy, people knew each other far too well to run any risks of public censure. The ladies, amiable and wise, presided over the making of shirts for their husbands and friends; the young girls, light-headed and amiable, sometimes exchanged clothing with their boy friends, whiling away the fair summer morning in these disguises and clapping each other on the back. But marriages were made at an early age and husbands were presented by their wives with numerous offspring.

People did not bother much about the intellectual life. Although Colonel Byrd in his manor at Westover possessed the largest library in the colonies (four thousand books in all), his neighbours made little or no use of it. Nor were there many free schools. The clergyman took the place of both doctor and pedagogue, but was not very gifted in either vocation. The most distinguished people sent their sons to England to be educated and to finish their studies at Oxford or in the Temple. As for the others, some auction sale would provide at the cheapest rate a cultivated servant who gave their children as much instruction as they had need of. In the end a college was founded at Williamsburg — 'William and Mary College' — but at first it was a sorry institution: 'a college without chapel, learned men, and charter,' as they said. [7]

If the great lords of Virginia were not great scholars, neither were they fools. After the year 1735, they were responsible for the best edited gazette of the New World; from their estates, they kept in touch with everything new that happened across the sea. They provided themselves with all the luxuries from England, where they did not fail to go regularly to superintend the sale of their tobacco or to find a wife. They brought back with them the spirit and the gaiety of this young England, so prepared to invade the world and so radiant with vitality. It was England that provided them with everything, from the nails of their shoes to the hair for their wigs, which, like William Byrd, they sent to be repaired in London. Their lives, now solitary, now social, were continuously luxurious and gay.

We can hear the echo of their laughter when we read from the newspapers of those days. In its issue of the 7th of October, 1737, the 'Virginia Gazette' announced:

'*Williamsburg, October 7*. We have advice from *Hanover* County, that on *St. Andrew's* Day, being the 30th of *November* next, there are to be Horse Races, and several other Diversions, for the Entertainment of the Gentlemen and Ladies, at the *Old Field* near Capt. *John Bickerton's* in that County, (if permitted by the Hon. *William Byrd*, Esq., Proprietor of the said Land), the Substance of which are as follows, viz.

I. It is propos'd, That 20 Horses or Mares do run round a Three Miles Course, for a Prize of the Value of Five Pounds, according to the usual Rules of Racing: That every Horse that runs shall be first enter'd by Mr. *Joseph*

Fox; and that no Person have the Liberty of putting in a Horse, unless he is a Subscriber towards defraying the Expence of this Entertainment, and pay to Mr. *Fox* Half a Pistole of it, at entring the Horse.

II. That a Hat of the Value of 20 s. be cudgell'd for; and that after the first Challenge made, the Drums are to beat once every Quarter of an Hour, for Three Challenges, round the Ring; on no Answer made, the Person challenging, to be entitled to the Prize; and none to play with their Left Hand.

III. That a Violin be played for by 20 Fiddlers, and to be given to him that shall be adjudged to play the best: No person to have the Liberty of playing, unless he brings a fiddle with him. After the Prize is won, they are all to play together, and each a different Tune; and to be treated by the Company.

IV. That 12 Boys of 12 Years of Age, do run 112 Yards, for a Hat of the Value of 12 Shillings.

V. That a Flag be flying on the said Day, 30 Feet high.

VI. That a handsome Entertainment be provided for the subscribers, and their Wives; and such of them who are not so happy as to have Wives, may treat any other Lady. And that convenient Booths be erected for that Purpose.

VII. That Drums, Trumpets, Hautboys, &c. will be provided, to play at the said Entertainment.

VIII. That after Dinner, the Royal Healths, his Honour the Governor's, &c. are to be drank.

IX. That a Quire of Ballads be sung for, by a Number of Songsters; the best Songsters to have the Prize, and all of them to have Liquor sufficient to clear their Wind-Pipes.

X. That a Pair of Silver Buckles be Wrestled for, by a certain Number of brisk young Men.

XI. That a Pair of handsome Shoes be danced for.

XII. That a Pair of handsome silk Stockings of One Pistole Value, be given to the handsomest young Country

Maid that appears in the Field: With many other Whimsical and Comical Diversions, too tedious to mention here.'

To make perfectly plain what the spirit of the fête was to be, the newspaper added:

And as this Mirth is design'd to be purely innocent, and void of Offence, all Persons resorting there are desir'd to behave themselves with Decency and Sobriety; the Subscribers being resolv'd to discountenance all Immorality with the utmost Rigour.

Such was Virginia in its gay simplicity at the beginning of the eighteenth century.

The Dynasty of the Washingtons [8]

Neither too high, neither too low — such was the social status of the Washingtons for five centuries in England. They belonged to a good family and they were landowners. Their lives were always led in contact with the peasantry and in contact with the higher aristocracy, to which latter, however, they never quite belonged. Theirs was a deep-rooted sense of honour, an irresistible love of the earth. But they did not store up great wealth; they bequeathed to their descendants neither great estates nor legends of heroic exploits. They were the sort of people whose legacy consisted only in coats-of-arms and account-books.

They retained certain of their old traditions: they named their sons John, or Lawrence, or Augustine; they were good Anglicans and faithful royalists; they respected the institution of the family. And God rewarded them: in the beginning of the seventeenth

century, they really believed that they were about
to climb the ladder at whose foot they had hereto-
fore languished, for two of them were knighted, Sir
William and Sir John. History, however, has been
pleased to leave them in their niches: dignified but
empty names.

Another brother became a clergyman. He went
through Oxford, as family tradition demanded, and
with more distinction than they had hoped; but less
satisfactory, indeed, was his marriage. He wedded
Amphyllis Rhoades, the daughter of a farmer or of a
servant — it is not known whether for love, by necessity or by accident. This did not prevent his holding a
good living but he was deprived of it later by the
Puritans on being accused of being a wine-bibber,
a libertine, and a royalist. So he and his wife and
children were relegated to a little parish where he
could barely scrape together enough to live on (1643).

He was forced to submit to circumstances, but he
and his family had a most difficult time of it. He
died in 1652, and his wife followed him in 1654. The
children, no longer able to keep going, emigrated:
John in 1658, then Lawrence and then Martha, the
daughter.

They went to Virginia. Throngs of Cavaliers had
in fifteen years patronized her shores so enthusiastically that between 1640 and 1670, the population increased from fifteen thousand to seventy thousand.

This was, indeed, a good time to settle there. The
eastern territory had been cleared and rendered
healthy to live in, the villages and the plantations

were organized and the Indians driven far from the coast. Civil institutions and the aristocracy had become well established there. For one who belonged to the ruling classes, life no longer presented too many difficulties, as the power of the Puritans was rapidly waning. The loyal Virginians could at last breathe freely.

John began well and adapted himself rapidly. He had tried the navy, but it did not please him as he was unlucky in this attempt and had had as associate a man whom he subsequently discovered to be a cheat and a fanatic. After this experience, at the age of twenty-five, he was glad to land in Virginia.

Without delay, he married Ann, the daughter of Nathaniel Pope, Lieutenant-Governor, a wealthy man who was both important and virtuous. Thus, John Washington was immediately able to own his plantation near the mouth of the Potomac, build his house there, and cut a fine figure as a gentleman.

At this time the important Virginian dynasties — particularly that of the Byrds — were being founded, and John's family took its place among them. By three successive marriages he established new relationships and became rooted in the soil. After Ann's death, John married the widow of two of his neighbours; when she died, he contracted a new alliance with the widow of Captain John Appleton (in this way becoming the possessor of fourteen thousand acres of ground in the County of Westmoreland), and built two houses there. This estate, for long a family centre, was known consecutively as 'Bridge Creek,' 'Pope Creek,' 'Westover,' and 'Nominy.' John Washington, furthermore, was elected Burgess and nominated Colonel of the Virginian militia.

He even conducted a war and led his troops against the Indians, an event which was perhaps the most notorious and the most disturbing in his life. He killed some Indians, but their brother Indians, and the jealous allies of the Virginians, the Maryland people, claimed that these Indians had not been killed according to rule, since they had come as plenipotentiaries. An investigation was held and the Governor of Virginia, Sir Thomas Berkeley, decided in favor of the Indians: he censured John Washington. Public opinion in Virginia, on the other hand, sided with him. For them, the important thing was not how the Indians were killed, but the fact that they *were* killed. And the Indians, in their artless fashion, showed that they were of the same mind, for they conferred upon John the title of 'Conocotarius,' which means 'destroyer of villages,' and bespeaks admiration.

In 1677 he died — a respected and honoured man.

At his death, he left a family very well settled and in fairly good circumstances. The four children by his first wife, Lawrence, John, Elizabeth, and Ann, were surrounded by all kinds of relatives. The land he bequeathed to them was worth seventy thousand dollars at the time of his death — a large amount in those days — and he had actually been far-seeing enough, through association with a friend, to obtain a concession of five thousand acres on the Potomac. Besides this, he left two thousand dollars' worth of personal property in America, and other property in England.

He had reëstablished the Washington dynasty and on a higher rank.

Nor were his efforts wasted: purchases of land and speculations in tobacco continued to provide as well as Providence.

Lawrence, the eldest son, married Mildred Warner, the daughter of Augustin Warner, a wealthy man and a member of the King's Council. When Lawrence died at the age of thirty-six in 1697, his widow married George Gale, but died shortly afterwards in England, where she had gone to look after her inheritance.

Augustine, Lawrence's second son, was left the family lands, while the eldest son, John, took over those of his mother. For one hundred and eighty pounds Augustine bought back the land on the upper Potomac from his sister and, in this way, reconstituted his grandfather's estate.

Augustine began as a navigator but as this was not a vocation which suited the Washingtons, he soon lost interest in the sea and began to till the soil from that time on. He was an active, enterprising man who knew how to advance himself. With a good family name and useful relations to lean upon, he soon reached the top.

At the age of twenty-one, Augustine married Jane Butler, who died thirteen years later, leaving him with two sons, Lawrence and Augustine, besides a daughter, Mildred. Shortly afterwards, on the 16th of March, 1731, he married again, this time Mary Ball, by whom he had six children: George, Elizabeth, Samuel, John Augustine, Charles, and Mildred. The

Balls were good, simple people, and their origin was more common than that of the Washingtons; Mary Ball Washington never allowed her husband to forget it during her lifetime. Otherwise she was a good wife to him.

In the meanwhile, Augustine was not wasting his time. He was renewing on a more intimate basis certain relationships which were to unite his family with the powerful Fairfax dynasty. He decided to make gentlemen of his two older sons and took them to England himself, placing them in Appleby's School, patronized by the Fairfaxes, using the occasion to make certain arrangements for the importation of servants, while his wife remained in America to look after the house and the younger children (1737).

It was his intention, on his return, to fit the estate for his eldest son and to install himself on the upper Potomac on the land acquired by his grandfather and which was known successively as 'Hunting Creek,' 'Epsewasson' and 'Mount Vernon.' He built a house there, became one of the important personages of the neighbourhood, and was chosen vestryman of the Truro Church and member of the House of Burgesses. He took rather a good deal of power into his own hands in forcing upon his colleagues a certain Charles Green as vicar, a man who was neither esteemed by them nor was worthy of their esteem.

This accomplished, he launched into a speculation. In Virginia had been discovered some iron deposits, and a company — 'The Principo Company of Virginia' — was formed to exploit them. Now at this time the colonies produced almost no iron and England herself very little, so this was a rare and precious commodity, useful both in civil life and for the army; the Principo Company, backed by its patriotic enthusiasm and its desire to make money, rushed to the fore. It would appear that Augustine played an important rôle in it as twelfth part owner. In order to keep an eye on his interests, he went to live near the centre of this exploitation, or close to Fredericksburg, a hamlet which had just been laid out and which already boasted a number of houses. He brought his entire family to this spot called Ferry Farm (or River Farm) on the Rappahannock and, in 1742, he was made a trustee of the town. As for the company, it developed well and, in 1751, exported three thousand tons of iron at a time when Pennsylvania produced only two hundred tons, and England, only seventeen thousand tons in all.

Augustine, however, was destined not to enjoy for long the devotion of his little family nor the promises of wealth, for on the 12th of April, 1743, he died of an attack of gout which went to his stomach, as gout did in those days. He was forty-nine years old and his second wife, thirty-nine.

He had been a good husband, a good father, a good worker, and a good Virginian. But he died too young. To be successful in Virginia, a man had to outlive his rivals, his neighbours, and his wives.

The Education of George Washington, A Younger Son

Augustine Washington left a family which, though prosperous, was far too numerous; each member did its utmost, however, to get on.

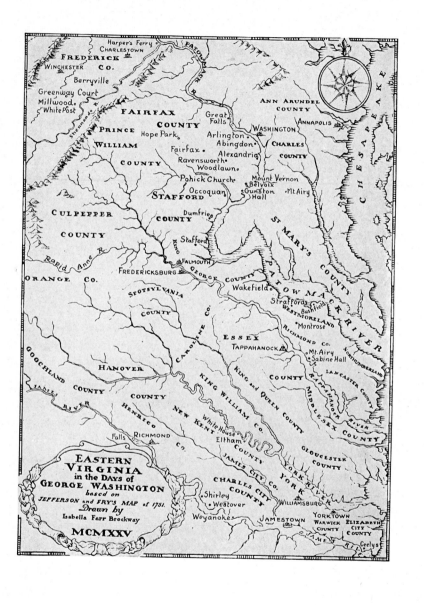

His eldest son, Lawrence, once his formal education was finished, returned from England; he was given the land on the upper Potomac, and settled there.[9] For an eldest son he seems neither to have been very strong in body nor in character, but at least he knew enough to marry well; he wedded the rich and radiant Ann Fairfax, the Honourable William Fairfax's daughter.

The second son, Augustine, also returned from England at the end of his schooling, and he established himself in the old estate on the lower Potomac, where he contracted a most judicious alliance with the wealthy Ann Aylett. So much for these two sons.

The fate of Mrs. Washington, the widow, was a less prosperous one. She continued to live at the Ferry Farm near Fredericksburg. She had her own fortune and also the interest on the portions left to her eldest son George and to her other children by their father.

Her eldest son, who was his father's third son, was really left very barely provided for. His portion consisted of a farm on the Rappahannock, three morsels of ground near Fredericksburg, some fields on the Deep Run, and a few slaves; actually the whole of it only enough to endow a very small farmer.

Destiny, which in the seventeenth century, so it seems, marked out two Washingtons as the founders of a noble line and the legators of wealth to their children, in the eighteenth century appointed the two sons of Augustine's first marriage as the actual maintainers of this noble line of Washingtons; whilst Mary Ball's children, less fortunate and too numerous, were once more relegated to that inferior status from which the family had taken so much pains to extricate itself forever.

The social advancement of the Washingtons between 1650 and 1743 seemed only to benefit Lawrence and Augustine — not the little George. On the contrary, for upon him devolved the rôle of younger son without land in a country where land was everything.

There was nothing for him to hope for but luck.

He had it.

He was born on the 11th of February, 1732, at ten o'clock in the morning on the lower Potomac property. In 1735, he went with his father and the rest of the family to the estate on the upper Potomac. In 1739, he took part in the new migration which was to settle them on the Rappahannock. He was with his mother when his father died and he remained with her.

Would he be a Ball or a Washington? There was, on the one hand, the house near Fredericksburg, filled with children and scantily supplied with money, where a widow struggled sullenly against discomfort, very inadequately helped, so it would seem, by the merchants, the lawyers, in short, all the prosperous family connections. On the other hand, there were the two gentlemen as prosperously established on their estates and surrounded by as highly respectable families as any in the colony.

Mary Ball Washington was not very particular about her person or her manners or her style. What mattered to her the most were her material interests, the importance of which she exaggerated, perhaps,

and she never succeeded in hiding her disdain for all
the special preoccupations involving military honour
and glory. For the rest, she was a mother more
anxious than tender, more tender than intelligent,
more intelligent than courageous, more courageous
than gentle. She liked to have her children gathered
round her and was afraid of seeing them stray.
Thunder terrified her. Her education was but slight.
In fact, the dawning history of the United States
reveals her illuminated by a hard and simple life
about which it can record nothing discreditable. By
its obscurity, this history even has the tact to leave
us the privilege of assigning to her all the charm that
it is natural to imagine in women.

But she was decidedly plain.

The two Washington sons, brought up in England,
had excellent manners.

After his schooling, Lawrence lived the life of
a gentleman. During the War of the Austrian Succession and the contests between Spain and England, he
took part as second commanding officer of the Virginian troops in the English expeditionary army
which, under General Vernon, attacked Cartagena
(1741). Truly, this was a miserable campaign: the
Spanish defended themselves too well and the climate
achieved what the Spanish cannons had begun. The
English were forced to retreat, leaving many of their
men on the field and only taking back with them as
trophies all sorts of contagious diseases.

Lawrence lost his health there, for he contracted
the germs of consumption (pulmonary tuberculosis)
which never left him. He just missed losing his good

name also, for, on their return, certain of his companions in arms told unfriendly tales about him, although two centuries later, it is impossible to distinguish slander from truth. Whatever may have occurred, public opinion was with Lawrence, since, on his return and immediately after his father's death, the Fairfaxes,[10] who could *choose* whom their daughter was to marry, did not refuse him her hand.

He must have had a free conscience, because he called his new house 'Mount Vernon' in memory of this campaign which he must have looked upon as the most striking and glorious event in his life. He lived like a great lord, without any cares, on his twenty-five hundred acres of ground. Quite near to him, on their estate, 'Belvoir,' was his wife's family, the Fairfaxes, with whom he continually exchanged visits. Young couples abounded at Mount Vernon and Belvoir, and life in both places was elegant and lordly. They formed a clan. Lawrence saw to it that he was elected Burgess and for the short time that God granted him life, he must have been one of the great figures of Virginia.

What a contrast between the existence little George led at Fredericksburg and the life he saw at Mount Vernon when he visited in his brother's house! Unfortunately, he clung closely to his mother. She was responsible for his name of George, which was not a traditional one with the Washingtons, for he was called after her guardian, George Eckeridge. It would also appear that he owed his slightly heavy physical appearance to his mother as well as certain traits of character. Like her, he was obstinate, and, like her, he seemed more fitted for an active physical life than for intellectual pursuits.

He was not urged, really, to apply himself to these.

They did not send him to England to receive the elegant education of the English aristocracy, nor was he sent to Williamsburg to be instructed with the sons of the Virginian gentlemen.[11] He received the first rudiments from a servant bought at the market. In the Rappahannock house, he studied the sermons of the Bishop of Exeter and pored over 'The Young Man's Companion,' one of those copious lesson-books such as were given to children in those days, teaching them the three 'R's' as well as supplying them with a mixture of useful lore: how to draw up a will, to sail a ship, to make ink or cider, to cure illnesses, or to write letters to a fiancée.

Following upon the death of his father, he went to school at the house of Mr. Williams in Westover (he was then living with his brother Augustine), and at that of the Reverend Marye in Fredericksburg. The only appreciable gifts of these professors were some of the rudiments of Latin, fairly good handwriting, and faulty spelling. He must have learnt a great deal more from his innumerable cousins and little friends with whom he played, fought, swam, rode horseback, rolled on the grass, and who helped him to build up his strong, resistant, active body, perhaps the most important possession he was to acquire during these youthful years.

Thus, like his training and his learning, all that he was taught was simple and limited: no fine manners, very little Latin, some exact and practical ideas —

these were engraved upon the child's receptive mind.
Unlike most of the great men of the eighteenth century, he learnt first of all, not words, but how to act,
how to calculate, how to reason, and this discipline did
not shatter the character of the silent, strong-minded
child.

Since no one knew whether the youth would turn
out beggar or king and since everybody believed that
he would merely be the younger son in a needy family,
such an education was not a hindrance, but seemed
highly suitable. They did not insist upon his having
ample instruction, as they hoped to place him early
in life. Lawrence thought of sending George to sea;
many others before him thus either made their fortunes or lost their lives, to the great relief of their
families. And as George was robust, brave, and
capable, he would no doubt have been a success. It
was a hard life, however, in which he would have had
to begin at the humblest work; he would have had to
set out on a trading-vessel where, although the wages
were rather good, he would have risked being forcibly
pressed into the navy. Since the Washingtons were
in far-away Virginia, their influence at Court would
not have been sufficient to obtain for young George
an officer's commission. The Ball uncle wrote a forceful letter from England stating his disapproval of the
plan, and Mrs. Washington, who was already terrified
for her son, refused to allow George to leave, and he
does not appear to have insisted. For these young
provincials of Virginia, wholly attached to their lands
and to the world they lived in, the sea had not the

same attraction as it had for the children of Boston and other American ports who all turned naturally to salt water.

What could they do with George Washington?

His brothers were decent fellows and very fond of him. Also, although he was a younger son, he had certain special rights, for in his father's will it was written that, in case of the decease of Lawrence, George was to inherit the Mount Vernon estate. So his brothers took up his cause. Instead of leaving him in Fredericksburg to lead a sluggish life with his mother, Augustine took him to Wakefield; previously, Lawrence had invited him to Mount Vernon and introduced him to Belvoir. The Washington cousins had received him at 'Chotank,' where he made life-long friends with Lawrence and Robin.

Rich or poor, George was perfectly at home in Virginia — an instinct which seemed deeper-rooted in him than any desire for change. Lawrence, who began to notice the ravages of his disease, decided to have his young brother live with him. So George was installed in the midst of the Fairfaxes. He rather veered towards the trade of land-surveyor, in which he was sure to succeed, protected as he was by families so influential and so richly provided with lands. Moreover, this trade suited the young man's character, for these lengthy circuits over deserted tracts required moral energy and reserve; precision, also, was needed for the marking of boundaries and honesty was an integral part in such work. As a reward, he would acquire an understanding of the people, the country, the Indians. And his day's wages would be good.

This was the first stage of George Washington's career and the first sure guarantee his class was to give him that they would hold by him. His decision united him with Virginia as well as with the Fairfax and Washington clans.

Now that we have left him for the moment to dwell in the bosom of his family — a grown-up, awkward youth — we may presume to pause a little to consider this person whose fame was to spread so far and whose career was to confine itself to such precise and narrow limits.

At sixteen, George Washington did not evince the same brilliant ingenuity shown by Franklin, a printer of Boston, at the same age; nor were his the divine gifts of Voltaire — that favourite of the most refined society which ever existed. Even so, he was neither a fool nor a bumpkin: the character and the precision of his mind were apparent from the days of his earliest training. If he was not quick to seize an idea, if dreams came seldom into the province of his imagination, if he was practically unable to define or to express his feelings, at least from an early age he was able to recognise and appreciate things as they were. Indeed, upon this, his entire life and all his actions were hinged so rigidly and exactly that he inspired sympathy in everyone he met. The young Franklin, the young Voltaire, the young Rousseau were uprooted: the young Washington was solidly rooted in a soil he loved and which suited him. In his peregrinations as a boy from one Virginia manor to another, he learned more than Latin, French, and fencing. He learned to know his own country, its climate, its seasons, its yield, the disposition of its inhabitants, the character of its notables, the value of its Negroes, in fact, the import of every cloud on its horizon.

It would seem as if all the great men of the century strove, in so far as their strength, their intelligence, and their resources permitted, to adapt themselves to the mightiest possible social scheme. Voltaire, Franklin, Rousseau, Frederick, would have liked the world as theatre and all humanity as audience. George Washington was instinctively prompted to adapt himself in the best possible way to a limited scheme of things. He was perfectly at home in Virginia: he would be a perfect Virginian. And upon this single card he would risk his entire life and fortune.

Directed, like all his family, by a feudal instinct rather than by the customs of the times, he did not try to exceed his capabilities. He was not obsessed by the longing for novelty nor troubled by the unknown in this century of great discoveries. The verbal intoxication to which humanity had been given over since the Renaissance was alien to him. For Washington, words were enemies to be battled with before they were conquered, while *things* were near and intimate friends which he could resort to and control.

Upon his silence and realism, Puritan society and official writers have built up the holy legend of a devout and over-sensitive child obsessed by moral ideas and given to preaching. All the documents and all the traces he left of his childhood disprove this, but when he became the national hero, this legend followed the evolution of the national idea. Before they created Prohibition, the preachers of New England created a type which they called Washington. Now, in the age of jazz, a new national idea seems to be in process of formation: we are shown a Washington who, from his childhood days, was both cynical and brutal; a young under-officer absorbed by love-affairs, drink, and cards; an ignoramus as foolish as a goose. Never would Washington's silence lead us to believe these things nor would the unskilful and stammering literary efforts he has bequeathed to future generations show him up as inferior in any way to his age or times. These are only rendered ludicrous by harsh investigation and are, in fact, but the extremely touching efforts of an already developed male mentality and a still clumsy body to adapt themselves to the imbecility of his day.

In the days of his youth, his modesty, his moderation, and his self-restraint are evident, and the joy with which he grew active and silent in that rich and happy Virginia of the Fairfaxes and the Washingtons.

George Washington's Ideas

It is no longer possible for us to know how he rode a horse or how he dressed his hair, but we do know how he thought. This is worth taking into consideration, because in the space of seven years this youth, with the mere aid of his prudence and luck, was to join the first ranks in his part of the country.

Amongst the papers of his childhood days has been found a carefully preserved pamphlet given him by his teachers to copy, study, and learn. It is entitled: 'The Rules of Conduct and Politeness.' In substance this book is taken from a treatise of decorum composed by the Jesuits of La Flèche in 1595. As instructors of the nobility and the ruling classes of France, these good fathers had chosen to codify and summarize all that a young man should know in order to conduct himself properly in society. As these fathers have always taken pains to adapt themselves to the world of their day, they looked at things from a practical point of view. Their rules were based on usage and expediency rather than upon fundamental principles, and these, even if mentioned, were never developed. The treatise was little concerned with God, but mostly with men.

To this pragmatism the success of this little book was no doubt due, for, in the seventeenth century, it was translated into Latin, Spanish, German, English, and Bohemian, and went into numerous editions in all of these countries, particularly in England, where a later Jesuit, Hawkins, spiced it to suit the taste of that country. It was this work they drew upon for Washington's education. The summary of good manners and aristocratic precepts of the Old World served as a model for the behaviour of this younger son of Virginia. It pleased them to abridge it still further, rendering even more concrete its information.

Thus, out of one hundred and ten maxims (a few of which apply to several subjects) only one mentions God, one conscience, and two kindliness, while twenty-one of them are consecrated to cleanliness and fifty-seven to politeness.

Before all else is placed the social spirit: the first maxim proclaims: 'Each action performed in society should show some sign of respect for those present.' [12]

And then George Washington was instructed in great detail as to cleanliness: 'Rule 100. — Do not clean your teeth with the table cloth, the table napkin, the fork or the knife but, if others do so, use a toothpick.' 'Rule 95. — Do not put your meat into your mouth with the knife, at hand; do not spit out the fruit-stones of tarts into the dish, and throw nothing under the table.'

Politeness was insisted upon at length: 'Rule 77. — Talk business with people at opportune moments and do not whisper in company.' 'Rule 42. — Adapt your bowings and scrapings according to the rank of him you address, for it is absurd to speak in the same fashion to a clown and to a prince.' Then followed tact and artfulness: 'Do not be a flatterer; do not play with those who do not desire that you play with them.' 'Rule 23. — When you see a crime being punished, you may feel satisfied within yourself, but always show the semblance of pity for the guilty man who is about to submit to his suffering.' These took up much more space than the virtues, although the latter are not forgotten either, especially those which procure social advantages for man, such as acts of kindliness: 'Rule 22. — Do not show pleasure in the misfortunes of others, even if they be your enemies.' 'Rule 44. — If a man does all that he can, do not blame him.' 'Rule 50. — Do not be quick to welcome unfavourable gossip about your neighbours.'

Certain other of the Christian virtues are included amongst these recommendations:

Chastity: 'Rule 7. — Do not undress in the presence of other people. And do not leave your room half naked.'

Humility: 'Rule 63. — A man should not prize himself for his successes nor for the qualities of his mind, still less for his riches, his virtue or his family.'

Benevolence: 'Rule 89. — Speak no ill of absent ones, for it is unfair.'

Respect for God, for parents, for conscience: 'Rule 108. — When you speak of God or of his attributes, let it be seriously and with reverence. Honour your natural parents and obey them even if they are poor.' 'Rule 110. — Strive to keep alive in your heart that little spark of celestial fire called Conscience.'

Thus the spiritual life was neither denied nor systematically ignored, but relegated to the background, while practical, realistic considerations came to the fore and the social instinct dominated. Rule 82 says prudently: 'Do not enter upon that which you cannot carry to a successful finish and be careful to keep your promises.' 'Rule 48. — Where you blame others, see that you yourself are without reproach, for example carries more weight than precept.' And Rule 69 teaches: 'In important matters remain on the strongest side.' — We no longer know whether we are listening to Machiavelli, Cardinal Mazarin, or the Reverend Father Suarez!

But all this was useful knowledge to a young aristocrat destined to live in a society at once feudal, narrow, hierarchic, and proud.

Washington never forgot these things.

He did not know so much that he could forget them. His spelling was barbarous, his style unformed, his manners clumsy. He had a heavy face, a heavy body, a heavy mind. And they hurried to finish his education so that he would be able to earn his living as land-surveyor and take his place with the best people of Virginia. In Fredericksburg he studied fencing with Van Braam, the Dutchman, for whom he conceived a great admiration, for Van Braam spoke several languages and was of some importance. Sergeant Woods instructed him in the art of war. He also took music lessons. And his desire to please carried him even further: when he visited the Fairfaxes at Belvoir, and later Lord Fairfax at Greenway Court, he read from the best authors in order to give form to his style or to his thoughts, but, above all, to learn to please. At sixteen, he made the discovery of the 'Spectator,' through which at the age of fourteen the young Franklin had formed his style.

His real school, however, was life. He abandoned himself to it without reticence, for he was filled with the joy and the excitement of youth. The restlessness which oppresses so many existences or sends them astray at the beginning does not seem to have burdened him. Although he displayed extraordinary physical activity, no document or tradition can show us a single instance where he was influenced by dreaming, by vain or unsettled desires, by remote aspirations. The immediate and concrete present absorbed him. From 1748 to 1751 he was continually moving about, whether to visit his family, to survey land, or to go in quest of such persons whose beautiful eyes enticed him. His centre was Fredericksburg, where he owned some property and met his young brothers, especially his favourite, John Augustine, to whom he confided his disappointments in love and his secret adventures. There was also Westover, where he went to see his brother Augustine; Mount Vernon, forty-three miles to the north and the family seat because Lawrence lived there and which in turn became the centre of George's interests because so many beautiful young women were to be found in the vicinity; Belvoir, neighbouring on Mount Vernon, where the Fairfaxes welcomed him so generously; last, Chotank, where he went to meet the true friends of his childhood, the Washington cousins, and to imbibe their advice as older and more experienced lovers.

He went backwards and forwards between each of these points as perfect brother, perfect son, perfect cousin, perfect and ingenuous lover, and always, as perfect gentleman. He would stop to rest at inns, to take a drink or to listen to the chatter of other travellers. With his brothers, cousins, friends, or protectors, he was gay, played at cards, whist or loo. He amused himself with billiards, lost or gained, but always carefully marked the amounts in his notebook. On all these occasions, he bore a serious air, which makes us realize how faithful he was to the Rules of Conduct.

Better, he endeavoured to apply them, and to improve upon them.

Although literature was not his strong point, he began to write a diary in March, 1748. He was then sixteen years and one month old. In it he meant to

set down all the beautiful sights and all the useful
information connected with a trip in Western Virginia
with his new friend, George W. Fairfax, seven years
his senior. Accompanied by several surveyors, the
two had gone to mark the boundaries and subdivide
Lord Fairfax's huge estates. George felt quite a
'grown up gentleman' in such good company and on
so important a mission. He recorded these discoveries
faithfully and with amusing solemnity, and, even today, a certain youthful fragrance emanates from
them. Three of them deserve to be related here.

He learned how he must sleep on a campaign:

Tuesday, March 15th. — [After a long day's surveying
in the rain.] We set out early with Intent to Rune round
ye sd. Land but being taken in a Rain and it Increasing
very fast obliged us to return, it clearing about one o'Clock
and our time being to Precious to Loose, we a second time
ventur'd out and Worked hard till Night and then return'd
to Pennington's. We got our supper and was lighted into
a Room and I not being so good a woodsman as ye rest of
my Company, striped myself very orderly and went into
ye Bed as they called it when to my Surprize I found it to
be nothing but a Little Straw-Matted together without
sheets or any thing else but only one thread Bear blanket
with double its weight of vermin such as Lise, Fleas, &c.
I was glad to get up (as soon as y. Light was carried from
us) I put on my Cloths and lay as my Companions. Had
we not been very tired I am sure we would not have slep'd
much that night. I made a Promise not to Sleep so from
that time forward, chusing rather to sleep in y. open Air
before a fire. [13]

This anecdote, related by himself, shows us George
ever faithful to his school-book. He courts cleanliness, he shuns filth, and he observes Rule No. 7: 'Do

not undress in the presence of other people. And do not leave your room half naked.' It also shows his ability to learn and his promptness in acquiring experience. He was sixteen; he looked at things as seriously as a man of forty, combined with the artlessness of his years.

On the 23d of March, 1748, he made another discovery, which he tells as follows:

Rained till about two o'Clock and clear'd when we were agreeably surpris'd at y. sight of thirty odd Indians coming from War with only one Scalp. We had some liquor with us of which we gave them part, it elevating their Spirits put them in y. Humour of Dauncing of whom we had a War Daunce. there manner of Dauncing is as follows viz. They clear a Large Circle and make a Great Fire in y. middle then seats themselves around it. Y. Speaker makes a grand speech telling them in what Manner they are to Daunce. after he has finished y. best Dauncer jumps up as one awaked out of a Sleep and runs and Jumps about y. Ring in a most comical Play. ye. Muzick is a Pot half (full) of Water with a Durskin Stretched over it as tight as it can and a goard with some Shott in it to Rattle and a Piece of an horses tail tied to it to make it look fine. Y. one keeps Rattling and y. other Drumming all y. while y. others is Dauncing. [14]

This spectacle was as good as a circus. It delighted the young George, but he soon had enough of it, for, the following day, he notes:

Friday, March 25th. — Nothing Remarkable on thursday but only being with y. Indians all day so shall skip it.

And finally on Monday, the 4th of April, Providence taught him still a third lesson:

This morning [he writes], Mr. Fairfax left us with Intent

to go down to ye. mouth of ye. Branch. we did two Lots and was attended by a great Company of People, men, women, and Children that attended us through ye. Woods as we went showing their I really think they seemed to be as Ignorant a Set of People as the Indians. They would never speak English but when spoken to they speak all Dutch....

So it was, in 1748, the young Virginian became acquainted with the three categories of human beings composing society: Anglo-Saxons, Indians, and *others* who are neither Anglo-Saxons nor Indians. He found the Indians comical and pleasant if there was alcohol to give them, the others merely ridiculous and not even deserving the honour of description.

As for the Anglo-Saxons... they surveyed the earth and they owned it.

There was no further need to prompt him in this particular lesson nor to repeat it. The love of the earth which had brought the white man to Virginia, which had created and established feudalism in Virginia, was as deeply rooted in George Washington as the instinct for life.

At the age of sixteen, he began to earn money.[15] In 1748, the Fairfaxes paid him a doubloon, or six pistoles a day (seven dollars or twenty-two dollars), for surveying. Even if he did not work every day, he earned quite enough. In July, 1749, through the influence of his brothers and the Fairfaxes, he was appointed official surveyor for Culpeper County at one hundred pounds sterling a year.

This money did not go for warlike concerns nor for amorous attentions nor for literary frivolities. With

the first hundred pounds sterling, George Washington
bought five hundred acres of uncultivated land in
Frederick County, and, as this money had been earned
by his surveying, he named his property 'Bullskin
Plantation,' because of the cowhide trousers he had
worn when riding.

From 1748 to 1750, George Washington rushed
from one end of Virginia to the other; he surveyed the
land and did his best to lose his heart. All his biographers have discoursed at length upon his various
amours, upon his sighs and his rebuffs, but of all this,
nothing has come down to us but vague, confused
echoes and a few love-letters with muddled dates
and names. On the other hand, his account-books —
precise and undebatable — are at our disposal to
prove to us that even while sighing, the young George
Washington never forgot to think, and that his
thoughts were precise and practical. In July, 1749,
his social position was good, and, in 1750, he purchased more land, four hundred and fifty-six acres,
from James MacCracken, for one hundred and twelve
pounds sterling; in 1752, he acquired five hundred and
fifty-two acres from Captain Johnson, next to his
Bullskin Plantation.

So, thanks to surveying and thrift, this younger son
was in a fair way of becoming a landed proprietor. At
the age of twenty, he owned fifteen hundred acres of
land in Virginia.

We must not make the mistake of judging according
to our estates today; George Washington was a very
small squire, indeed, with his fifteen hundred acres of
wild, uncultivated, unproductive land. It was at this

time that his two brothers, together with some influential friends of Virginia and important English merchants, organized the 'Ohio Company,' which obtained a concession of *half a million acres* of land in West Virginia. At least this was worth something, and Lawrence Washington, as the president of this company, was somebody.

George Washington was well brought up; he knew how a great lord should conduct himself. All the instincts for domination and ownership in him had been developed, but the power to satisfy these instincts was not yet his.

Fate was to take charge of that.

The Luck of George Washington

One after the other, each of the three children Lawrence's wife had borne him died young, leaving only a frail little girl to survive. As for himself, the illness he had brought back with him from Cartagena became aggravated by the moist climate of Virginia. When the crisp autumn days of 1751 came, Lawrence's condition became so much worse that the doctors, seized with alarm, advised him to go for a cure to the Barbadoes, well-renowned for their mild and equable climate. Ann Fairfax Washington, worn out by many pregnancies, was unable to accompany her husband on such a long and arduous crossing. George was available. His precocious solemnity, which bored the youthful, won him the sympathy of the older Virginians. Lord Fairfax treated him with familiarity, Augustine Washington received him joyfully, and Lawrence depended upon him. So George was entrusted to conduct the ill man to sun and health.[16]

Without a doubt, the healthiest man would have been made very ill by the discomforts of such a voyage. It often took more than a month for the sloops of the eighteenth century to go from Chesapeake Bay to the Barbadoes over extremely rough seas often visited by tornadoes, cyclones, or dead calms. On board the Fredericksburg, Lawrence and George Washington experienced the varied emotions of a long sea voyage. They were submitted to every possible shock; they expected to see the ship's masts crack in the wind, and, at the very last, one beautiful morning at four o'clock, when they still believed they were far from their journey's end, the pilot was amazed at the sudden apparition of the Barbadoes coast line. It was a mere chance that they did not miss it!

Lawrence felt extremely unwell, but the doctor assured him that the climate would cure him. George felt perfectly well, but the island was to become nearly the cause of his death, for they were taken in by a Massachusetts family, living in the Barbadoes, whose children had the smallpox. George did not fail to catch it. His youth and good health threw off the disease, but not without leaving livid and ugly scars on his face. Little, indeed, did he enjoy this heavenly climate nor the pretty island women (whom he found a little too slovenly to his liking) nor the exquisite, tropical produce: alligator pears, pineapples, and tangerines. He left suddenly on the twenty-second of December for Virginia, to devote himself to his brother's and his family's interests which could not be allowed to lapse any longer. He returned as his brother's representative and, under this title, went to Williamsburg to visit the new Governor, Dinwiddie, recently arrived from England and who was also interested in the Ohio Company. So, in a single stride, George Washington came in touch with the great of the earth.

Fortune seemed to waver between George and Lawrence: during February and March, 1752, George was very nearly carried off by a dangerous attack of pleurisy contracted a few days after his return.

Meanwhile, Lawrence was struggling and hoping in the Barbadoes, but, in the end, Fortune condemned him. As he was becoming more and more ill, he hurried back to his house in Mount Vernon which he had just completed and so named in order to hand down to his descendants the memory of his painful and glorious campaign with Admiral Vernon. The pitiless Virginia climate and the bad sanitary conditions of the times were enough to kill off the weakest.

Lawrence continued to struggle for several months, but, during the torrid days of July, 1752, he died of pulmonary tuberculosis.[17]

His remaining daughter followed him a few months later. And his widow hastily married again, marrying Colonel Lee.

He confirmed in his will the arrangements already made by his father: George, the younger son, as heir, to receive the property of Mount Vernon, the use of which was to go to Lawrence's widow during her lifetime. But Ann Fairfax Lee was little concerned with it: she ceded her usufruct to George for an annual income: for the value of fifteen thousand pounds of tobacco paid each year, George Washington became the proprietor and lord of Mount Vernon (£ 95 in 1755; £87 in 1756, 1757, and 1758; £81 in 1760). In 1761 the death of Ann Fairfax Lee freed the estate from all encumbrance; the family property, the seat of the Washington dynasty, was his.

CHAPTER II

THE LEGEND OF COLONEL WASHINGTON

A War of Blind Man's Buff

AT THE time that Destiny made of George Washington one of the great men of Virginia, Virginia became the centre of the world and attracted universal attention.

France and England, face to face, were watching one another. An intense commercial rivalry possessed them, an age-long national jealousy exasperated them, and the difference in their religious beliefs sharpened their antipathy. Meanwhile, the Governments knew very well that, once begun, the war would be atrocious, long, and costly, and would probably be the end of one or the other nation. Perhaps it was due to laziness that Louis XV desired peace. His ministers endorsed his policy through submission, integrity, or snobbishness. For had not the Marquis d'Argenson, his Minister for Foreign Affairs, written in 1746 that he wanted 'to make France prevail in Europe through her sense of justice and her good works'? Had he not also said that 'the King would rather be deceived than deceive'? (January 10, 1746) [1] Monsieur de Machault, the skilled financier, and Monsieur Rouillé, eager to reconstruct the French Navy, badly damaged by the late war, gave themselves to the same pacifist ideas and used all their influence to prevent conflicts.

Nor was the English Government looking for them.

King George II was attached to his Hanover; he was fearful lest a war with France would bring it to ruin or even take it from him. His Prime Minister, the Duke of Newcastle, knew that his Ministry was tottering and entertained no doubts whatever that a war would be its downfall. He wished to remain in office. Besides, he was not a leader of men; he was too whimsical to be popular. The most improbable stories were told about him. On one occasion it was reported that one winter day, when he was obliged to confer with Pitt about an important matter, he found his colleague in an icy room confined to his bed with the gout. While he was descanting, he noticed the bed which Lady Chatham had just left as he was coming in. He jumped into it, settled himself comfortably, pulled up the sheets and blankets, and thus the two statesmen continued without interruption to discuss the fate of nations from one bed to another. Such a man could only be dangerous owing to his bursts of humour and his foibles.

He allowed himself to be influenced by events and public opinion, and these it was that, step by step, led him into war. Undoubtedly the intelligentsia and the philosophers kept up friendly relationships on both sides of the Channel, but the lesser nobility, the middle classes, the Army, the Navy, and, above all, the tradesmen indulged in a profound mutual hatred. This would have led to nothing had it not been organized. But in France as in England, the very wealthy merchants concentrated upon it.

French trade, conscious that it was still weak in spite of the hasty reconstruction of the Navy, was none too assertive; it maintained, nevertheless, a threatening attitude. The commercial English upper classes which, since 1748, had witnessed a rapid rise of its French rivals, could no longer contain itself. This class, so powerful, active, and well organized, ranked just below the landed gentry and was bound to it by a thousand ties; its slightly inferior position was atoned for by its wealth and influence. There were in the English commercial upper classes an over-abundance of adventurous men, and consequently this class engaged largely in colonial enterprises in the East and the West Indies.

They embarked easily upon these bold speculations, for, besides, there was more breathing space in these still untouched territories, where every opportunity had not been exhausted beforehand, as in Europe, and where no government put stumbling-blocks at every turning. In America this class was hand-in-glove with the Virginia aristocracy, which, like itself, was greedy, ambitious, and daring.

It was these two classes which precipitated the Seven Years' War.

No one, not even the most astute, understood anything of all this.

A few years later, Voltaire wrote, 'These two nations have gone to war over a few acres of snow in Canada and, in it, they have spent a great deal more than Canada is worth.' He never ceased to be astonished that 'two civilized nations' should cut each other's throats in Europe over a few acres of snow and ice in America.

Monsieur Rouillé, the French Minister for Foreign

Affairs, agreed with Voltaire. He remarked sadly to the Duke of Mirepoix, the French Ambassador to England: 'We should hardly have imagined, sir, that anything of so little importance in itself as the present issue could have occasioned a war.' (March 17, 1755.)[2]

Everything relating to this conflict was obscure — its origin, its causes, and the conditions under which it was fought all seemed ridiculous to the general public in Europe.

How would one anticipate that the only requirement to set the two most powerful kingdoms of the world at variance was the decision of a group of English and Virginian capitalists to exploit the banks of the Ohio?

Such was the case, however, and it was precisely the precautions taken by two Crowns to avoid an outbreak that made it inevitable. The makers of the Treaty of Utrecht (1714) were most desirous of avoiding trouble, and, not seeing a way of doing so, left the frontiers of America undefined, guaranteeing to the holders — French, English, or Indian as the case may have been — the land which they already owned. The makers of the Treaty of Aix-la-Chapelle (1748), even more eager to avoid trouble and seeing even less clearly a way of doing so, left the frontiers in question in as undetermined a state as before, but, nevertheless, established an international commission of arbitration for the purpose of defining them. This commission was to sit in Paris: the commission sat, but that seems to be all that it ever did.

While it was deliberating, the Virginia colonists,

the Washingtons, Colonel Cresap, George Fairfax, Thomas Nelson, Thomas Lee, and others, in conjunction with prominent English business men, and particularly with the wealthy Hanbury family of London, agreed to ask the Board of Trade and Plantations for a grant of half a million acres on the Ohio. Most discreetly, this request was at once accorded (1749–1750). The Virginians believed they had a right to occupy this land since their Charter of 1609, granted by the English Crown, had given them a strip of territory stretching from the Atlantic to the Pacific and included this land. The English Government did not question its right to dispose of this land as it pleased, the more so as the Treaty of Utrecht had established the *status quo* for the lands lying in the centre of North America. At the time of the Treaty of Utrecht, the banks of the Ohio, the 'Beautiful River,' belonged to the Indians of the Five Nations — territory which they later ceded to England.

All of these negotiations were carried on in secret, for the new masters were afraid of arousing jealousy. The concession was to be complete and final only after seven years' occupancy, and then solely on the condition that the Company establish a hundred families and build a fort upon these lands. There was the ever-present fear that the capitalists of New York and Philadelphia might attempt to ruin their enterprise in order to take their place. Secrecy was so well maintained that little was known of the undertaking in America, almost nothing in England, and absolutely nothing on the Continent.

France heard not a word about it. The war over

(1748), relations with England had not been very actively resumed and it was generally believed that the possession of Ohio was a settled thing. For did they not own this region by 'right of discovery'? Since 1679 this land had been considered as theirs by the French; since that date the Treaty of Utrecht had guaranteed the existing *status quo* for the plains of the Ohio. Thus each side was convinced it was in the right and that its claim was incontestable.[3] Here, indeed, was a matter for a never-ending lawsuit, and that the affair would never be disentangled seemed certain. Each side reasoned logically from its diametrically opposed premises and was always bringing out contradictory facts. The two Governments understood nothing whatever of the matter and were well aware of it. French and English maps showed differences of three hundred leagues and the various French maps did not agree. Monsieur de Lisle, on his map of the Ohio basin, traced the course of one river, and upon his, Monsieur d'Anville presented two. Monsieur de Mirepoix, the French Ambassador to London who was engaged in examining into these questions, had altogether forgotten the names of the rivers to which France laid claim. 'One of them, as nearly as I can remember,' he said, 'is called the Audouche.' He meant to say Wabash! But, certainly, war was not brought about by such silly things.

The kings of the two countries involved would have been pleased enough with a diplomatic discussion, but nothing short of a fight was needed to satisfy the people. What seemed in Paris, and even in London, vague enough was very definite in the minds of the people of Williamsburg and Quebec. The English had come to the New World with the intention of finding land to exploit and they wanted a great deal of it. The French, too, feeling the need for expansion and adventure in a new country, had come to Canada, and had no intention of being frustrated. In the American wilderness, the English colonist and the French trapper stood face to face, both continuing along their chosen paths without troubling much about their respective Governments. Between 1650 and 1750, eleven Canadian brothers named Lemoyne [4] had made Louisiana French territory with practically no assistance from the Versailles Government; only after accomplishing their task did they ask for the approval of the King.

The English and Scotch farmers, when they felt cramped in their quarters, merely pushed on further into the wilderness, leaving to the King of England the privilege of shifting his troops, his frontiers and his government, if it should so please him. What they the farmers, wanted was land, and, from distant London, it was impossible to oppose them. The Government would have abandoned them had not the rich merchants of London interfered, for as capitalists they were interested. The war was indeed started by the colonists, but it was forced upon the English Government by the English merchants — especially by the Hanburys, members of the Ohio Company.

This was a war of people against other people, not one of those graceful aristocratic battles which were still the fashion in Europe, where everything which took place was according to strict and chivalrous

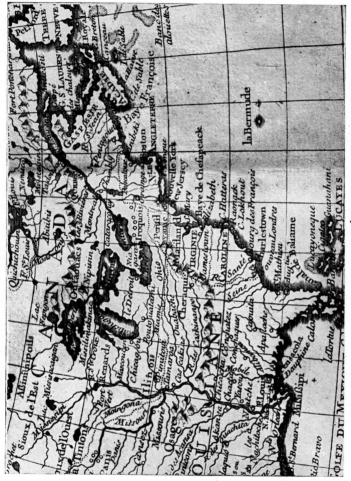

A PART OF GUILLAUME DELISLE'S MAP OF AMERICA, 1722

This was the map used by Mirepoix in his negotiations with the British Ministry

rules. But how could an obscure struggle have any connection with grace and elegance?

The battle-field was tremendous — a continent. The combatants scarcely knew it. They hadn't the time to name it. They used the vague names furnished by the Indians, a people of low intelligence, or else they invented pretty names themselves, for the scenes of action. In this way each battleground of that war bears three names, an Indian, a French, and an English one. To the Indians, Pittsburgh was 'Shannopin,' to the French 'Fort Duquesne,' and to the English 'Fort Pitt.' Often, the French knew the name of a place only by the translation into Norman-French of an Indian word, half understood, and reproducing or translating an English word, which, in its turn, had been but half understood by the Indians. This applies to the post known as 'Loyal Hanna': the French commander called it 'Royal Arni' while Washington refers to it variously as 'Loyal Hanning,' 'Royal Amnon,' and 'Royal Hannon'; and, a short time later, this spot became known as 'Fort Ligonier'! The English and the Indians also made errors in the matter of French names: in October, 1753, Washington speaks of the 'Black Islands' where the French, according to some deserters, had established forts. In reality it was *Illinois* which was referred to and was as yet unknown to him. He did not distinctly understand the word, mistaking it for 'Iles Noires' and translating it literally into 'Black Islands.' [5]

The same confusion prevailed in regard to persons as well. Washington speaks of a certain officer named 'Riparti.' There was no person of that name in the region. Doubtless he was alluding to Legardeur de Repentigny, whose name had come to him in that twisted form. Nor was it certain where or against whom the fighting took place. The vast unknown that lay between the French and English was a kind of immense barrage and the only intermediaries were the Indians. They, alas! had none too precise notions and, besides, they did not particularly care to proffer a light for the white men's lanterns. They had everything to gain by leaving the French and the English in ignorance and many times even took pleasure in fooling them.

Ever since the invasion of the white man in North America, war had become the main resource of the Indian, and the taking of scalps the most prosperous industry. Any outbreak of hostilities afforded excellent occasions for pillaging, and brought all sorts of advantages with it, both great and small. Besides the herds, the provisions, the clothing, and the weapons each expedition along the English or the French frontiers yielded, the English offered premiums for French scalps, while the same advantages were to be obtained from the French for similar services. To tell the truth, the wisest of the French commanders did not enjoy this traffic and the most astute among the English mistrusted it. An English scalp looked so much like a French scalp, and, then, the Indians were none too scrupulous! So, in 1758, we find Washington shaming the Crow,[6] an Indian brave who, having returned from an expedition, presented two scalps which he claimed were French when such was not the case at all. In order not to ruffle the Crow too much, however, a little gift was made to him.

The presence of the Indians made it impossible to keep to the ordinary rules of warfare. Here, there were no grandiloquent and formal declarations of war, no solemn treaties of peace setting down definite conditions. Here, in the forest, there was no means of knowing whether it was a time of peace or a time of war. It was always wise to carry a gun. Doubtless, at the conclusion of war the King of France notified his Indian allies that hostilities had ceased, and the King of England certainly did likewise, but, as means of communication were very uncertain, the news most probably failed to reach a tribe in course of migration. Or else the tribe was as apt as not to pay no attention to the new order. Actually, a peace bound the Indians as allies to the kings of Europe, but as allies they remained a strictly independent people (for the Indians were still this). Peace seemed to them an excellent occasion in which to settle quarrels among themselves. So, from 1750 to 1753, France's Indian allies, who had been roughly handled by the Catawbas during the last war, avenged themselves by expeditions and military operations against the latter — measures which greatly resembled war. The dividing line between war and peace in these virgin forests and prairies was ill-defined.

War, too, was carried on without any definite rules. The agreements with the Indians were made verbally over the peace pipe. Mere smoke! And the wind dissipated it all the more quickly, as, on those most important occasions, the Indians were given over to strong drink. On such occasions they became so thoroughly drunk that they had no idea what they were doing. It would have been a simple matter to persuade them to sign a treaty, but, alas! they could neither read nor write, which made the possibility of their observing a written covenant extremely uncertain. The Indians had a liking for killing and a highly developed technique in killing. And they never missed a chance to kill. Besides, they cared nothing whatever for the opinion of Europe. Under such conditions, had a European insisted upon a scrupulous observance of the rules governing the conduct of war, he surely would have paid very dearly for it. During the eighteenth century, war as conducted in the vast forests of America seemed much more like a hunt for wild beasts than a civilized struggle.

In the midst of so much confusion, the French appeared to grasp the situation better than the English. From the very beginning of the period of colonization the French were more interested in pushing forward while the English were bent upon establishing themselves. The English remained in the coast settlements where their commerce and agriculture flourished; the French, on the contrary, pushed on towards the interior, incited by the love of adventure and the hope of discovering marvels. Their missionaries and woodsmen had long since left behind them the peasants established along the banks of the rivers of the North. In order to accomplish something useful in the forests, either in pursuit of converts or the trapping of fur-bearing animals, the presence of the Indians was essential, whereas the English farmer desired nothing so much as the absence of the Indian, for he wished to cultivate his fields in peace. Thus, from the beginning the French missionary and woodsman had learned the Indian language and had studied his psychology, while the English farmer had devoted his energy to clearing the soil and perfecting his marksmanship. In 1750, the French had a goodly number of officers and traders who were acquainted with Indian customs and who were in constant and close communication with the Indian people, whereas, at the same time, the English possessed only five or six men sufficiently expert in Indian lore to be relied upon: Conrad Weiser and George Croghan who worked for Pennsylvania; Christopher Gist, agent for Virginia; Johnson, agent for New York; Glen, agent for South Carolina, and the French renegade who called himself 'Captain Montour.' These six men were employed either by the large companies or by the colonists themselves to act as intermediaries with the Indians; but, while they constituted a valuable staff, their number was too small to be really effective. Many of the set-backs of the English were due to this.

On the other hand, they were better stocked with manufactured articles and sold them cheaper than the French. Instead of French cognac, the Indians preferred English rum, which, according to them, was more efficacious. If the overwhelming superiority of numbers was to be added to this (more than 1,200,000 English as against only 65,000 Frenchmen), it would seem that the ensuing struggle might surely have been brief and its outcome certain.

Such was not the case, however. The English were divided among themselves, while, comparatively speaking, a spirit of coöperation united the French.

The English spent more time and energy quarrelling among themselves than in fighting the common enemy. Each colony had rival territorial claims encroaching upon its neighbour: Pennsylvania against Maryland, Maryland against Virginia, Virginia against Pennsylvania. Each protested loudly and appealed to London. The Governors, who were officers of the Crown and held an imperial point of view, might have arranged the matter between themselves, but the colonial assemblies refused to come to any agreement. They were chiefly engrossed in preventing the Governor, who represented either the Crown or the Proprietors, from playing too important a rôle in their affairs. This conflict between the Governor and the provincial assemblies of New York, Pennsylvania, and Virginia was very acute from 1750 to 1755. Then, discord reigned in the provincial assemblies themselves. On the one hand, the members representing the rich element of the colony were anxious not to crush the Indians, for they found in them a fruitful source of commerce, and, on the other hand, the members representing the less prosperous element of the colony were in favour of exterminating the Indians. Those speculating in lands in the West maintained that their grants from England were unquestionable and sacred; those whose interests were bound up in the East looked upon the Western expansion with disfavour and doubted the validity of royal grants. Each time that the subject of credits for providing the Indians with gifts arose, a bitter conflict ensued.

These differences in point of view made any effective military organization impossible. There were even undercurrents of hostility such as those which were inspired by the Irish Catholics (still few in number) and the Catholics from the Palatinate and the Rhine (who, since 1730, had begun to come to the colonies in great numbers). Both of these elements harboured a secret sympathy for France. Then, again, there were the Quakers, rich and influential, and opposed to any kind of strife or warlike preparation.

Such was the chaotic and divided condition of America where all was confusion and disruption, excepting only the flaming passion which possessed the Virginian aristocrat for the acquisition of more and more land. It was this flame that was destined to set two continents on fire.

GEORGE WASHINGTON'S FIRST MILITARY EXPLOITS

At first, all went well. The Ohio Company was firmly established and favourably looked upon in London; the new Governor, Dinwiddie,[7] a patriotic, crafty, energetic Scotchman, was pleased to take an interest in it. The neighbouring colonists — the Penns in particular — dared say nothing in spite of a certain prevailing jealousy. So the Company, directed by Hanbury, pursued a policy at once redoubtable and prudent, and went on its way rejoicing.

George Washington had an opportunity of seeing Dinwiddie in January, 1753, in connection with the affairs of which he had charge for his sick brother. They understood each other at once. In this tall silent young man the Governor recognized manly qualities bound to develop, and the kindness of the Governor won the confidence of the young Virginian.

After the death of Lawrence, the authorities, anxious to mark the importance of the change in the position of this young man, did not hesitate to bestow upon him the title of Adjutant-General for the Southern District of Virginia. It seemed natural enough to commission the young surveyor, inspector, and defender of this territory, for was he not well known as confidential agent of the Washingtons and the Fairfaxes whose possessions spread into the West? His family's and his friends' lands were in the north of the colony, and thanks to diplomacy and the influence of William Nelson, Washington obtained the control of the northern district in 1753.

At the same time another honour and a not less profitable one was conferred upon him. He was not yet twenty-one when the Masonic lodge of Fredericksburg initiated him Apprentice Mason. The 4th of August, 1753, he became a Master Mason.

What did it matter, we might ask? It mattered a great deal in the eighteenth century. Freemasonry in the colonies was the centre around which were grouped all the fashionable young men. After coming through a sort of crisis, the society became then firmly established. It gathered together its members to make them drink, to teach them to consolidate their commercial interests, and to promote in them a certain ideal of 'enlightenment and good-will.' It was not in direct opposition to the reformed religions, although it had already begun its campaign against Catholicism. In its tendencies and its origin, it was Anglo-Saxon.

Its fame spread the world over; in the English colonies of America, where social organization was still in a rudimentary state, it constituted the most important intercolonial network. In Virginia, Philadelphia, New York, and Boston, it attracted the most prominent persons. Numerous journalists, such as Franklin in Philadelphia, Zenger in New York, were Freemasons, and the entire press all over the colonies was under its influence. In this way, Freemasonry did much to aid and promote the young worshipful brothers.

It happened, then, that in 1752-53, George Washington won his place amongst the leaders of the Virginia dynasty, without opposition, while as a Mason he came into contact with an even more inclusive society. From that time forward, his doings greatly interested his brother Masons in the other colonies.

The moment had come, he now felt, for him to establish a family. He loved the ladies — especially pretty and young ladies. So he fixed his choice upon a neighbouring Betsy Fauntleroy [8] and carried on his lover's campaign in as lively a fashion as he could with the aid of advice from the Washington cousins at Chotank. She refused him, but he was not to be put off; he became insistent, tried to win over her parents to his cause. But the beauty no doubt was more impressed by the pocks on his face and the awkwardness of his manners than by the moral and physical force which graced the young man. She threw him over. It would be better to say that Fortune threw her over so as to give all its attention to him.

Events moved rapidly, and the Ohio Company was forced to act with precipitation for fear of losing the game. The rival capitalists in America set to work, and, in London, the influential Thomas Penn was roused to action. The Company could waste no time in constructing its fort and collecting its farmers. Unfortunately, there was an unexpected fly in the ointment; in the South, a little war was going on between the Creek Indians and the Catawbas which Carolina was not able to quell. In the North, the Six Nations and the Catawbas were exchanging blows, despite all the efforts of Virginia and the other colonies to reconcile them. Behind this barrier of tumult and bloodshed, no one any longer knew what was going on in the wilderness. Disquieting rumours, however, were circulated. The Indians were robbing and killing the English traders. In Pennsylvania, it was pretended that the emissaries from Virginia were inciting the Indians against the Pennsylvania merchants, at the same time that the press — patriotic and pro-Mason — was openly attacking the French. The latter, as a matter of fact, alarmed by all the commotion they had noticed throughout the Alleghanies and west of the English frontiers, hurried forward to define and establish their earlier claims (dating from the discovery) in the regions of the Ohio. Céloron de Blainville was ordered to reconnoitre the country (1749); the French expelled the English merchants from their trading centres near Pickavillany (1752) and, by order of the Governor, constructed a chain of forts to join up Canada with the Ohio.

As a royal Governor and as a member of the Ohio Company, Dinwiddie took fright. He realized that to keep his grant from being taken from him by other

English capitalists, the Company must act at once, take immediate possession of the territory, and establish colonies there. In order to do this he must get rid of the French without delay.

Someone would have to cross the Indian wilderness to find out just where these mysterious French outposts were. The ambassador he decided to send would at the same time spy out the land, deliver an ultimatum to the French to evacuate the territory, and find out how, if they refused to go, they could be forced away. For this delicate and dangerous mission he chose George Washington. The young man was not to be frightened. Moreover, so much of his family's interest was involved that he was certain to act with zeal.

On October 31, 1753, Major Washington set off towards the Ohio, taking with him a letter from Governor Dinwiddie which was a polite summons that the French Governor evacuate His Britannic Majesty's lands and a testimonial to Dinwiddie's ardent love of peace. Washington was accompanied by two advisers and guides, two servants and two woodsmen. He described in the following manner this historic departure marking the beginning of the Seven Years' War:

The next [day, 1st November] I arrived at Fredericksburg, and engaged Mr. Jacob Vanbraam, to be my French interpreter....[9]

This was a mistake. In the well-regulated and exceedingly judicious life of Washington can be found few blunders of this kind. While Mr. Jacob Van Braam had been his instructor and, as such, had a claim to his gratitude, he was neither very brave, a very good officer, nor was he an expert in French. And he soon proved it.

The others were better chosen: Mr. Christopher Gist was a good guide and thoroughly accustomed to the Indians' languages and habits; Barnaby Currin and John MacQuire as woodsmen, and Henry Steward and William Jenkins as servants, have left no mark in history, but they did their duty well.

The journey was interesting, successful, and, on the whole, pleasant, in spite of the snow already covering the mountains, the rain swelling the rivers, and the impassable roads.

The Indians, whom Gist had been in touch with beforehand, refused neither their friendship nor advice. So they came to terms with Tanacharisson, the Half King of the Seneca Indians (so named because his sway over his subjects was not total, the Six Nations being their sovereign); with Monakatoocha, his friend; with Shingiss, King of the Delawares, and others. George, adopting the title which his ancestor, John, had gained through killing Indians, insisted that they honour him by the name of Conocotarius, the 'Destroyer of Villages,' which inspired them with respect and sympathy towards him. And so he succeeded in weaning these people from the French. He was also lucky enough to meet six French deserters who confirmed the information the Indians had given and furnished still more — unfortunately interpreted in a topsy-turvy fashion by Mr. Van Braam, who did not know the difference between Illinois and 'Iles Noires'!

From here they went on to Venengo, arriving December 4. This was the first French post to be reached, and Captain Joncaire, the French and Indian half-breed commander, served them a good supper well supplied with wines which did away with all constraint and encouraged a discussion as frank and friendly as it was far from the point. Washington, who could stand a good deal of wine, drew out of Joncaire certain useful facts about the French forces in the West. On December 11, the party reached Fort le Bœuf, under command of Colonel Le Gardeur de Saint-Pierre.

Washington, who was politely received, wasted no time, at once delivered his message, and waited. This is how he describes these days in his diary:

The chief Officers retired to hold a Council of War; which gave me an Opportunity of taking the Dimensions of the Fort, and making what Observations I could.[10]

Thus, he was able to reproduce to perfection the plan of the fort, gather an exact idea of its buildings, its staff, its cannon; he was able to obtain information about the English woodsmen scalped in the neighbourhood, or taken prisoner and sent off to Canada. After two exceedingly full days he received a polite but negative reply from the commanding officer. Saint-Pierre declared that this territory belonged to the King his Master, and, as for the rest, he would leave it to his chiefs, to whom he was reporting Washington's message. He gave the young Virginian 'a plentiful store of Liquor, Provisions, etc.,' and then dismissed him, scheming at the same time to make the Indians stay.

The return was difficult because of the snow and the cold. As the horses could hardly endure it, Washington and Gist were forced to cover a part of the way on foot and the first day they walked about twenty miles. Washington's strong constitution served him well. The journey was made with no further incident save a royal interview, which the young Major noted down:

I went-up about three Miles to the Mouth of Yaugh-yaughane to visit Queen Aliquippa, who had expressed great Concern that we passed her in going to the Fort. I made her a Present of a Matchcoat and a Bottle of Rum; which latter was thought much the best Present of the Two.[11]

On January 16, 1754, Washington reached Williamsburg and handed the French officer's reply to Dinwiddie. He turned in his report, which was sent forthwith to London and immediately put into print there. There was a Williamsburg edition of it as well. The patriotic and pro-Masonic newspapers at the time made a great deal of the whole affair. Here is the paragraph that appeared on February 5, 1754, in the 'Philadelphia Gazette':

Extract of a Letter from a Gentleman in Virginia, *to his Friend in* Annapolis, *dated* Jan. 16. 1754.

Mr. Washington, the Ambassador sent to the Indian Country, is returned, which affords us new Conversation. It is undoubtedly affirm'd for Truth, that the French have settled and fix'd several Forts near the Ohio Tract, especially one upon French River, which Mr. Washington was at, and that proper Officers, and 500 men, are in each Fort, chiefly French and that they have 12 cannon mounted on each of them, and that great Numbers of French and Indians are close at Hand, to assist at a small Warning.

Mr. Washington was received in a polite genteel Manner, by the Commandant of the Fort, who read and answer'd our Governor's Letter, and at the same Time told Mr. Washington, that it was his Instructions from the King his Master, to keep Possession, and advance farther and fight those that should oppose them, &c. And added, that he had expected an Army to be sent for twelve Months past by the English, and that they were prepar'd for them; for he suppos'd they must knock it out, and he did not care how soon. Mr. Washington is gone to Williamsburgh, and 'tis suppos'd the Assembly will meet immediately, and that Men will be raised, &c.[12]

We can measure how much the press exaggerated this news when we remember that Washington had found only two French forts, each occupied by one hundred and fifty men at the most, and that all his conversations with Joncaire and Saint-Pierre had been peaceful, hearty, and good-humoured. At all events, this press account gave the impression it was intended to give. He was ready to fight; the Ohio Company had made up its mind to this, and in the publication of the report of the mission America and England took fire. This mission and its results immediately decided Virginia to make a move against the French and to engage in a private war, while, under the influence of the great merchants (Hanbury in particular), the English Minister began to take energetic measures. France and England now stood face to face.

The first mission of Major Washington was not unsuccessful.

It was no longer a laughing matter. The Assembly

ceased quarrelling with the Governor and voted the
necessary credits. The Ohio Company decided to
build a fort. Washington was promoted to the rank of
colonel as a reward for his services and put in command of a party sent to construct the fort on the Ohio.
They hoped by acting quickly to gain an advantage
over the French.

So Washington, on April 2, 1754, departed in haste
with two companies of infantry, one hundred and
twenty men in all, commanded by Captain Peter Hog
and Lieutenant Jacob Van Braam, five non-commis-
sioned officers, two sergeants, six corporals, one drum-
mer, one surgeon, and one Swedish volunteer. Two
wagons, in charge of a lieutenant, a sergeant, a corpo-
ral, and twenty-five soldiers, followed. The little
army plunged into the wilderness. It advanced but
slowly, for roadways had to be cut for the wagons, and
sometimes their advance was no more than two miles
by the time the sun had set. The cutting of trees, the
levelling of roads, the building of bridges exhausted
the men, who performed these tasks with bad grace.
The officers, dissatisfied with their pay, thought only
of returning and did their best to annoy Washington.
The young commander became bothered and wrote
letter after letter to the Governor, from the depths of
the forest, saying that his dignity as a gentleman
would not permit him to serve much longer for such
small pay.

Bad news poured in from everywhere. The Indians
began to disappear, including the Half King. The
French had surprised the Virginians, who were building the fort at the fork of the Ohio River, had made

them capitulate, and now, on the same site, they were engaged upon the construction of an even larger fort. Some Indians brought news of a garrison of six hundred Frenchmen; others spoke of eight hundred; and all agreed that very soon eighteen hundred Frenchmen were to be stationed there. Tales of a sudden descent of the Ottawas and the Chickasaws, allies of the French, were circulated. French scouts scoured the country; their agents outbid their rivals whenever the Indians hesitated. The English trappers began to retreat in panic. Overcome with fright, Washington's soldiers deserted. Washington himself was worn out repeating his demands to the Governors of Virginia, Maryland, and Pennyslvania for help which should have been forthcoming. He begged for Indian auxiliaries, blankets, provisions, and rum. To make any use of the Indians who had come to him, Washington found himself obliged to buy the rum from his own purse.

However, he continued to advance and at last reached Great Meadows, in the neighbourhood of the French, where he pitched camp. From here he observed the enemy. The Half King and his followers joined the camp. A bit of rum, the hope of booty and of a few scalps steadied their wavering fidelity. The Indians between the French and English were like a thick, ever-shifting veil, always about to be torn asunder, yet ever there, and behind which French and English groped in the dark. It was always impossible to foretell who would be betrayed by the Indians: the French or the English, the allies or the enemies.

On this occasion, the French were betrayed. A

small body of French troops advanced along the river-
bank, slowly and awkwardly. They had the ill-luck
to fall upon the Half King and his followers, and were
clumsy enough not to know either how to intimidate
them or win them over. The Indians fell back upon
Washington's camp and warned him that the French
were at hand. So, in spite of the darkness of the night
and a heavy downpour, Washington set out at ten
o'clock. He was accompanied by forty men and later
joined by about ten Indians, who led the way to the
French camp. Tanacharisson and Monakatoocha
were among his Indians. A common plan of action
was not readily agreed upon. The Indians, however,
were entirely willing to allow the English to attack the
enemy on their right and gave them the privilege of
leading the assault. They reserved for themselves the
left, and the glorious finish, if necessary. And so it
happened that at the break of day on May 28, 1754,
Colonel Washington fell upon Captain de Jumonville
and his detachment of thirty-two men. Captain de
Jumonville had come to this region in the name of the
King of France to order the English off His Most
Christian Majesty's lands. Captain de Jumonville
and his followers were still asleep, but were awakened
by the sudden discharge of rifles. While some hastily
reached for their guns, others as hastily seized the important papers which were their credentials as agents
of the King of France. The English fired two volleys,
then stopped, as was the custom. After the firing had
ceased, Jumonville, wishing to make use of the momen-
tary cessation of hostilities, stood up in the midst to
read his paper aloud. The English at once interrupted

his recitation by discharging their guns directly into
his face and he dropped to the ground, dead.[13]   A
skirmish then ensued. The French answered the shots
of the English, killing one of their officers and wound-
ing several men. Had not the Indians interfered and
surprised them in their rear, they might have continued longer. While the white men were attacking each
other so gallantly, the Indians engaged themselves in
finishing off the victims and torturing the wounded
with their tomahawks. Realizing that they were lost,
the little company of French surrendered. Ten of
them, including their commander, lay dead on the
ground, and one man was dangerously wounded. Another, Ensign Monceau, and he alone succeeded in es-
caping, made his way, barefooted, through the forest
and reached Fort Duquesne, the French base of operations. The twenty-one survivors, after surrendering,
protested against the violation of the diplomatic
character of their mission and demanded their immediate release.

Washington was far too proud of his victory to think
of doing any such thing. He denied the diplomatic
character of their emissary. Why, then, had they hidden? Why, then, were there thirty-two of them? Why
had they been out spying for several days? In truth,
they were spies; nothing more. When they showed
him the summons which was drawn up according to
rule, he only grew the angrier and said: 'The summons is so insolent and savours so much of gascoigny,
that if two men only had come openly to deliver it, it
was too great indulgence to have sent them back.' [14]
The only terms he would grant the prisoners were

to return them to their homes without doing them harm. He then notified Dinwiddie, his family, and his friends of his first battle. Washington was greatly excited. 'If the whole Detachment of the French,' he said, 'behave with no more Resolution than this chosen Party did, I flatter myself that we shall have no g't trouble in driving them to the d — Montreal.'

And, for the benefit of his brother he added: 'I heard the bullets whistle, and, believe me, there is something charming in the sound.'

He was certain of his glory. But he was mistaken. While the news of this lucky encounter filled the English colonies with joy, it seemed nothing short of an atrocity to the French in Canada. To kill an emissary without so much as listening to him was a thing that did not happen in civilized war. People talked about the 'Jumonville murder.'

Washington affirmed that Jumonville could not be regarded as an official emissary. He was a spy. His instructions had been to watch and spy upon all Washington's movements; his summons was the merest insolence; he was accompanied by far too many soldiers for a mission of that character; his men moved about with all the caution of enemies, a thing not usual with diplomatic missions. All this was true.

The French said that Jumonville was the bearer of a diplomatic summons in legal form; that he was attacked by surprise; that the English did not listen to what he tried to tell them; further, that all this occurred during a time of peace, before any bloody military operation had begun. All this was true like-wise.

Had Washington killed Jumonville in Europe, he would have been dishonoured, punished by his supe-riors, and shamed by public opinion. But this hap-pened in America, in the heart of virgin forest.

Jumonville was the bearer of a summons neither more ridiculous nor more insolent than that given by Washington to the French six months before; Jumon-ville indulged in a little spying at the same time, ex-actly as Washington had done six months before; Jumonville was accompanied by a strong escort of Frenchmen in crossing the woods, precisely as Wash-ington had been accompanied by a detachment of English and savages when he had gone on his mission to Fort le Bœuf six months before. Jumonville had hoped to be treated with the same respect as Wash-ington had received.

However, Washington, having delivered his sum-mons, considered that the period of negotiations was past. The French (without shedding any blood, it is true) thereupon expelled the English from the fork of the Ohio and this, he considered, was the beginning of hostilities. Another thing, he did not know French, and Van Braam understood it too little to determine what Jumonville was trying to say. He knew that in the shadows of the woodland and the unspeakable confusion of Indian warfare, he who was caught off his guard was lost and that the winner of the first vic-tory would have the greater influence over the Indi-ans. He acted, therefore, as a good patriot. He obeyed the laws of the forest rather than the rules of

European warfare. He was a gentleman from Virginia and not a regular officer. He had done his duty to his colony, his class, and the Ohio Company.

The Trials of Colonel Washington

Continue he must. A victory such as his would have had no meaning unless practical advantages were to follow in its wake: helping to rally the Indians to the English cause and entrenching themselves strongly along the Ohio by means of a fort and a good road. Washington at once began to make use of his success.[15]

The Indians, those faithful devotees of victory, began to swarm into his camp. The Half King Tanacharisson and Queen Aliquippa were amongst the first to arrive, and thirty families accompanied them (June 1). Aliquippa had not forgotten the taste of good rum given her by the handsome soldier. Monakatoocha did his best to bring other families. Decorated with the scalps of four Frenchmen, he explained to the Six Nations and the Wyandots that England was great and good and that the hour had come to show their zeal in her cause. There was at once an exchange of necklaces, belts and strings of wampum — the traditional symbols of friendship. Councils of war took place; that is to say, much rum was consumed and there was a free flow of compliments. Reënforcements began to arrive. Gist, then Montour, came into camp followed by a company from Carolina. The trail began to be clear and the fort to take on form. Washington felt himself a leader.

But alas! there was scarcely time for rejoicing, for

COLONEL GEORGE WASHINGTON
By Charles Willson Peale, 1772

difficulties immediately began to present themselves. To entice the Indians to the camp was indeed a good move; but after that they had to be supplied with food and rum. Washington was no longer in a position to do this. The Great Council which took place in his camp from the 18th to the 21st of June and brought together the Half King, Shingiss, chief of the Delawares, representatives from the Mingos, the Six Nations and the Shawanees, had no other result than to exhaust the supply of provisions. He tried in vain to persuade them to move into the interior of Virginia and place themselves under the Governor's protection. The Indians had not the slightest desire to become hostages nor to withdraw from this field of battle where they could always hope for plunder in raids and also have the pleasure of taking some scalps. They declined to go.

Washington had no less trouble with his American collaborators. Though expected, the promised reënforcements did not arrive. God willing, they did come from North Carolina, these same volunteers, and although willing enough to fight, refused to take part in the work on the road and on the fort except for special pay: a shilling a day. The Virginians, forced by Washington to do manual labour for the ordinary pay, felt disgraced and jealous. Moreover, the men from Carolina were commanded by Captain Mackay whom, because of his King's commission, Dinwiddie had begged Washington to treat with the greatest respect. In the heart of the forest, when you are surrounded by enemies and Indians, respect can become a most annoying thing! It is useful, also, to know who

is doing the commanding: Mackay never for a moment doubted that the colonial greenhorn, Washington, would be unable to command *him*, and *Colonel*
Washington refused to admit that *Captain* Mackay
might give him orders.

Meanwhile, the French had received reënforcements. Jumonville's death had surprised, infuriated,
and instructed them, so they made up their minds to
get even as cleverly as possible. They lay in wait for
Washington, who, to follow his plan, had advanced
with a small body of men and was more and more isolated, badly provisioned, and surrounded by spies.
The Delawares and the Shawanees had deserted him.
The Senecas actually declared themselves hurt by
his severity and were making up to the French, telling
them extravagant tales of Jumonville's death to incite
them against Washington.

The young Colonel saw the danger. He retreated
quickly to his base, Fort Necessity, which he had established at Great Meadows. There he arrived on
July 1 with his weary and discontented troops who
had broken no bread for eight days. His Indians too
had deserted him, having decided that there was neither food nor advantage to be gained with Washington. Almost no provisions existed in the camp and the
entrenchments were miserable. There in the middle of
a clearing the forest surrounded them on all sides —
that forest, so doleful and hostile during those rainy
summer days. He was accompanied only by his Virginia regiment, about three hundred dissatisfied and
badly disciplined men, and by the Carolina Company
of one hundred men who were thoroughly exasperated

with him. But he awaited the New York troops; the knowledge that they were on the march to join him kept up his hopes.

During the night of the 2d–3d of July, 1754, the French, having been well posted by their Indians, crept stealthily around the English fort. Coulon de Villiers, Jumonville's brother, was the head of a detachment of five hundred French soldiers. He wanted to avenge his brother's death and counted upon complete success. Nor did he fail to take every precaution: he brought with him a great crowd of Indians, who stripped themselves naked to fight the better; from the black depths of the wilderness all the savages flocked to join his band; his advance was slow during the night and the following morning, but when Fort Necessity came into view shortly before eleven o'clock, his Indians were in perfect form and their numbers assured him of success.

They began to fire from a distance on the Virginia troops, then ranged in fighting order in front of their fort. The French and the Indians, however, were pleased to fire as they approached slowly, never leaving the shelter of the woods which protected them from the enemy's bullets and the torrential rain. Washington, realizing that he would never be able to keep up his fight in the open, ordered his men into camp, where they lay on their bellies in the mud under a heavy downpour, replying as well as they could to the French fire. This went on from eleven in the morning until eight at night, and, by this time, it became evident that the English were lost. Their reënforcements had not arrived. Blockaded by the French

with their Indian allies, cornered in this clearing, surrounded on all sides by the forest, devoid of every
means of transport, since their horses and cattle had
been the first and easiest targets for the French, there
was nothing left for them but death. To prepare for
it and to console themselves for having nothing to eat,
the English soldiers swallowed all the liquor they
could get hold of and many of them were drunk; they
were all the less able to fight, for most of the guns were
in bad condition: the rain had made them useless.
And to cap the climax, the presence of twelve dead
and forty-three wounded completed the discourage-
ment of the living.

Under these conditions they were amazed and delighted to have the French offer them an honourable
capitulation. Could it be possible that their enemies
were letting their prey go off so easily?

Coulon de Villiers had accomplished his mission
with thoroughness and adroitness. The King of
France did not want war, but diplomatic successes; he
would have preferred to receive news of a capitulation
rather than the announcement of a massacre. The
Governor of Canada wanted to expel the English
from Ohio and establish the authority of the French.
Therefore, to this manœuvre had to be given the
semblance of a police raid. It was Villiers's plan to
accomplish this and at the same time to give the
Indians striking proof of the power and magnanimity
of His Most Christian Majesty. And, above all, he
wanted to present the French Government with irre-
futable evidence of the unlawful intrusion of the
English in America, their unfairness and their violence.

The capitulation of Fort Necessity would serve to stress these points. So, with great care, Villiers drew up a paper and very politely submitted it to the English.

Under the continuously falling rain, with the twilight gradually closing in upon them, amongst their soldiers stupefied with rum and weariness, the little group of English officers held council by the flickering light of a candle. Washington appealed to his schoolmaster and friend, Van Braam. The Dutchman was very wet, very nervous, his French had never been good, his English was not much better. He deciphered it as best he could. But all his wishes as well as his efforts tended more towards conciliation than towards a clear interpretation. Washington had no control over him. The paper was plain, brief, apparently; the French officer's tone very agreeable, Van Braam very hasty. He asked that a few details be changed and they signed.

On the morning of July 4, 1754, a French detachment took possession of the fort, while the English troops, with their wounded and the heavy burden of their baggage, filed out before the French. From the forest came new sounds; an Indian contingent, attracted by the blood and victory, was coming up to reënforce the French. A little more trouble occurred, as the Indians were eager for plunder and scalps. The English quickened their pace and left behind them their ten cannons, a big flag, their dead, and the rum intended to placate the Indians. The well-satisfied Villiers had the barrels of rum ripped open, not wanting to see such a perfect and comfortable victory spoiled by a scandal. He had the cannons destroyed and picked up the flag, which he sent to his commanding officer along with the precious capitulation.

And this was truly a work of art!

Nothing possible could be more courteous than the preamble: 'As our intentions have never been to trouble the peace and good harmony subsisting between the two Princes in amity, but only to revenge the assassination committed on one of our officers, bearer of a summons...'[16] Nor could anything be more terrible for the English claims and for Washington: in a few words they recognized the sovereignty of the King of France over the region; they admitted having murdered Jumonville; in short, having been the first to begin warlike measures in America. And this was signed: 'Mackay, Washington, Coulon de Villiers.'

Washington returned to Williamsburg, saddened but not discouraged by his defeat and proud of having obtained the honours of war after such a defeat.

Suddenly, like wildfire, the terms of the capitulation spread throughout the length and breadth of the country. It was jabbered about in the taverns, the inns, the assemblies. Washington felt that he had lost all dignity or else that they were trying to lose it for him!

In Philadelphia, New York, and Boston the Virginians became a general laughing-stock. In September, having obtained the text, the Dutch gazettes were surprised and shocked at it. The King of France used it as a pretext to approach the King of England with the object of obtaining the evacuation of Ohio and the punishment of Jumonville's murderer. 'The murder reported by the official news is an insult to the rights, most sacred amongst civilized nations,' said M. Rouillé, French Minister for Foreign Affairs, to Boutet, French Chargé d'Affaires in London, and, in January, 1755, Robinson, Minister for the Colonies in England, promised the French Ambassador, Mirepoix, 'that such an act should not remain unpunished, and that no matter how difficult it would be to throw light on these problems, owing to the great distance and the conflicting reports made to the two Courts, His Britannic Majesty would exert himself to the utmost to discover and punish the guilty parties.' [17]

Disgraced in Canada and in France, jeered at in America, suspected in England, Washington became the centre of a whirlwind. Many blamed him for placing England in a ridiculous and unfavourable position, whereas the fact of the matter was that he had rendered more service to England than he dreamed of: he had shaken her out of her apathy. While the French were satisfied with the results and, to a certain extent, looked upon the matter as closed, the enraged Americans were preparing for action. The alarmed Anglo-American merchants brought pressure to bear on their Government and with all speed, on Thursday, September 26, the King's Council met in Kensington Palace and decided to take extraordinary measures and to send troops immediately to Virginia. These troops were to help the colonies, incapable of standing alone.

They were steering straight into the war, both un-wished for by the Newcastle Government and feared by the French Government. But what could be done? Neither Newcastle nor Robinson understood any-thing, and the only fact which seemed clear and de-cisive was the determination of the big Anglo-Ameri-can merchants to keep Ohio. They had stirred up public opinion. The Government followed.

The Government, however, was quite willing to negotiate with France. But these negotiations were as tangled as a jungle. How come to an agreement? Everybody was fooling himself and fooling his neigh-bour. The Indians had fooled Contrecœur, the com-mander of Fort Duquesne, by telling him that Wash-ington had come to terms with Jumonville before killing him; Contrecœur had fooled the Canadian Governor by delivering the same report to him. Con-trecœur had doubly fooled his Government by send-ing it despatches containing this statement, and add-ing that it took place 'on the King's dominions, along the Ohio River where England had never had a settle-ment, nor claims.' Thus fooled by its agents and its own ignorance, the French Government fooled its Ambassador at London, Mirepoix, by leading him to believe that the English and French claims in the legitimate possession of Ohio could be easily recon-ciled. Again, Washington fooled Dinwiddie when he told him that Jumonville resembled in no way a plenipotentiary; Dinwiddie transmitted this error to his Government, which was pleased just as he had been pleased with the false idea that its title to Ohio was indisputable. The English Ministry also fooled the colonies of Pennsylvania and of Maryland and the French Government in keeping secret the concession made to the Ohio Company. And by the reluctance they felt at accepting the idea of war, when their respective peoples were all ready to join up, the two Governments fooled themselves, and each other.

Before the eyes of millions of French and of many neutral persons, Washington passed as a traitor and a coward. Nothing could have been more unjust. But even so, he was tricked by the Indians and carried away by his desire for fame; he may have attacked the French too hastily on the 28th of May; it may have been wrong to choose Van Braam and confide in him, or to sign a compromising paper without verifying it closely. These are all facts. We might even reproach him for having proved stiff and awkward in his dealings with the Indians, with Mackay and with the men from Carolina during the month of June preceding the battle of Great Meadows. And then, it seems that if he had taken the trouble to cut a larger clearing around his camp, Fort Necessity, he would have been in a better position to fight.

He was only a colonel of twenty-two, lost among undisciplined troops, surrounded by officers with little conscience and little experience; his only scouts were dishonest and cowardly Indians, his enemies the French, whose language, characteristics, and manner of fighting he knew nothing about. We can only feel astonished, not at his failure in his first campaign, but that he did not lose his life with his honour.

Quite the contrary; he was very much alive and his

name, blown about on an ill wind, was known the entire world over. The reputation which he seems not to have been able to attain through some brilliant action followed unresistingly upon his misfortunes.

Yet everyone did not go back on him. The English colonies in America believed him to be right, for they knew far better the difficulties of Indian warfare and the lack of value of such papers! His brother-Masons, who were printers and publishers of gazettes, particularly Benjamin Franklin, were the first to defend him. In August in Philadelphia, then in September in Boston, they published an account of the battle sent them by Lieutenant Stephens, to which he had added this preamble:

Sir, As the Articles of Capitulation mentioned in your Philadelphia News Papers, are censur'd, and thereby seem to reflect Dishonor on Col. Washington, who is a brave and worthy young Gentleman, able to answer any thing that can be expected from one of his Age and Experience, as well as on all the Corps then present, I have given you an Account of the Circumstances we were in about the Time of the Engagement.... [18]

Nor did his own class abandon him. In August, the Assembly (where the big planters held sway) gave him and his troops a vote of thanks 'for their bravery and gallant defence of their country.' They were presented with a reward of one pistole per head. Only Trent, the Regimental Major, and Van Braam were left out, the one because of his cowardice, the other because of his mistakes in French.

And last the Governor defended him to the British Government. He even did more: to punish the French for their treachery, he refused to abide by the text of the capitulation; he detained the prisoners taken at Great Meadows and, without further delay, sent the Virginia soldiers to the frontier with the young Colonel at their head.

But the wary Governor did not care to compromise himself by showering too many favours on the defeated Colonel. After having ordered him to pull his regiment together, complete it with three hundred men, and march on Fort Duquesne, he failed to furnish him with the means necessary to carry out this dangerous task. During the autumn he decided to replace the two phantom regiments by ten companies of one hundred men each, fully equipped, each company to be commanded by a captain. The ten captains were to be equal in rank — no colonels, no majors, no quarrels over precedence, and, when the English troops should arrive, no doubt as to who would be in command. The Governor sighed with relief.

Colonel Washington could not see things in this way. He was a good patriot and a good soldier, as brave as his sword and in love with fighting; he had given up an entire year of his life to his colony, he had risked death and had lost his baggage, he had borne up under bad weather and a thousand insults, but he was a gentleman and could not submit to such humiliation. Rather than bow down and accept so humble a fate he preferred to retire and lose the opportunity of having his revenge. He sent in his resignation (the end of October, 1754).

Nothing could make him change his mind — neither Dinwiddie's letters, nor the entreaties of

Colonel Fitzhugh, who, in the name of Governor
Sharpe of Maryland (the new commander of the
royal forces in America), offered him an arrangement
whereby he would have retained his commission as
colonel, relinquishing, however, his pay and his command. Washington's reply was not without a touch
of insolence:

This idea has filled me with surprise; for, if you think
me capable of holding a commission, that has neither rank
nor emolument annexed to it, you must entertain a very
contemptible opinion of my weakness, and believe me to
be more empty than the commission itself.[19]

His vanity as a gentleman of Virginia had been
sharpened by his sufferings and insults. Furthermore,
he was tired and ill after the hardships of war. He
needed rest; he must make up his accounts, devote
himself to Mount Vernon and his future. He reflected upon marriage as a consolation for his defeat,
and of the great love he bore towards Mrs. Fairfax
— his friend's wife — who was forbidden him. Indeed, in the exaltation of war and suffering, this
sentiment had become all the stronger and had added
to his misery. He passed a gloomy winter between
Williamsburg, where he stayed for some time, and
Fredericksburg, where he paid a visit to his complain-
ing mother and to his brother, John Augustine, the
confidant of his love-affairs. He went to Belvoir only
to find sweet anguish again. To distract his mind, he
busied himself with practical matters, sold the land
he still owned at Fredericksburg, found some solace
playing at cards or billiards and drinking a bowl of
punch from time to time.

But all this was very drab for a young man thirsting for love, and who had only tasted war.

In March, 1755, he received a new invitation to take up war as a profession.

General Braddock had landed on American soil on February 20, having been sent from Gibraltar by the English Government which was anxious to see the last of the troublesome and impertinent little war being so awkwardly conducted by its colonies. The English Minister still wanted peace. He would have liked to come to terms with the King of France — after having occupied the territories he claimed. In this way the merchants would be perfectly happy and the peace of Europe undisturbed.

Braddock was a good general with a brilliant career behind him; he had a precise mind, a sense of discipline, rough good nature, and a great deal of courage. The Americans were very favourably impressed by his appointment. At last they were to have a real war with a real chief! And they were delighted most of all by the thought that England would pay for it. Tradesmen, farmers, landowners, felt in duty bound to profit by it.

Braddock was dumbfounded by their welcome; and in spite of his good temper, he was angry. He seemed to be surrounded by snares. He could procure neither horses, wagons, nor guides except for gold, and then he had to beg for them. Colonel St. Clair, in whom he was imprudent enough to confide, made arrangements for him to reach his destination by way of Maryland, although this was a far longer way — but the Colonel had interests in Maryland.

So Braddock invited Washington to join up with
him, promising him a place as aide-de-camp, without
pay and without command, to tell the truth, but with
no expenses and with the privilege of giving orders to
everybody. He had set his heart upon this young
man, whom he took to be naïve but, at least, honest
and courageous. Washington accepted in spite of
his mother's disapprobation and his brother's misgiv-
ings. The straightforwardness of the Virginian pleased
the Englishman. The young Colonel, who knew the
wilderness by heart, had the right to speak freely
with the old General who had never penetrated into
it, and soon Washington was entirely at home with
the staff — 'the General's family,' as they called it.

As bad luck would have it, he was not well. The
rough life he had led since 1748 and the terrible campaign of 1754 had weakened his health. He dragged
along with fever, needing medical care. But no one
was there to give it him. All was complicated, difficult, uncertain. One after the other his horses fell
lame. He dragged along until the 23d of June, but
was then obliged to give in to Braddock's entreaties.
In consideration of a promise from the General, who
pledged himself to send for him before the attack on
Fort Duquesne, Washington consented to follow the
advancing army at a distance, to rest, and to over-
take it again by short stages in a wagon.[20]

He was filled with hope. On the 14th of May, he
wrote to John Augustine:

As to any danger from the enemy, I look upon it as
trifling, for I believe the French will be obliged to exert
their utmost force to repel the attacks to the northward,

where Governour Shirley and others, with a body of 8000 men, will annoy their settlements, and attempt their forts.[21]

As a matter of fact there was talk of French reën-forcements near at hand, but Washington hoped that they themselves would get there first. On the 15th of June at the council of war, called by Braddock at Little Meadows, Washington urged with all his might that they push forward quickly and fearlessly. He succeeded in convincing his fellow officers and they prevailed upon the General.

I urged it, in the warmest terms I was able [he wrote], to push forward, if we even did it with a small but chosen band, with such artillery and light stores as were absolutely necessary.... As one reason to support this opinion, I urged, that, if we could credit our intelligence the French were weak at the Forks at present, but hourly expected reinforcements, which, to my certain knowledge, could not arrive with provisions, or any supplies during the continuance of the drought....[22]

So the council of war disregarded Braddock's fears and, encouraged by Washington, decided to push forward.

Their heavy baggage, the less good troops and the women, they left behind with Colonel Dunbar. The best soldiers (twelve hundred men) set out in haste across the forest, taking with them the best horses and a number of pieces of light artillery.

They could never hurry enough to please the impetuous Colonel, ill on the floor of his wagon and impatient to take Fort Duquesne and his revenge, after which he would return to his pretty ladies again.

The pace was much too quick to please the English soldiers; though excellent fighters in Europe, these regular troops were quite unprepared for this new calling that had been forced upon them. Besides, the burning summer heat and the drought were almost unbearable. To advance, trees had to be cut, bridges built, even the roadway laid. Not a living being in sight except a few Indians, always to be feared, for the English had been deserted by almost all the friendly savages. Not even any way of stopping to do the cooking. Oppressed by the mystery and hostility of the forest, led by a general who had not much assurance and encouraged by colonial troops, who inspired neither confidence nor sympathy, the English troops marched forward, always more and more sullenly.

At last, on the 8th of July, 1755, they came within ten miles of Fort Duquesne. They were told by their patrol that the French were already trembling. Colonel Washington was ill; his teeth chattered with fever, but he burned with hope, and came up to join his General.

Suddenly, while they were finishing their lunch, the woods came to life. The English vanguard had fallen upon a column of French and Indians coming out to meet them. A fusillade followed, the French Indians and the Canadians took flight, the French regulars dispersed into the wood. Were the English already victorious? The officers who had run forward, their napkins still tied around their necks, believed so. They were wrong, however. This first defeat saved the French just as this first victory defeated the English. Scattered through the woods, the French

soldiers were rallied by their officers, who then proved
reckless courage. They returned to the skirmish in
dispersed order, hiding behind trees; all the while, the
English, in full view on their road, were easy marks.
The Indians, by now encouraged, rallied to the French
one by one and, clambering to the top of a neighbouring hill, they fired on the English, howling. As they
moved about in the dim light, their dark, naked
bodies resembled demons. The English regulars and
the young recruits from Virginia had never before
seen such a spectacle nor heard such music. So worn
out, depressed, enervated were they that they lost
their heads. They crowded together ten or twelve
ranks deep, one on top of another, reassured by their
proximity, which, however, was the cause of their
downfall. They then began to fire volleys into the
forest, at random, and wildly in any direction. These
never reached the enemies, who were scattered and
safely hidden behind the trees; they succeeded only
in killing their own chiefs and comrades. Braddock
and his officers repeatedly tried to assemble them, to
get them into formation, to make them advance or retire, but in vain. The regulars would listen to nothing.
Reprovals, threats and blows from the flat of the
sword had no effect. A column of Virginia trappers
who had tried to manœuvre against the French in the
forest were caught between these wild volleys and the
well-directed fire of the enemy. One after the other
they fell. The guides, the drivers of the horses and
wagons, all fled, sowing panic, and were soon followed
by the regulars. Braddock had received a death-
wound; Washington, after having had three horses

killed under him, continued to fight on, while those of the officers who still had legs to carry them, ran away.

On the ground lay more than three hundred of their dead, their cannon, all their horses, all their flags and stacks of weapons.

The panic had not died down even by the time they reached the camp of Little Meadows, where the fugitives discovered Dunbar and his men. In spite of the exhortations of Washington, and even though the French were no longer pursuing them, they all fled. Dunbar joined in the retreat — a horrible retreat, with three hundred wounded in its train.

Three hundred men made up the attacking force and thirteen hundred the conquered army. Braddock died of his wounds. Beaujeu, the French chief, had been killed at the beginning of the action, but the command was taken over by an excellent officer, Dumas, who was responsible for the victory.

Braddock was right when he showed hesitation in plunging into the forest. His army was not well prepared, was not a unit, was not used to this kind of fighting. He paid with his life for his mistakes. He paid with his honour as well, for throughout the colonies the people all called him 'the stupid, blundering Braddock.' All the sins of Israel were heaped upon his head! The Pennsylvanians were enraged at having lost their soldiers and wagons, the English at having had such bad leadership, such bad support, and such a badly managed battle. Everybody was discouraged, annoyed, humiliated. Dunbar, who took over the command, decided to retreat as far as Philadelphia, leaving all the western frontiers at the mercy of the French and the Indians.

On July 14, 1755, the order to return immediately was sent from Versailles to the Duke of Mirepoix, the French Ambassador at London. War had come.

The French Government refused to countenance the armed attack and the seizure by the English fleet of two French war vessels [23] intended to carry reën-forcements to Canada. Newcastle might well repeat to Mirepoix: 'I assure you, we do not want war, but our colonies are shouting so loudly that they have stirred up public opinion here and the big Anglo-American merchants are forcing us to action; give us Acadia and Ohio and all will be well.' Mirepoix shook his head. The King of France could no more betray his Cana-dians than the King of England could abandon his Virginians.

The astonished universe had its eyes fastened upon Virginia where this new war had been conceived. Everybody talked about Colonel Washington, who had been the first to pull the trigger. Every news-paper in the universe quoted his name. In France he became the synonym for treachery. Thomas, the poet, published in 1759 a long patriotic poem entitled 'Jumonville,' to recall that terrible outrage. He said in the preface: 'The assassination of Jumonville is a perfidious monument which should anger all centuries to come.' All the French historians took up the theme. In England public opinion waxed vehement in con-nection with this drama, and, in August, 1754, the 'London Magazine' published George Washington's letter to his brother in which he gave an account of the fight and lauded the music of the bullets. The King shrugged his shoulders, saying: 'He would not say so if he had been used to hear many.' [24] Fashionable folk poked fun at the young hero, and in the workshops their jokes were repeated. The Government finally engaged in the war, but not without being considerably exasperated with the colonies which had begun it so hastily and clumsily. People enjoyed stories at the expense of the colonies. And no one had the least confidence in them. During the winter (1755–56), the English Minister was greatly disturbed by mysterious letters, which came from America to the French Ambassador in London; he intercepted them. Traitors, with accomplices in America and Ireland, were proposing to organize a mutiny in the American colonies. The centre of the plot seemed to be somewhere in Pennsylvania or Virginia. These missives were issued by an American commissioned officer, holding a command sufficiently important for him to have an aide-de-camp. This officer was in intimate communication with the Cherokee Indians. He boasted of being able to lure them, as well as his contingent of troops, away from the English cause. This was an act of high treason and was of the utmost danger.

Suspicion fell upon many American officers: Lydius, George Croghan, Washington's name, were mentioned. Had not his behaviour been unrestrained and troublesome for two years? When General the Earl of Loudoun, sent in the name of the King of England to organize the defence of America, reached

Miniatures of the French and Indian War

These little prints are from a curious series of miniature prints entitled 'French and Indian War. A short History in Miniatures of the Origin and Progress of the late War from its Commencement to the Exchange of the Ratification of Peace between Great Britain, France and Spain, on the 10th of Feb'y 1763,' probably published in London in 1765. The series comprises fifty-eight miniatures and as many legends. They are fastened together and fold up so as to go into a small silver box. On the top is a portrait of George II and on the bottom a portrait of George III. The first print shows the English traders dealing with the Indians before the French 'encroached'; the second shows the Marquis Duquesne, French Governor of Canada, sending the Sieur de Saint Pierre to command on the Ohio; the third shows the French invading the English territory — possibly the battle at Great Meadows, as Washington is mentioned in the legend — (a village is burning on the right and a fort bombarded on the left); the fourth shows further battles on the Ohio, possibly including Braddock's defeat. This rather rare set belongs to the French-American Museum at Blérancourt, to which it was presented by Miss Anne Morgan.

MINIATURES OF THE FRENCH AND INDIAN WAR

those shores, the first thing he did was to look into the matter. As soon as he arrived, he sent for Franklin and asked him who in America was sold to the French: Lydius, Washington, or Croghan — especially Croghan.

Franklin, who knew the colonies well and who had already penetrated the character of Colonel Washington, pointed out to Loudoun that this hypothesis was ridiculous. He mentioned the name of an Irish Catholic. The Earl of Loudoun listened to him. He made a note of it. He always made notes. But he seems to have done nothing decisive. He rarely did anything decisive. In short, on this occasion, he had not the time.

Such was Washington's position in the universe in 1756.[25]

But in the colonies he was a hero. Far from hurting him with the Americans, the hatred of the French and the jeering of the English stimulated his compatriots' admiration for him. He had become a national symbol. In the middle of the blood-stained glade, in the disorder and panic which seized the English regulars, the young Colonel — calm and heroic — stood out as a symbol of all America. His praises were sung from Charleston to Boston, while Braddock was mocked.

Moreover, he was a gentleman of Virginia. His equals — in other words, his relatives and friends — flocked round him, and, once again in Williamsburg, he found that he was the heart of his clan. In August, 1755, he was appointed Commander-in-Chief of the Virginia forces.

The Education of a Leader

The newspapers of the entire world recorded this decision as once more a defiance of France and an indirect lesson to England. In the country where an Englishman had lost everything for them, the Virginians had chosen one of their own people to save as much as possible from the ruins. The 'Gazette de France,' the 'Courrier d'Avignon,' the Dutch and English gazettes vied with each other in quoting the American newspapers: 'The Governor of Virginia has raised with the greatest possible haste, a Regiment of 1,200 men over whom Colonel Washington will be in command.'

But the new chief was not rejoicing in his fame. His heart burned with indignation and disgust. The defeat had seemed to him absurd and ignominious, and the abuse, pouring in on all sides against his friend and old chief Braddock, who had died on the field of honour, angered him. But his hands were tied. He had been exhausted by that arduous campaign, his means were greatly reduced by his losses in the two unfortunate expeditions, his estate was running down, and his only distractions were his fame and that respectful but hopeless love which filled his soul for Mrs. Fairfax.

Accordingly, he was glad to set off, but his task was not an easy one. Unspeakable panic reigned in the West. The population, surging like a wave and certain that the worst was yet in store for them, saw disaster everywhere. Gossip even spread to the effect that the country around Winchester had been ravaged by the Indians. They had come with fire and sword;

from the town, it was said, one could hear the weeping and the shrieks of the miserable people. According to several, the town itself had been seized and looted. Washington dashed there in haste: 'When we came there, whom should we find occasioning all this disturbance, but three drunken soldiers of the lighthorse, carousing, firing their pistols and uttering the most unheard-of imprecations!' [26]

The people in the interior were apathetic. It was next to impossible to levy troops there and quite impossible to keep them under arms; as soon as they received their bounty, the soldiers deserted, with the easy assistance of the population in whose company they gaily drank up their five pounds, no doubt raising their cups to drink the good health of the Indians!

If the lowly agreed too well, those in power did not agree well enough. There were nothing but quarrels about precedence. Washington had hardly stationed himself at the frontier with a little group of men, collected with the greatest difficulty, before he was obliged to fight with his brother officers to uphold his rights and prerogatives. He occupied Fort Cumberland situated on the soil of Maryland and which was destined to defend the western portion of Virginia. His rank was that of colonel, but he held a brevet signed by the Governor of Virginia. As it happened, Fort Cumberland also sheltered Captain Dagworthy, who, although only a captain, tried to command Washington, for had he not two brevets — one from the King of England and the other from the Governor of Maryland? As 'regular' he would not agree to give precedence to a 'provincial.' Nor would Washington give precedence to a captain, one of whose brevets had expired, while the other was worth less than that which he, himself, had been granted.[27]

Dagworthy referred the matter to the Governor of Maryland, Sharpe, who said that he was right.

Washington referred the matter to the Governor of Virginia, Dinwiddie, who upheld him.

Sharpe's decision could no more affect Washington than could Dinwiddie's impress Dagworthy. Things grew bitter. As commander of the fort, Dagworthy took it upon himself to distribute to all the troops of the fort alike the provisions sent from Virginia for the soldiers of Virginia. Washington objected that it was unfair to give the food of those who had paid for it to others. Dagworthy replied that, as in war danger was common to all, so should supplies be common to all.

Washington decided not to endure so much insolence any longer. He begged Dinwiddie to allow him to go to Boston to meet Governor Shirley, the Commander-in-Chief of the English forces, while waiting for the arrival of a new general from England (Loudoun). Dinwiddie did not feel that he dared refuse. In mid-winter, while the frontier burned, while the Indians howled around every plantation, while the French held the region of the Ohio under bondage, Colonel Washington made a journey of sixteen hundred miles to find out who was to be the commander of Fort Cumberland. The expedition took him fifty days and cost him many pounds.[28]

It is indeed a picturesque memory when we recall the spectacle of this young colonel of Virginia, twenty-four years of age, followed by his aide-de-camp,

Captain G. Mercer, and his two grooms, T. Bishop and J. Alton, on his way to Boston to determine a quarrel of precedence. Washington was a gentleman, and he could bear suffering, even injustice, on the condition that it cast no reflection upon his honour and his rank. In spite of his noble Virginian ancestry, the mainstay of his life, in spite of the fact that he never made useless journeys — for he was the most sedentary of Americans, or, for that matter, of the great men of the eighteenth century — he did not falter before this long expedition.

He was right. If he did not command respect, he would have no influence in Virginia and would not be able to carry through the important work which he alone could execute. He was not a moralist but a realist, who perfectly discerned the conditions of life in his own circle and times — always remembering his 'Rules of Behaviour.' While he could tolerate all sorts of impudence, he drew the line at anything which might lose him the esteem of his own class.

This journey marks an epoch in American history. The Virginian was a local aristocracy. When the members of it were wealthy, they went to amuse themselves to England, where they always sent their children to finish their education. Not like the wealthy of Boston, Philadelphia, and Carolina, they had never had much intercourse with their own kind in the seaports of their own country or in those of the West Indies. His own plantation and London was the complete outlook of a Virginian. Washington was one of the first to turn toward the other colonies. The man who was to judge his question was a Bostonian.

In the course of this journey, Colonel Washington danced and drank punch at the Assembly in Philadelphia, then the most elegant social gathering on the continent. He conducted the most charming of the Quakeresses to see the 'Microcosm,' an importation from London which was the delight of the fashionable crowd. In New York he played at cards with the Governor, he frequented the club of the distinguished young men and contemplated marrying a charming young lady. In Boston he was the guest of the Governor and met all the prominent merchants. He was already known as a bold soldier. In the lodges he was greeted as a brother. He became a reality, a concrete being, a personage in his handsome blue-and-buff uniform, with his distinguished air, his silence and that gracious and embarrassed manner which showed how noble he really was. Only to see him revealed him a leader — the leader. Shirley ordered Dagworthy to obey.

Washington, by this journey in 1765, accustomed the other colonials to look upon the Virginians as leaders, and upon himself as *the* leader — a lesson which they did not forget.

WASHINGTON AND HIS SOLDIERS

Naturally enough, he found everything in disorder on his return; there was panic amongst the civilians, want of discipline amongst the troops and lack of cohesion in the government.

For two years he struggled in the midst of these difficulties. It was really here that he served his apprenticeship in the army and in the art of command; it was here that he appeared for the first time as a Virginian aristocrat, who, although never tiring of commanding his troops or of corresponding with Dinwiddie — his exalted superior — nevertheless kept in touch with his own class, depending upon it, fighting for it and defending its rights as well as those of the King and the British nation.

And he was an aristocrat in relation to his men, that cowardly, cunning, dishonest throng known as the Virginia militia, or those forcibly enrolled wretches constituting the Regiment of Virginia.[29] His real battle during these two years was much less against the French and their Indians (he seems not even to have seen one) than against the riffraff of Virginia which he had to put on its good behaviour. He was upheld, he was spurred on (sometimes even more than he liked) by his own class. Dissatisfied rumours reached him from the Williamsburg Burgesses, who refused to admit that the soldiers and officers should consecrate their time to swearing, drinking, card-playing, merry-making, and deserting. In April and again in December, 1756, the Assembly fumed and fretted and Washington's temper was upset. Even the 'Virginia Gazette' took part. The officers and their Colonel defended themselves as best they could. He, the Colonel, had his opinion of his troops, and what he says makes an unforgettable picture of the Virginia soldiers.

From April, 1756, he describes the state of mind of the civilians making up the militia. When they hear that the Indians are looting the neighbouring districts, they refuse to take the slightest trouble, and end up merely by saying that their neighbours are clumsy cowards. 'Let them defend themselves as we shall do if they come to us,' they say. And they stay at home. Somebody is certainly needed to receive the Indians if they take it into their heads to come there. Nothing has the least effect upon these men — neither promises, orders, threats; they remain in the chimney-corner. It is enough luck if they are not planning treachery. At first sight suspicion falls on those of German extraction or Catholic origin, but these are not the only ones whom the lootings terrify and who willingly would go over to the French were they allowed to do so, and if the Colonel were not behind them.

If the Indians were to retire a little, if some insistence was brought to bear, if the weather was not too bad, if the militiamen felt that they wanted a little exercise, they would perhaps set off — at the time of day it pleased them! Philosophically, they treated these marches as pleasant strolls. Washington said indignantly:

... The waste of provisions they make is unaccountable; no method or order in being served or purchasing at the best rates, but quite the reverse. Allowance for each man, as other soldiers do, they look upon as the highest indignity, and would sooner starve than carry a few days' provisions on their backs for conveniency. But upon their march, when breakfast is wanted, knock down the first beef, &c., they meet with, and, after regaling themselves, march on until dinner, when they take the same method, and so for supper likewise, to the great oppression of the people. [30]

Meanwhile, they advance more like a procession of

merry-makers than troops. They refuse to guard themselves, to march in step, to have scouts. Even when installed in a fort, they live as if they were at an inn. It is not a difficult matter to surprise them unawares and the Indians do not deprive themselves of this pleasure. Making a great deal of noise and spending money are their sole virtues; nothing could stop them. When they had had enough of these things, they went home on any pretext, without even listening to their officers: their wife was ill, their cow calving, a family anniversary had to be celebrated. If nothing of this sort happened at home to make an excuse to get them off before the end of their service (one month's duration!), they vanished the very moment this service was over, without bothering to discover whether the enemy threatened to attack or if any similar contingency might present itself. They simply went off.

The worst of all was their lack of social discipline. Each wished to be an officer and the majority of them succeeded in passing as such.

... They are obstinate, self-willed, perverse, of little or no service to the people and very burthensome to the country. Every mean individual has his own crude notions of things, and must undertake to direct. If his advice is neglected, he thinks himself slighted, abused and injured; and to redress his wrongs, will depart for his home.[31]

After several bad disasters had been caused by the militia, Washington thought it useless that so much money should be spent without other result than their afflicting the colonists or killing each other. So he tried to make use only of his own regiment. There, at least, he had his body of officers chosen by himself and his recruits levied by the colony. This plan should have worked, but the blossoms of hope and reality do not grow on the same bush — the officers gambled, drank, and made love or made debts. The soldiers devoted all their attention to deserting. Although they were not good for much, they knew all about the nine hundred and ninety-nine methods of deserting.

Even to enroll them was troublesome enough! A man really required a taste for both adventure and misery to serve as a Virginia regular. While the English regular drew eight pence a day and those of New England one shilling per day (with rum, dried pease, tobacco, ginger and vinegar), those of Pennsylvania the royal sum of one shilling and sixpence, the poor lads of Virginia only received sixpence, and twopence a day was withheld for their uniforms. With their remaining fourpence they had to provide their own shoes, shirts, stockings, tobacco, and the luxuries of life. They found this intolerable, and complained that this forced them to '... drag through a disagreeable service in the most disagreeable manner.'[32] Quite understandable, too!

Add, also, to such misery, the exploitation by profiteers. 'The rates of their liquor,' declared Washington, 'are immoderatly high, and the publicans throughout the country charge one shilling per meal, currency, for soldier's diet....' So it was almost a miracle when the poor boys managed to procure enough liquor. In the end, however, they seem to have been successful, for they passed the greater part of their time dead drunk, finding here, at least, some consolation.

Washington did everything in his power to better their lot and their morale. The most efficacious method, he believed, was a thousand strokes of the whip. This expression occurs so often in Washington's correspondence that it seems almost like a refrain. Although a remedy for many evils, it did not serve for all. So many of the recruits were in bad health, beating them would have been useless. Much better send them home — Washington sometimes did so. At other times he had Quakers to deal with — hard-headed, thick-skinned, invincible-hearted Quakers; all the whippings in the world would not have compelled them to fight, bear arms, work, or do anything, for that matter, which might contribute to the war. On these gentlemen he tried a certain kind of diet, very good for the health indeed!

Although the Quakers refused to obey, at least they remained in one place — not the case with the other recruits. There could have been nothing more flighty than a Virginia recruit. From Washington's description of them, we have a picture of a child pursuing a flock of sparrows scattered over a large field.

In May, 1756, the militia, by its bad example, had completely corrupted the regulars, who deserted *en masse*.[33] Washington stationed certain officers at the cross-roads and caught a few of the fugitives; he took great pride in having captured two! This was really an exception, for, usually, the gallant fellows vanished in pairs and nothing was ever heard of them again. And this went on during the entire summer of 1756. In August, sixteen of them departed in a single group on a single day — 'The more the merrier!' Those who had a relish for enrolling and then deserting joined up with the Pennsylvanians who received better pay and a good enlistment bonus. In September, more deserters and a horse-thief amongst them. In December they poured out in a stream. During the night of the 3d–4th, eighteen soldiers disappeared, not because of any particular disgust for army life, but because of a lust for change. They deserted the Virginians to enlist with the Royal American Regiment, for which they then raised recruits in the district, and this, with the consent of the Governor of Virginia too! Washington, infuriated by such conduct, by this 'flagrant instance of unnatural, unjust and dishonourable proceedings,' [34] at once sent a platoon of twenty-six men with a captain to search them out. Sixteen men were caught; they confessed to having been persuaded by the recruiting officer of the Royal American Regiment, an individual who had actually pledged them to kill any of their officers who might attempt to detain them or bring them back to the Virginia Regiment!

In 1757, the evil increased. In January, renewed sedition.... Driven to extremity, Washington put them under court-martial; they were soundly beaten and some even condemned to death. Nothing had the least effect, however; the desertions continued.

The Colonel tried gentleness on them, but no more successfully. In July, everything was about as bad as it could be. Washington wrote despairingly:

This infamous practice, wherein such numbers of our men have deserted... has been wonderfully successful; and is now arrived at such a height, that nothing can stop its scandalous progress, but the severest punishments, and most striking examples. Since mine of yesterday, no less than 24 of the Draughts (after having received their money and clothes) deserted.

Although he had taken every precaution and the roads were guarded, the deserters were so bold that they wounded an officer detailed to retrieve them, and one of the soldiers on patrol. Out of four hundred recruits, one hundred and fourteen deserted within the space of a few days. Washington finally decided to have a gallows erected, forty feet in height, with the intention of really scaring them. He then resolved to hang two or three of the thirty men whom he had recaptured. This event was celebrated on Thursday, July 27, 1757, before the front line, although Washington greatly regretted having to hang soldiers instead of shooting them, as was both seemly and according to rule. His intention, however, was to play upon the troops' imagination and produce a profound impression. This was his only alternative. The faces of the onlookers during this performance promised hopefully for the future.

After that he was able to meet his men with that friendly and lofty attitude which he preferred to all others.

Alas! he did not maintain it for long. In September, desertion *en masse* commenced again. Out of twenty-nine Luneburg recruits, fifteen deserted. Washington was worn out.

Your Honour may observe [he wrote to Dinwiddie], by the enclosed list of deserters, all of whom have left the regiment since the last return I sent, and after having received too their clothes, arms and bounty-money, how

prevelent still is that infamous practice among the das-
tardly drafts, especially at this garrison, where I indulge
them in every thing but idleness, and in *that* I cannot, the
nature of the work requiring the contrary. Lenity, so far
from producing its desired effects, rather emboldens them
in these villainous undertakings. One of those who were
condemned to be hanged deserted immediately upon
receiving his pardon. In short they tire my patience, and
almost weary me to death. The expense of pursuing them
is very considerable, and to suffer them to escape, without
aiming at pursuit, is but giving up the point, altho' we
have had little success of late.[35]

His limit of vexation was reached some days later
when his adjutant deserted after having sold to the
civilians and squandered a large portion of the regimental food and stores. Washington would have
liked to bring all these rascals to justice, but the laws
of Virginia offered no such facilities. After fighting
against the deserting soldiers, he had to fight against
the civilians, who rendered them help and profited by
their desertion, and against the tribunals which protected the civilians.

Washington was sick with disgust and weariness.
Another might have weakened, but he was determined
not to give in. Monotonously and stubbornly, he returned to the fray. He prevailed upon the Assembly
and the Governor to take measures against the desertion, persuaded his officers to watch their men closely,
and brought his soldiers to a better understanding of
their duty. After the early part of 1758, he began to
have his troops under control and had perfected their
discipline. Thanks to his patience and his anxious and
untiring care for every detail, he had won out, al-

though not the least reason for his success was his great, personal dignity.

COLONEL WASHINGTON AND HIS CHIEFS

Washington should at last have been able to take an offensive stand instead of defensive. That boon, longed for by all military chiefs as reward for much hard work, should have been granted him; in other words, a brilliant, active, and decisive campaign.

Nothing of the sort happened. Even as colonel, instead of being able to prove his courage, Destiny seemed bent upon making him exploit his peaceful and civic qualities.

As commander of the First Virginia Regiment, he was under the direct command of the Governor, Dinwiddie.

As officer in charge of the defence of the frontier of Virginia, he was obliged to follow the instructions of the Virginia Assembly.

As a colonel of British troops, face to face with his French and Indian enemies, he was expected to obey the military orders of the general appointed by His Majesty as commander of his troops in America.

Thus, Washington carried on three correspondences: one with Dinwiddie who despatched orders to him, in the beginning friendly enough; one with John Robinson, the President of the Assembly, his friend and protector, through whom Washington often persuaded the Assembly to give orders to Dinwiddie; one with Stanwix, then Loudoun, then Bouquet, by whom he was to be guided.

If these three authorities had been in agreement,

obedience would have been simple enough, but, as they never appeared to be, Washington's rôle became all the more difficult, responsible, and ticklish. Most often it happened that when the Assembly was for him, the two functionaries of the King, Dinwiddie and the English general, were against him. Ordinarily he defended the British interests and those of Virginia at the same time. As the English general had only general matters to trouble him, his rôle was easy enough. Nor was the position of the Assembly too trying; its attention was first of all concentrated on local interests, or on those of its electors. Dinwiddie's situation, however, was a complicated one; his duty was to please his King and Master, who had sent him to America, without too much displeasing the Virginians, his subjects, who were quite capable of making his life odious. This, they had tried at first, even going so far as to send a delegate to London with complaints against Dinwiddie. The exertions of the Governor and the rude welcome tendered to the delegate calmed the zeal of the Assembly. It fell back upon a sort of bad-tempered cordiality — none too charming; the letters from Washington, for all that, disseminated still more bitter feeling.

Above all, the Assembly wished to protect its electors, while Dinwiddie wanted to cleave the French asunder. Washington was the arbitrator. From every standpoint he, and only he, would be capable of drawing up the plan of battle. At first, he was wholly in favour of the defensive. He insisted that a chain of little forts be constructed along the entire Virginia frontier. Dinwiddie ended by seeing wisdom in the project, and agreed — also the Assembly. Everything was going well (summer, 1756).

Unfortunately, the question of Fort Cumberland hinged upon this. This fort, on Maryland territory, was an advanced post holding the most important position on the southern frontier. Although of great value as a strategical point, it had little value as a protection for the Virginians, who thought it useless to appropriate funds or to mobilize their forces to guard it. At least, this was the opinion of Washington, of Robinson, and of the members of the Assembly. It was not, however, that of the English Government, and Dinwiddie was forced to order Washington not to abandon the fort, but, on the contrary, to concentrate his troops there and to discontinue the work on the little Virginian forts. ✓

William Fairfax had said to Washington in the name of his associates and friends in the Assembly:

The Council and the Burgesses are mostly your friends; so that if you have not always particular instructions from the Governor, which you think necessary and desire, the omission, or neglect, may proceed from the confidence entertained in your ability and discretion to do what is fit and praiseworthy.[36]

Thus encouraged, he made headway. His letters to Robinson had the effect of sending the Assembly on the highroad to opposition. Much to Dinwiddie's annoyance, it demanded the evacuation of Fort Cumberland. Both sides grew stubborn and ended by being pig-headed. Dinwiddie wrote to Washington:

As to Fort Cumberland, it's a King's Fort and a Maga-

zine for stores. It is not in my power to order it to be deserted... at present it must be properly supported with
men.

In a letter to Robinson, Washington interpreted this
reply, saying (5th August, 1756):

The following is an exact copy of his answer. — 'Fort
Cumberland is a King's fort, and built chiefly at the charge
of the colony therefore properly under our direction, until
a governor is appointed.' Now whether I am to understand this ay or no to the plain, simple question asked,
viz: — 'Is the fort to be continued or removed?' — I
know not. But in all important matters I am directed in
this ambiguous and uncertain way .

This conflict of principles turned into a conflict of
individuals. The person to whom he wrote on June
10, 1754 — 'Believe me, Hon'ble Sir, when I assure
you, my breast is warmed with every generous sentiment, that your goodness can inspire. I want nothing but opportunity to testifie my sincere regard for
your person, to whom I stand indebted for so many
unmerited favours' [37] — this same person had become
an enemy. Dinwiddie and Washington, carried away
by their contrary ideas of strategy, had come to blows.
Their conflict began by indirect thrusts and then continued by direct stabs. In December, 1756, after having received from Dinwiddie the urgent order to
conduct one hundred men to Fort Cumberland, Washington wrote to him:

Your Honour's late and unexpected order has caused the
utmost terror and consternation in the people, and will, I
fear, be productive of numberless evils, not only in this
place, and the public works erecting here, but to the

country in general, who seem to be in the greatest dread of
the consequences.

This is the spirit in which the young Colonel addressed
the old Governor.

The latter replied, however:

You seem to charge neglect in me, not having proper
conductors. This charge is unmannerly, as I did what I
thought proper, though disappointed by the villainous
traders...

So, paying less and less heed to the Colonel's opinions, Dinwiddie issued orders which became more
and more summary and imperious.

It was impossible for them to agree; the one spoke
with the haughtiness of a superior functionary, the
other with the pride of a gentleman supported by his
own class. This being so, Dinwiddie scrupulously defended the British Empire against the French and
against the evil tendencies of the English colonies;
Washington regarded himself as the earnest defender
of British liberty as opposed to French barbarity and
English invasion.

He endeavoured to point out to Dinwiddie the
absurdity of the orders he received from him:

I am a little at loss to understand the meaning of your
Honour's orders, and the opinion of the Council, when I am
directed to evacuate all the stockade forts, and at the same
time to march only one hundred men to Fort Cumberland, and to continue the like number here to garrison Fort
Loudoun. If the stockade are all abandoned, there will be
more men than are required for these two purposes, and
the communication between them of near eighty miles,
will be left without a settler, unguarded and exposed. But

I mean nothing by asking this question than to know your Honour's intentions, which I would willingly pay strict obedience to.[38]

Meanwhile he gave out a message to the colonists:

You may assure the settlement, that this unexpected, and, if I may be allowed to say, unavoidable step was taken without my concurrence and knowledge; that is an express order from the Governor, and can neither be evaded nor delayed.

He protested at the same time in energetic terms to the President of the Assembly.

Surely, he said, his Honour and the Council are not fully acquainted with the situation and circumstances of the unhappy frontiers thus to expose so valuable a tract as the Branch, in order to support a fortification in itself (considering our present feebleness) of very little importance to the inhabitants of the Colony [i.e. Fort Cumberland]

And he added also:

My orders are dark, doubtful and uncertain; *today approved, tomorrow condemned.* Left to act and proceed at hazard, accountable for the consequences, and blamed without the benefit of defence, if you can think my situation capable to excite the smallest degree of envy or afford the least satisfaction the truth is yet hidden from you and you entertain notions very different from the *reality* of the case.

Well supported as he was by public opinion and the Assembly, Washington might have been in a very strong position. But he had rough customers to deal with. If the Governor did not quite dare to attack him directly, knowing him to be upheld by the Virginia aristocracy, the discontented subordinates and jealous colleagues did not entertain the same scruples. With them lay the danger for the young chief. In the Assembly the word went round that he managed his regiment badly. They circulated the news that, in disobedience to Dinwiddie's orders, he had remained at Winchester, being less exposed to danger there, instead of going to Fort Cumberland, where, in his absence, the Virginia troops had become shockingly undisciplined (December, 1756). Worse, from Winchester, where the population finally became harassed by the presence of troops, all sorts of unkind rumours reached the Assembly, and Washington wrote mournfully:

I am convinced that it would give pleasure to the Governor to hear that I was involved in trouble, however undeservedly, such are his dispositions towards me.[39]

In the autumn of 1757, the Governor was to have this pleasure. Actually, Washington heard that Mr. Carter had said, that Mr. Charles Robinson had said, that Colonel Richard Corbin had said, that Colonel Peachy had said, that he, Washington, had said in private — according to gossip — that there was not a single imminent danger, not a single Indian in the neighbourhood. (This referred to that entire period of the spring of 1756 when he was wrangling with Dinwiddie about maintaining the Virginia troops along the Virginia frontier, and when he begged Dinwiddie to send him recruits and money.) Judged by this gossip, Washington would have *admitted* that all his recriminations were scheming tricks! This rumour took wing and greatly harmed him with Dinwiddie, the Council, and even certain members of the Assembly. He found himself on trial before Virginian morals and public opinion, not, as before, with the chance of attacking Dinwiddie, but having to defend *himself*. This he did vehemently, but, in the process, he was forced to depend on Dinwiddie's loyalty — which he found most unpleasant.

It is uncertain in what light my services may have appeared to your Honour, but this I know, and it is the highest consolation I am capable of feeling, that no man that ever was employed in a public capacity, had endeavoured to discharge the trust reposed in him with greater honesty and more zeal for the country's interest, than I have done. ... On the other hand, it is hard to have my character arraigned, and my actions condemned without a hearing.

I must therefore again beg in *more plain*, and in *very earnest terms*, to know, if Colonel Corbin has taken the liberty of representing my character to your Honour with such ungentlemanly freedom as the letter implies? Your condescension herein will be acknowledged, as a singular favor done your Honour's most obedient, humble Servant.[40]

Which gave Dinwiddie the opportunity to reply with polite and stony-hearted indifference:

Your other letter of the 17th I perused. I would gladly hope there is no truth in it. I never heard of it before, or did I ever conceive you would have sent down any alarms without proper foundation. However, I shall show it to Colonel Corbin when he comes to town; but I'd advise you not to give credit to every idle story you hear; for if I was to notice reports of different kinds, I should be constantly perplexed.

My conduct to you from the beginning was always friendly; but you know I had great reason to suspect you of ingratitude, which I am convinced your own conscience and reflection must allow, I had reason to be angry, but this I endeavor to forget; but I cannot think Colonel Corbin guilty of what is reported. However, as I have his Majesty's leave to go to England, I propose leaving this in November and I wish my successor may show you as much friendship as I have done.[41]

And, to emphasize this, he refused the Colonel the permission, so warmly solicited, to go to Williamsburg to give an account of himself and make up his accounts.

You have no accounts that I know of to settle with me, [said Dinwiddie] and what accounts you have to settle with the country may be done at a more proper time.[42]

Thus parted the Governor and the Colonel. They were destined never to meet again. Dinwiddie carried away with him the memory of an obstinate young officer, hard to manage and much too given over to political intrigue. He cherished less ill-will towards Washington's ingratitude than towards that mixture of military stubbornness and political cunning, which he thought he detected there. But when all was said and done, he shrugged his shoulders, only too glad to leave the shores of Virginia behind him.

This trait of obstinacy in Washington, together with his talent for understanding his own kind, assured America's future. And notwithstanding all these incidents, the country looked upon Washington as the Military Hero of Virginia.

The Last Campaign of Colonel Washington
Officer of His Britannic Majesty

After the exceedingly hard winter of 1757–58, during which Washington, completely worn out, exasperated and ill to the point of needing medical care, thought his last hour had come, Spring appeared like a Messenger of Hope.

In Europe, the King of Prussia had covered himself with a mantle of immortal glory; on the seas, the English fleet held supreme sway; in America, the French had been driven back on all sides and the colonial troops — well organized and well commanded at last — took the offensive. They could see the dawn of victory rising before them. Washington, whose gaze had been riveted upon Fort Duquesne for four years, dreamed only of the day when he would enter it at the head of his troops, liberating forever the Virginia frontiers from the Indian menace, and restoring its patrimony to the Ohio Company.

Washington no longer dreaded the daily desertions of his soldiers, and his officers were well in hand. The departure of Dinwiddie left the land free to be administered by its aristocracy and the country was governed by the President of the Council. All promised well.

Unfortunately, they began by wasting time. Then, as leader of the expedition against Fort Duquesne, Colonel Bouquet prepared his plans of attack. The hottest days had come. It was August. Washington was feverish. And what a disappointment when he learned that Bouquet intended to approach Fort Duquesne by the north road across Pennsylvania instead of making use of the south road over which Washington had passed in 1754 and Braddock in 1755. Bouquet preferred the north road; it was shorter, less unfrequented.

Washington was dismayed. Since 1754, he had been fighting for England and the Ohio Company. For them, he had nearly been killed, worse, nearly disgraced; and now that success was in sight, they would approach Fort Duquesne by the north, would open up a new road, thereby placing these rich lands within easy reach of Pennsylvania and depriving the Virginians of the just fruits of their labours!

In spite of all his former troubles and the fatigue fast overcoming him, he was not, however, too tired to do battle. On the 8th of August, he sent Bouquet a long letter to dissuade him from carrying out the journey in this way: the south road had even been picked out by the Indians themselves and was already a track. What useless effort to construct one in the north across the forests and mountains! This alone would take so much time that they might as well give up the attack on Fort Duquesne this year. And how discouraging for the Southern colonies, already tired by their protracted effort.... He even went to confer with Bouquet, but unsuccessfully. On his return he wrote:

If Colonel Bouquet succeeds in this point with his general, all is lost — all is lost indeed! |Our enterprise will be ruined, and we shall be stopped at the Laurel Hill this winter; but not to gather *laurels*... [43]

He fought with and against everyone, even to the

point of exasperating General Forbes, who wrote in criticism of him, 'His behaviour about the roads was no ways like a soldier's.' Once the orders were given, he obeyed them scrupulously, but, in his reports to Bouquet, he never left off extolling the advantages the other road would have offered:

Every one knows what could have been done on the old road — few can guess what will be done on the new, there being not only the difficulties of the Road to encounter, but the chance of a French reinforcement also, but it is useless to add on this head. I should rather apologise for what I have said.

He was more open with the President of the Assembly:

My dear Sir, We are still encamped here, very sickly and quite dispirited at the prospect before us. That appearance of glory, which we had once in view, that hope, that laudable ambition of serving our country, and meriting its applause, are now no more; but dwindled into ease, sloth, and fatal inactivity. In a word all is lost.... The conduct of our leaders... is tempered with something I do not care to give a name to P-i-v-n artifice, to whose selfish views I ascribe this miscarriage of this expedition; for nothing now but a miracle can bring this campaign to a happy issue.

The worst, or, at least, the most trying, fact remained that this infernal and hateful road was to be constructed, its trees cut, its soil levelled, its bridges built, by the Virginia troops — those exploited and victimized gulls were, in short, destined to endure a thousand sufferings. Washington had never anticipated that his campaign of revenge against the French would be so impregnated with bitterness against his English chiefs and American collaborators. He fought the French, served his King loyally, but his attitude of mind towards his companions-in-arms was bitter.

When, on the 13th of September, 1758, Major Grant, sent with an advance-guard of eight hundred men to observe Fort Duquesne, was beaten by the French under its very walls, Washington, in spite of his patriotic regrets, could not suppress a certain satisfaction. This intelligence he called 'news of a very interesting nature.'

From all the accounts... it appears very clear, that this was either a very ill-concerted or ill-executed plan: perhaps both...[44]

Still, the Virginians fought bravely. They could claim the honour of having been the first to fell trees, the first to advance to the front, the first to risk their lives; in these things, as in everything else, it was Colonel Washington who set the most chivalrous example of courage, even while showing his disapproval of every plan and of all the movements of the army. On the 30th of October, 1758, he wrote again from Loyal Hanna:

My march to this post gave me an opportunity of forming a judgment of the road, and I can truly say, that it is indescribably bad.

He arrived on the 25th of November in sight of Fort Duquesne, experiencing, at the same time, the joy of surprise and a sort of disappointment. In the black night-skies of autumn, the red reflections danced above the tree-tops. The French had set fire to their

forts. Their canoes glided along the waters of the
Ohio River bearing away those five hundred defend-
ers of the fort who, for four years, had held in check
all the English troops of the Southern colonies, and
who now under cover of the night disappeared into
the mysterious depths of the forest. They had been
expelled, but not conquered.

On the following morning, November 25, the
English troops, numbering over four thousand soldiers, took possession of the smoking ruins of the
fort.

CHAPTER III

COLONEL WASHINGTON AT HOME

WASHINGTON left Fort Duquesne almost at once. He
went back to Virginia to take care of his health. A
few weeks later he resigned his commission.

He had done his work. He had given his country
the service that it had expected of him. The frontier
was safe, the Ohio lands solidly held.

He had won a unique position for himself in Virginia, where his courage, dogged obstinacy, and remarkable understanding of the art of leading men were
fully recognized. He was a hero to his own class,
which had always supported him, well knowing that
he was entirely devoted to their cause.

Washington had gained for himself a great reputation in England; the generals and government officials
spoke of him as a resolute soldier and an able politician. In Europe, too, he had his reputation; the
French considered him as a perfect type of the coarse
and treacherous Englishman.

He had certainly learned a good deal since 1753.
He found out very soon that in order to have the
pleasure of hearing the bullets whistle past his ears,
he would have to pay dearly in the interminable bore-
dom of training, feeding, clothing, disciplining, and
leading his men. He had learned all too well that
there were brief moments of joyous excitement and

weeks of tedious preoccupations. Washington was
one of the first great men of the eighteenth century
who had come to know by personal experience how
dull and laborious war could be. He had kept his
gentleman's love of hazard, but he had now no illusion
that war was, as the youth of Europe dreamed, a
thing of lace and ruffles.

These four years had spread his name all over the
world, formed his character and made him a great
man. But most of all they left him even more deeply
rooted in his native Virginia.

Virginia, from 1753 to 1759, a storm centre of human passions and anxieties, interested all the world.
Her situation forced Washington to the front. If it
ever comes to pass that she has again her predominant
place, she could never deny to her great son the re-
vival of his glory. But in 1759, Virginia appeared to be
simply a rich, distant, and unreal colony of the vast
British Empire.

The Great Love of Colonel Washington [1]

For the next ten years Virginia seems to have been
lulled to sleep; the vast plantations and leisurely
towns were bathed in silence. Washington, too, took
refuge in silence; he was weary of all the disputing,
of all the turmoil which accompanied a military
campaign; he was tired of forever quarrelling with
others. And he needed all his energy for a much
greater struggle — the struggle with himself.

He had met Sally Cary in 1748; she was tall and
willowy, not as beautiful as she was charming in her
proud way; her gaze was direct and penetrating, her

words just and profound; she was utterly different
from all women George Washington had up to then
found attractive. She was eighteen years old and had
just married the young officer's closest friend, George
William Fairfax of Belvoir, whose father had been
Washington's affectionate protector. All the Fairfaxes were his friends, but Sally was dearer to him
than all the Fairfaxes put together.

He saw her, loved her at first sight, and gave himself to her unresistingly, but without abandon. In his
notebook he scrawled:

> ' 'Twas perfect love before,
> But now I do adore...'[2]

She was the queen of his thoughts and ruled over
them quite as if he had been one of the faithful,
chivalrous knights of the Middle Ages whom he so
closely resembled. There was everything to bring
them together; his intimacy with George William
Fairfax, the benevolent attitude toward him of the
entire family, the manners of the time, the habit of
constant visiting and extensive entertaining, the common interests and tastes, as well as the pleasures and
the courtesy with liberty of the eighteenth century.
But more than all this, their natures were profoundly
similar; they both had an instinctive liking for grandeur, and there existed between them that subtle
mutual understanding which sometimes unites two
people before they have even dreamed of understanding each other and which, in their case, established a tie that nothing could destroy. But at the
same time, Fate had irrevocably separated them, for

they had not met each other until after Sally had married George Fairfax (December, 1748).

Washington, then a tall awkward lad, whose education had been much neglected gave her every mark of favour and attention which he could offer to a woman capable of amusing herself by acting classic tragedies, and conversing brilliantly. Sally Fairfax had grown up in one of the most opulent manor houses of Virginia, and her father, Colonel Cary, possessed one of the finest libraries in America. Her family had been an important one in England, and consequently held a very high rank in the colony. She had been well educated, could converse in French; she knew how to smile at the right moment or not smile; she understood the art of gentle teasing which charmed men and disarmed them, and possessed the still more subtle accomplishment of questioning them in such a way that they could not answer. She was a dignified and faithful wife to George William Fairfax, whom all regarded as the future Lord Fairfax, and who united with a tendency toward liberalism the generosity of a great gentleman and the benevolence of a good man.

Washington counted George Fairfax as his best friend; in his small beginnings it was the Fairfaxes who had helped him; at critical moments in his military career it was they who supported him; in politics he and Fairfax helped each other to become Burgesses, and the labour on their neighbouring plantations was divided between them. George Fairfax would look after the work of Mount Vernon in the absence of George Washington; George Washington managed Belvoir when George Fairfax left on long voyages.

They lent each other carpenters, woodsmen, wagons, carriages, boats, slaves, tools of all kinds, and all sorts of comestibles. Their friendship filled their life.

Sally Fairfax was Washington's only love. It was not that the two friends loved the same woman; George Washington simply loved the wife of George Fairfax. He could not help himself, he could not even hide his love. His brother, John Augustine, knew about it, for he was Washington's messenger during campaigns; George Fairfax knew about it, and once, when he was leaving on one of his travels, he advised his wife to avoid any indiscretion; the Fairfax family knew about it, for they were anxious to see Washington married (some of them, it is said, even took Sally to task); the Washington family knew about it, because so many other people did, and the colony knew about it, for it was small, and because in the eighteenth century it was the habit to be interested in your neighbour's love affairs.

Everybody knew about it, but no one knew it as bitterly as George Washington. During these tragic years, when his life was constantly in danger and his honour so often assailed, and when several times he risked losing everything, George Washington lived in an almost continual state of exaltation, alternating hope and despair; he never stopped dreaming of Sally Fairfax and compared the wild surge of his heart toward her with her unbroken reserve. Had he been really wise, he would have guessed that she was more on guard than he, but without having escaped the contagion of love; for the teasing with

which she overwhelmed him, and which she interrupted by long intervals of silence, her enigmatic
notes, were all not without a certain skilful and careful coquetry, which revealed not only a need to please,
but the desire to defend herself against others and
against herself. All the love letters which George
Washington sent to her, Sally Fairfax treasured all
her life. But he never knew it.

He begged her to speak; he did not realize that a
confession would have separated them forever —
or, perhaps, he did not worry about that. She knew,
and she did worry. She set him an example of silence
at a time in his life when he was constantly berating
the French, the deserters, the militia, the Indians,
the Governor, the other colonies, and the British
generals. She remained silent, but the lesson in
silence which she gave him was eloquent enough, and
he was sufficiently discerning to comprehend it.

He, too, tried to forget, he made attempts to ar-
range his life well, but Destiny mocked his feeble
efforts; in 1752, he proposed for Miss Fauntleroy, a
good match for Virginia, but she did not find him
enough to her liking to marry him; in 1756, a Miss
Philipse of Yonkers was not sufficiently attractive, he
thought, to enable him to forget the woman who had
become his obsession. So he remained close to Sally,
separated from her by his sense of honor, and tortured
by the impetuosity of his violent disposition, which
the unnerving military events had still further over-
excited.

Finally she succeeded in making him understand
clearly what he ought always to have known. In

September, 1757, William Fairfax died, leaving to his son George and to his daughter-in-law the estate and manor of Belvoir, as well as properties in England. George had to leave in 1757 to take up his rights of succession; he left Sally behind him. In November, Colonel Washington, whose unhappy love and wearing campaigns had finished by exhausting him, arrived at Mount Vernon, wasted by fever, stricken with consumption, and condemned by the doctors. His house was uncomfortable, as he had had neither the time nor money to add conveniences, and from November, 1757, to February, 1758, he shivered and lay near death. In his extremity, he appealed to Sally, asking for her help, for green China tea, Canary wine, and hartshorn.

He did not ask her for her pity, but he needed it more than all the rest.

It is certain that she gave it to him — she coddled him, took care of him, and made him shirts, as her account-book still shows. Finally, after long winter weeks and when they had despaired of saving him, he got well. But she had given him more than care, well-tailored shirts, and courage; she had given him a lesson; when he was at last on his feet again (February, 1758), he made a final decision and betook himself to visiting a young, pleasant, plump, and rich little widow, Martha Custis, née Dandridge (March, 1758).[3] She was a year older than he, and had just lost her husband, who had left her two children and much valuable property — an estate of one hundred thousand dollars for her, and one equally large to be divided between her two children — a large sum for the eighteenth century. She was a practical woman, and having had an old husband who had left her his fortune, she was now looking for a young one who would keep it and manage it for her. She was a clever woman, and although she had had but little formal education, she was a good housekeeper, a lady, and attractive and neat in appearance. She would be a completely satisfactory wife and was well considered by her neighbours. This was, doubtless, Washington's impression. Like a good knight, he was ready to defend the widow and her children, and to give them his loyalty and protection. It was not hers or his to give any deeper emotion.

Because of the legal privileges and rights entailed by an estate, a marriage in an important family during the eighteenth century was much more of a public responsibility than a personal pleasure, and so it was considered. Washington made his decision with calmness and courage.

This was the moment that Sally Fairfax chose to break her silence; she lost no time in congratulating Washington — and teasing him. She who had never answered his letters and scarcely, it seemed, even read them, now sent him two, one right after the other. Perhaps she was not really willing that he should lose sight of her forever. Washington almost went mad with grief and joy. She asked him if his hurry to see the war ended was because he was so eager to return to his fiancée. Her question was easy to answer; he would only have had to send her a copy of the letter he had just written to Martha Custis on July 20, 1758:

MARTHA (DANDRIDGE) CUSTIS
BEFORE HER MARRIAGE TO WASHINGTON

July 20, 1758

We have begun our march for the Ohio. A courier is starting for Williamsburg, and I embrace the opportunity to send a few words to one whose life is now inseparable from mine. Since that happy hour when we made our pledges to each other, my thoughts have been continually going out to you as another self. That an all-powerful Providence may keep us both in safety is the prayer of your ever faithful and affectionate friend.[4]

This letter would not have failed to satisfy Sally Fairfax, woman as she was. The letter he sent her was one which must, indeed, have contented her. It read:

Camp at Fort Cumberland
12th Sept. 1758

Dear Madam:

Yesterday I was honoured with your short but very agreeable favour of the first inst. How joyfully I catch at the happy occasion of renewing a correspondence which I feared was disrelished on your part, I leave to time, that never failing expositor of all things, and to a monitor equally faithful in my own breast, to testify. In silence I now express my joy; silence, which in some cases, I wish the present, speaks more intelligently than the sweetest eloquence.

If you allow that any honour can be derived from my opposition to our present system of management, you destroy the merit of it entirely in me by attributing my anxiety to the animating prospect of possessing Mrs. Custis, when — I need not tell you; guess yourself. Should not my own Honour and the country's welfare be the excitement? 'Tis true I profess myself a votary of love. I acknowledge that a lady is in the case, and further I confess that this lady is known to you. Yes, Madame, as well as she is to one who is too sensible of her charms to deny the Power whose influence he feels and must ever submit to. I feel the force of her amiable beauties in the recollection of a thousand tender passages that I could wish to obliterate, till I am bid to revive them. But experience, alas! sadly reminds me how impossible this is, and evinces an opinion which I have long entertained, that there is a Destiny which has control of our actions, not to be resisted by the strongest efforts of Human Nature.

You have drawn me, dear Madame, or rather I have drawn myself, into an honest confession of a simple fact. Misconstrue not my meaning; doubt it not, nor expose it. The world has no business to know the object of my love, declared in this manner to you, when I want to conceal it. One thing above all things in this world I wish to know, and only one person of your acquaintance can solve me that, or guess my meaning. But adieu to this till happier times, if I ever shall see them... I dare believe you are as happy as you say. I wish I was happy also. Mirth, good humour, ease of mind, and — what else? — cannot fail to render you so and consummate your wishes....[4]

And so for the first time in his life, Washington had said what he needed to have said, and he had asked directly the question which had haunted him for ten years: 'Do you love me?' Sally Fairfax was not offended; on the contrary, she answered the letter by return mail — but she did not answer the question. And Washington wrote again on September 25:

Do we still misunderstand the true meaning of each other's letters? I think it must appear so, though I would feign hope the contrary as I cannot speak plainer without — but I'll say no more and leave you to guess the rest.[4]...

Having declared his love to Mrs. Fairfax (12–25 September), George Washington married Martha Custis, January 6, 1759.

Then all four, Sally Fairfax, George Washington, Martha Washington, and George Fairfax, began living side by side. The lives of George Washington and Martha Custis from now on were inseparably bound together, but Sally Fairfax was mistress of his heart — so completely that he could not even want to resist her. George Fairfax and Martha Washington, who knew everything, were determined to know nothing, as long as their lives were lived with comfort and distinction.

The couple of Mount Vernon and the couple of Belvoir were close and ideal neighbours.[5] Their intimacy was frank and free. Not a week passed without their visiting each other. George Washington at first went alone, but he avoided staying the night at Belvoir; he would visit and dine, and then, at a late hour, would ride back home over the fields which separated the two estates. Gradually he formed the habit of taking Martha with him to Belvoir. Finally, the whole family went visiting there together, they would stay there, they would take the children there and as the years passed, Washington often spent the night at Belvoir — with Martha.

Sally and Martha became great friends. Both were queens of their respective domains, and they exchanged good services just as did their husbands. George Washington took care of George Fairfax's mare during his absence (the mare died); Martha Washington lent Sally Fairfax her Holland quilts or else they would exchange salt pork, little casks of port wine, and white earthenware chamber pots. But what they did more as time went on, and they all grew richer, was to go hunting together, galloping over the vast fields of Virginia — accompanied by a band of friends and neighbours, the Triplets, Magowans, Colvills, Alexanders, Poseys; these hunts always wound up with enormous dinners of all sorts of good food, and were as gay as they were fatiguing.

They lived their lives as George Washington had indicated he wanted them to be lived, in his letter to Sally Fairfax in 1755. They lived this life freshened by a thousand of these 'tender passages,' which give lovers the certainty of being loved, and ruled by 'Destiny which has control of our action not to be resisted by the strongest efforts of Human Nature.' There was nothing there for the world to see and nothing there for it to understand.

George Washington was rich, important, and re-spected; his career in very few years had made him famous. He had married extraordinarily well and was considered by everyone to be one of the very great lords of Virginia. Nevertheless, the word which oc-curs the most frequently in his diary — kept so meti-culously during these years — was *alone*. He would travel untiringly from one of his farms to another, from a gathering of the Burgesses to a meeting of stockholders, from a watering place to a distant plantation, moving constantly over this land of Vir-ginia which he knew so well, and over which he went always — 'alone'; or he would shut himself up alone in his study to write his interminable business letters to England or to his comrades-in-arms; or he would simply remain there *alone* to think and dream. He noted in his diary sometimes during a whole week that he had remained at home *alone* — although Martha Washington was living under the same roof and in the same house.

Washington armed himself with solitude and silence against his dangerous delights and wasting sorrow, 'the silence which so often speaks more clearly than eloquence.' The glory and joy of the eighteenth century was in writing, speaking, and in telling stories; Voltaire, Rousseau, Franklin, and even Frederick the Great were more writers than they were men; what they did is not worth so much as the way they told what they had accomplished; their words often gave the sole value to their actions. Washington, on the contrary, saved his life and enjoyed it only because he kept it within himself, hidden, concentrated, repressed, inexpressible.

COLONEL WASHINGTON STUDIES SILENCE AND AGRICULTURE

The learning of silence is not accomplished in a day. Tormented by the strong emotions which he had to hide, and harassed by the innumerable trifles to which he had to attend, Colonel Washington had a hard time of it in the beginning at Mount Vernon. During the first few years he was in a constant state of irritation or indignation. He had nothing but disappointments and troubles.[6]

How long the days of Mount Vernon were! There was no use galloping along the river-banks or even the hills; everything was a burden to him, everything conspired to make his life difficult, men, objects, and himself. The estate, having been neglected all through

the war, was in unbelievable disorder, while the
climate, damp in winter and dry in summer, was un-
healthy. His health, which had been shattered by
overwork, was poor. He was ill, and believed without
regret, but also without eagerness, for, after all, he
was normal, his life could not last much longer. Beside, he had still to take care of Mrs. Washington who
was rather sickly. His overseer, Hardwick, broke his
leg; the darkies had pleurisy in the winter, smallpox
in the spring, mumps in summer; the horses stumbled
and broke their legs, the pigs were thin, the oxen were
not much better, the sheep invaded and destroyed the
newly planted field of peas, the tobacco grew poorly
because of the humidity, while the corn in a drought
dried on the stalks. What he could harvest did not
sell well; his tenants of the upper farms did not know
how to pack tobacco and it arrived spoiled. Washington had had to buy so many things to install his house-
hold, to house his slaves, to clothe all his people and
himself, to repair his mill, to own a carriage, and enlarge his house that, when the accounts were made up
in 1765, he, one of the richest lords of Virginia, found
himself in debt.[7] Thus what was the good of working,
or of marrying?

He complains of everything. On January 1, 1750,
he is violent against a Mr. French who had tried to
deceive him about the price of salt pork, denounces
his 'cupidity,' but he finally patches up his quarrel
with him, for they could not live at Mount Vernon
without salt pork; on the 3d and 6th he quarrels with
an oysterman who comes to install himself on Washington's private wharf and there conducts himself in-

decently; Washington gets upon his high horse and threatens the fellow for his outrageous behaviour, but with little success; on January 8, he begins a suit against John Balladine who in selling him some iron bars falsifies his weights; on January 28, he finds fault with his overseer, Stephen, whose son is a good for nothing, and over whom the father has no control. Washington tells him some home truths.

To distract himself from all these annoyances, he goes to a ball at Alexandria on February 15, but there he only finds new opportunity for sarcasm.

Went to a ball at Alexandria, where Musick and Dancing was the chief entertainement. However in a convenient Room detachd for the purpose abounded great plenty of Bread and Butter, some Biscuits with Tea, and Coffee which the Drinkers of coud not Distinguish from Hot water sweetned. Be it rememberd that pocket handkerchiefs servd the purposes of Table Cloths and Napkins and that no Apologies were made for either.

The Proprietors of this Ball were Messrs. Carlyle, Laurie and Robt. Wilson....

I shall therefore distinguish this Ball by the Stile and title of the Bread and Butter Ball.[8]

He was deep in his troubles. Does he not have Clifton, from whom he wished to buy lands, try to make a tool of him? Washington speaks of him in the beginning as not being a responsible person, with a 'great love of money,' he then sharpens his tone and calls him 'a thorough pac'd Rascall,' but when he cannot manage him, as he badly wants the land, he comes to an understanding with him, to get the better of those who had wanted to use Clifton against him.

On March 18, he breaks out against his overseer, Hardwick, for not having taken care of the horses; he was 'Rascally' too. On April 9, Doctor Laurie, the good Doctor Laurie, comes to Mount Vernon to attend to Mrs. Washington. And the Colonel notes in his diary: 'Doctr. Laurie came here. I may add Drunk.' The following morning, before bleeding Mrs. Washington, Doctor Laurie must have had a conversation with Mr. Washington. Whatever happened, at no time in the future is it ever mentioned that he comes to Mount Vernon in such a condition.[9]

On August 10 and September 28, Washington shuts himself up in his study to write his business letters to his agents in London, and he does not mince matters with them. He complains that his tobacco was being sold much too cheaply, while, on the contrary, everything he ordered was paid for at extravagant prices and that, moreover, his orders were not carefully followed: his purchases were being sent to him in unheard-of ways; half the time they did not arrive at all or arrived spoiled, worthless, or broken. He was not getting his money's worth.

Life seemed hard and strange to him: men were nothing but puppets. On January 12, after a long, rough, and fatiguing trip on horseback he arrived at Mr. McCrae's to dine there, only to hear the Colonel Cocke was 'disgusted' with Mount Vernon and had not wanted to stay to 'see an old Negro there resembling his own Image.' Washington shrugged his shoulders.

But he would begin again. Though he saw the shortcomings of others clearly, he was not blind to his own faults, and he did not want to drag on indulging his poor health and his indolence. By a powerful effort of will and the effects of a few visits to Belvoir he recommenced his former activity. He took up agriculture with a vim; it became for him a distraction and a discipline. It was at once a pastime and a profession. In his America, farming was as much the fashion as in Europe where Monsieur Rousseau of Geneva and Monsieur le Marquis de Mirabeau had both given agriculture an enormous impetus, one by his 'discourses' (1751–55), the other by his 'Friend of Men' (1755). Agriculture was the thing, and the greatest men of the time praised it without stint.

Washington began by studying it. Surveyor and soldier, he was familiar with nature, but he had never tried to cultivate the soil. Now, in this Virginia, which had been so hastily colonized and where labor was always lacking, he wanted to create a productive plantation. He had a sense of order; he was efficient and progressive while around him agriculture was in a miserable state; the surface of the ground was hardly scratched, it was exhausted by always raising the same heavy crops of tobacco and corn; everyone bought as much property as he could, not expecting to pay for it, and the estates, which were extended indefinitely, brought in less and less and cost more and more; no matter, the Virginian gentlemen plunged happily into debt in London, New York, Philadelphia, and Williamsburg, they consoled themselves with lively hunting parties — until they came a cropper.

Washington did not lead a different life from the others, but he was more intelligent about it. His bitterness at least gave him the advantage of seeing clearly. He refused to live on illusions and wrote:

Our gazettes afford but too many melancholy proofs of it in the sales which are daily advertised; the nature of a Virginia estate being such, that without close application, it never fails bringing the proprietors in Debt annually, as Negroes must be clothed and fed, taxes paid, etc. etc. whether anything is made or not....[10]

All this was too evident all about him. Almost all his good neighbours, even the Fairfaxes, were ruining themselves gradually, not so much through laziness and stupidity, as by neglect. They knew neither how to work nor how to keep accounts and they imperceptibly arrived at a point where they possessed nothing but a valueless estate. As a matter of fact it was exceedingly difficult to do anything else, for the art of keeping accounts in the eighteenth century, especially in Virginia, was complicated and exhausting. One seldom knew what one owned, and never what one owed. The principal product of the country, tobacco, was negotiated in London, and all necessary articles came from there. The market prices of tobacco varied constantly, the trend generally being downwards; the price of commodities changed just so often, but their trend was upwards. Whoever depended on the quoted prices was sure to be ruined. Furthermore, it was impossible to calculate the expenses of a plantation. The initial cost of Negroes was not high — they averaged fifty pounds in 1765; but they were expensive to house, feed, and clothe, and almost ruinous to have properly watched. Most of the master's time was spent in just such activity as

well as the time of his best overseers. Undoubtedly
the Negroes lived by the soil as well as on it, but in
the great tobacco plantations it often happened
that both wheat and corn had to be bought in quantities to feed the too numerous slaves. The black
and white workmen which were hired from neighbours and elsewhere had to be paid in cash. These
employment contracts of the eighteenth century were
fantastic. The overseer, Turner Crump, was paid
thirty pounds sterling per annum for managing the
six carpenters of Mount Vernon, plus a sixth of the
cost of the work accomplished by his men. William
Powell, who was the overseer for the property of
Washington's mother on the Rappahannock, received yearly three hundred and sixty-five pounds
of salt pork, the milk of one cow, and the seventh
part of the annual harvest of wheat, corn, and tobacco
grown on the plantation. He had to provide himself
with his own furniture, buy his own clothes, and
promise to keep 'no horse or other creature on the
Plantation.' The following year, when Powell was
given one or two men more to aid him in his work as
well as five horses, he agreed to a salary of an eighth
part of the season's harvests.[11]

Under such conditions, when the largest part of
wages was not paid in money but in provisions, when
tobacco, salt pork, and salt were as good a medium of
exchange as gold or silver, when settlements of accounts were extended over a period of two years,
when in the employment contracts financial clauses
were accompanied by exchanges which were remini-
scent of ancient feudal customs, exact book-keeping

was impossible. The gold standard was not practical.
A rich man could calculate only by guesswork. To
make his ground productive and keep it in good condition, and avoid sinking into debt, an extreme care and
assiduity were necessary, combined with a great deal
of common-sense. According to Washington himself,
only two qualities could save a farmer: 'leisure... a
competent knowledge of plantation business.'[12]

From 1759 to 1774, Washington devoted all his
time to agriculture and neglected nothing that could
aid him.[13] He sent to Europe for all important books
on farming. He read them, made notes and summa-
ries, followed the advice given with exactness and
verified his results by experience. His method was
slow but scientific and sure. The works of Tull,
'Horse-Hoheng Husbandry,' Duhamel du Manceau's
'A Practical Treatise of Husbandry,' 'A Farmer's
Complete Guide,' and Horne's 'The Gentleman Farmer' were books he frequently consulted from 1760 to
1799.

Moreover, they filled his imagination. When he
walked around the country, he meditated not only
upon his tragic and sublime love, but wondered how
his timothy and clover crops were coming on, if the
grain were not still too green for harvesting. He was
interested in manures and experimented with dung
and manure; he noted the relations between stallion
and mare, the more complex intercourse between his
bitches and his dogs or his neighbours' dogs, and filled
his diary with his observations.

In spite of all his efforts, he did not succeed in
making his soil fertile. God had not made it so and

nothing could be done about it. But he did the best he could and managed to make his cultivation profitable — a success that was almost unique in Virginia. Without ever being cruel, he obtained an excellent, carefully calculated result from the work of his Negroes and whites. He divided this labour skilfully, and, thanks to his authority and practicality, they got through a lot of work. It sometimes surprised even him, and when he would see his overseer, Stephen, toiling painfully in the middle of a field, he would exclaim in sympathy — though generally in a brusque sarcastic manner. He almost admired him for it, forgetting that Stephen's master had enough energy for two and that recently Stephen had received a reprimand.

Farming was a real pleasure when he was able to wrest harvests from the stubborn soil, but in reality this was not the source of Washington's wealth. At the most it was the concrete symbol of his fortune. To be considered rich in Virginia it was necessary to have money, lands, slaves, houses, and credit. In this country commercial exchanges were slow and difficult owing to the lack of currency; money because of its rarity had become a false standard and there was no security for the ordinary rich except in many forms of wealth. Whoever possessed but one of these forms of wealth was at the mercy of the smallest circumstance. Washington realized this immediately and prudently worked to round out his fortune in every way. By 1771, he had increased the extent of Mount Vernon from 1500 acres to a beautiful estate of 5500 acres, and at this date he paid taxes for 12,500 acres of ground in Eastern Virginia, while in the West he owned almost 25,000 acres. In order to safeguard the future, he looked for new grounds in Ohio, Florida, and Pennsylvania. He was cautious and persistent. He did not neglect anything. In Williamsburg he had a fine house with six chimneys, he built another at Alexandria, enlarged Mount Vernon, and erected a mill. In the beginning he owned a small sailboat; then he had a schooner built and finally acquired a brigantine. He was an influential member of the company which was draining the Dismal Swamp; he considered becoming interested in a foundry in Virginia and he invested money in England.[14]

Everything that he undertook he thoroughly accomplished and he superintended everything to the end. He never allowed himself to get confused. He was good and generous to his neighbours, but was careful of lending them large sums of money. He knew only too well the avalanches of bankruptcies which resulted from such dealings. His kindness towards the poor, the orphans, and friends in difficulties was untiring; he never went to see his mother without leaving her some money or helping her in some way. He was close to all his numerous family. He always acted as godfather for the children of his friends and he paid this honour to the young Ferdinando Fairfax, son of Bryan Fairfax, and to the son of Mr. Chichester. He undertook the education of young William Ramsay at Princeton. Upon the death of Thomas Colvil, he took on the heavy duty of administering his estate and liquidating the situation. When George Fairfax and his wife went back to Eng-

land, it was again Washington who had the task of
settling up their whole estate in America. He kept
track of all his old servants and their families, helping
them when it was necessary. He was kind and generous to his negroes, and had them well taken care of
when they were ill. On Sundays he would lend them
the big net to go fishing. He superintended their work
closely, and if any of them showed a bad disposition,
he did not hesitate to send him to the slave market at
the Barbadoes. Under his iron rule his little world
grew and prospered. In 1760, he had 49 slaves; in
1770, 87, and in 1774, 135. He now had a solid property, but as yet it was not magnificent. His red and
white liveries made a fine effect; his carriage was
gilded, but he had begun by buying a second-hand
coach. He ordered his clothes from London, but he
did not desire lace or ribbons, at most gold buttons
on a plain waistcoat. He always lived the life of an
aristocrat, but he did not begin to hunt assiduously
(hunts included huge receptions and feasts once the
hunting was over) until he had settled all his debts
and after the death of Anna Lee, his sister-in-law,
which relieved him of paying interest on Mount
Vernon. Until 1766, he had struggled upstream and
built up his reserves; after this date he felt secure and
lived at his ease. In 1768, he had a great hunting
season; in 1769, he ordered a fine new coach from
London; he had a full-length portrait of himself exe-
cuted by Peale in 1772; in 1774, he bought a beautiful
brigantine for one hundred and seventy-five pounds
sterling and finished the additions to Mount Vernon.
The well-arranged and ornamented manor house had

a fashionable appearance and life therein followed a
serene course.

Where at first so many pages in his diary were
taken up by his tempers, his difficulties and annoyances with his neighbours, clover, timothy, corn,
tobacco, and hogs finally occupied it altogether. He
noted nothing but the weather, the slow and sure
growth of wheat, the rapid passage of clouds...
Agriculture had taught him to come out of himself, to
be interested in the visible world. The victories he
won over the hard poor soil of Mount Vernon were
sweet. He enjoyed the creative struggle which had
taught him happiness and silence. One day he wrote
in praise of agriculture in these words:

The more I am acquainted with agricultural affairs, the
better I am pleased with them; insomuch that I can no
where find so great satisfaction as in those innocent and
useful pursuits. In indulging these feelings, I am led to reflect how much more delightful to an undebauched mind
is the task of making improvements on the earth, than all
the vain glory which can be acquired from ravaging it, by
the uninterrupted career of conquest.

And again he wrote:

I think... that the life of a husbandman is the most
delectable. It is honourable, it is amusing, and with judicious management, it is profitable. To see plants rise from
the earth and flourish by the superior skill and bounty of
the laborer fills a contemplative mind with ideas which are
more easy to be conceived than expressed.[15]

COLONEL WASHINGTON'S OTHER GREAT LOVE,
POLITICS

As Washington became more peaceful, he began to enjoy life once more and to interest himself in people. *lost* He kept open house at Mount Vernon, and every week a stream of visitors arrived there to lunch or dine or sup or stay the night. Sometimes Washington's guests would stay two or three days. Whenever Jacky and Patsy invited their friends to have a dancing lesson, the old house would be filled with the laughter of young people. Occasionally Colonel Washington would give a great reception for the officers of the frigate Boston which was anchored in the Potomac. Then, too, every day during the summer there was neighbourly visiting from manor house to manor house. Racing was a popular diversion; there were the local races, races at the capital Williamsburg and in the big cities near by, Philadelphia and Annapolis. During the racing season there was the theatre; and there were beside all kinds of balls and receptions.

Virginia, in spite of her debts and the low price of tobacco, became richer and more refined. The Governor at Williamsburg had a little court about him, especially when he happened to be a splendid and debonair nobleman as was Norborne Berkeley, Baron of Botetourt, or such a wily gallant gentleman as was James Murray, Earl of Dunmore. The Governors received the Burgesses and gave banquets for them. On great occasions there were fireworks, sometimes marionettes, or they might all go together to see the waxworks which some itinerant showman was exhibiting to the curious public. The Virginian aristocracy, which from small beginnings had risen to great heights, and was now a feudal order, very solidly established, had a well organized social life. The constant intermarriages between the families that had settled in Virginia a century or a century and a half ago, the Lees, Byrds, Carters, Fairfaxes, Randolphs, Masons, Bessetts, Carys, and Washingtons resulted in a sort of social and financial oligarchy, capable of dominating all the other classes of the population and managing the Governor. It was the heart of the colony; outside of it, in Norfolk, there was a group of merchants established, representing the only middle-class element in Virginia, and, in the barely colonized West, where democracy was being born, there was still a spirit of adventure; but for the rest there were only tiny towns in the centre of huge plantations, or great domains where poor people lived without worries and without rights. They lived in complete isolation while all pleasures, privileges, duties were for their masters who kept them under their control.

Of all the ties which bound these gentlemen together, however, and gave them such a strong homogeneity, none was of so much importance as Politics. Most Virginians had originally left England because there was no safety for them there, or because they disagreed with the majority of the government of the moment, or because they thought they had been badly treated. They were inclined to be rebels. They came from various parts of England, and at different periods and from very separated classes. Their principles and prejudices were often opposed (the Wash-

ingtons were Cavaliers, the Fairfaxes Roundheads),
and in consequence for a long time they had neither a
definite line of policy nor any concerted action.
The presence of the Indians on their frontiers kept up
their patriotism, while the menacing proximity of the
French, maintained their British, liberal, and Protestant spirit. The chief ambition of the Virginian
aristocracy was to imitate the nobles of England who
had won the praises of all the philosophers because of
their Parliament.

The French and Indian War and the complete
success of England in the New World changed these
conditions.[16] At the very moment that the Virginian
aristocracy realized that they were strong, united,
and sheltered from danger, England no longer seemed
to be an indispensable protector and appeared to be
rather a stepmother. The Virginians realized that the
population of the colony was increasing, the soil becoming impoverished and their debts mounting. To
remedy these evils, which menaced them with ruin,
they considered two possibilities, one economic, the
purchase and gradual conquest of the West; the other
financial, the emission of paper money.

For the Virginian aristocracy the acquisition of
the West was little more than a speculation. Few of
these gentlemen had any intention of settling there or
establishing farms there under their own control.
They wished to remain in their manor houses of the
East, but their plan was to purchase lands cheap and
sell them at high prices to immigrants and 'land-
jobbers.' The heavy risks which these speculations
entailed gave them certain claims; and as they chose

what they thought were the best lands, they were giving some service.

England was not of their opinion. She wanted the West for her own aggrandizement, not for that of her colonies. She also feared that dispossessing the Indians too rapidly would provoke them beyond endurance. She found these Eastern colonies enough of a nuisance without adding the doubtful pleasure of increasing and strengthening them. England considered as was the belief of the period, both of philosophers and governments, that they were too extensive, that they served only to depopulate the mother country. In the face of so many objections, and little realizing the advantages, the English Government decided to leave matters as they were and wait for events. By a proclamation of 1763, it forbade the Governors and the English colonies of America any colonization beyond the Alleghenies.

This proclamation would not have been enforced very strictly had not the leading merchants of London, Liverpool, and Glasgow insisted on its observance. These merchants were not indifferent or inattentive; they held persistently to their ideas, and the commerce of the Mississippi Valley was of capital importance to them, first, because of its enormous capacity for production (furs) and secondly because of its enormous capacity of absorption (rum and other products sold to the Indians). Consequently the merchants did all they could to hinder any colonization of the West in which they would not have a leading part. Thus they were in conflict with the Virginian aristocracy and were formidable enemies because of their opulence, their control of the press, the Government, and the Parliament, which they had the habit of making do as they pleased, as they did in 1755.

These same merchants from 1760 on, kept up a quarrel with the Virginians on the subject of paper money. They had drained the colonies of practically all the currency by means of their commissions on the sales of tobacco and by their exportations of manufactured products to Virginia; all the colonies owed them money, but the leading planters were the deepest in their debt. These knew of but one way to pay their taxes or their bills, either borrow money or print it. The second expedient seemed to them much simpler and more satisfactory. But the English merchant did not like it at all. These colonial banknotes which the planters sent to settle their bills meant nothing to them. They had no confidence in this money, which depreciated as soon as it was in circulation (the Virginian pound was twenty-five per cent below its face value in 1770, thirty-three per cent in 1774), and demanded that the Government forbid this American practice. The English Government petitioned by its subjects, who lived thousands of miles distant and who did not vote, and by those who lived right at hand and did vote, decided quite naturally that the latter were right. The Americans were forbidden to print paper money.

The Virginian planters — whether they went galloping over their impoverished estates or sat in their studies where the bills accumulated — keenly felt the oppression put over them by the English aristocracy. And they were all the more irritated because the

English aristocracy from 1760 to 1775 was lavish,
vain, and weak. Intoxicated by its success and infatuated by its importance, the English nobility
wasted its time in useless parliamentary discussions
which led to nowhere and resulted in disorder. Ministers succeeded one another in rapid succession without realizing their policies and sometimes without
even having had the time to formulate one. If a prede-
cessor had taken the trouble to frame one, his successor was more than apt to reverse all his decisions just
for the pleasure of doing so. The ministers prudently
took no action concerning any important question,
and let them lie dormant. America, with her surly
and mutinous attitude was just such a question, all
they did was to remind her of the suzerainty of the
British Parliament, the incarnation of the British
nobility.[16]

The Virginians could only turn to the King, who
was the supreme arbiter and their only hope. Such
was certainly the attitude they took from the very beginning, and which was reflected in the pamphlets,
newspapers, and correspondence of the time. There
was an increasing current of hostility against the
financial and parliamentary English aristocracy, and
there was a profound respect for the King, who was
always spared all the disputes, as the Americans
hoped to use him as an arbiter. The troubles of
America (1763–74) were simply the struggle of two
rival aristocracies, one established in England and
solidly entrenched in its privileges; the other, young,
lively, and anxious to procure the same privileges for
itself. The idea of natural rights which are found

constantly in the American writings of this period is nothing less than a generalization and systematization, natural for a philosophic age, of the rights which the English aristocracy had conquered for themselves. By adopting these conception of rights, they would destroy the British supremacy; to imitate was to supplant them.

The all-powerful and proud English aristocracy was drifting aimlessly without a leader; the youthful Virginian aristocracy was feeling its way, not knowing where to find its leader. There were orators in plenty, but no leader as yet. George Washington was in a fair way to become one.

He had all the requisite qualities. They felt that he belonged to them; like the others, he owned enormous quantities of poor land, and, like them, he needed Western domains to regild his coat of arms. Like the others, he had debts and was looking for a way to get ready money; like the others, he was a gentleman who felt keenly the disdain of the fine lords of London, and resented being exploited by the English merchants.

His superiority made itself felt. He was more circumspect, more cautious and stronger than the others. He acted more quickly and to better effect. While the others were thinking about the West, he had actually been there and knew the territory which lay the other side of the mountains. While the others talked of war and drilled their soldiers, he had fought. He knew how to manage his estate and people better than did his neighbours. They could count on him, not only for useful advice, but for actual aid at a critical moment. His friends were grateful to him.

But Washington also was feared. No one could make a fool of him. Among the easy-going gentlemen of Virginia he was a leader. He had too often, by his haughty manner and his violence, which struck cold, put men in their places. No one frightened him.

The carpenter, Askew, cheated on his hours and days of work. Washington asked him one day if 'he did not think himself one of the most worthless and ungrateful fellows that ever lived....'[17]

Captain Posey, his neighbour, tried to induce him to give security for his debts. Washington wrote him:

Having received your letter of Wednesday last and to-day, it appears very clearly to me... that you are not only reduced to the last shift yourself, but are determined to involve me in a great deal of perplexity and distress on your account also.

P.S. I have this instant been informed that you have declared you paid me all you owed me except about £20. Does such disingenuity as this, deserve any favor at my hands? I think anyone might readily answer for you, no.

Captain Dalton proposed a new way of organizing the parish of Truro. Washington answered him: 'The thought is absurd!' Then he went on to explain that he believed Dalton to be a thief.

Captain Weggener complained of not having received his share in the distribution of lands given to the veterans of the French and Indian War, under Washington's direction. Washington sharply retorted, reminding Weggener that he had not paid his share of the expenses; then he added:

I have no power to redress the complaint, even if I had

adjudged it reasonable, which in truth I do not, as I have declared upon this, and shall do upon every other occasion, when call'd upon.

William Black had signed with Washington a deed of sale for certain mills and at the last moment he wished to extract a few more advantages for himself; Washington wrote:

Is there honor, justice or equity in such kind of proceedings? No, sir, there is not, and to cut the matter short, I have directed Mr. Hill to wait upon you, and before evidence to demand immediate possession of the two Mills.

Colonel Muse complained of having been badly treated in the distribution of lands to the veterans and sent a letter to Washington which was far too insolent to please him. He answered:

Your impertinent letter of the 24th ulto., was delivered to me yesterday.... I am not accustomed to receive such from any man nor would have taken the same language from you personally, without letting you feel some marks of my resentment; I would advice you to be cautious in writing me a second of the same tenour; for though I understand you were drunk when you did it, yet give me leave to tell you, that drunkenness is no excuse for rudeness; and that, but for your stupidity and sottishness, you might have known, by attending to the public Gazettes... that you had your full quantity of ten thousand acres of land allowed you;... I wrote to you a few days ago concerning... an easy method of dividing our lands; but since I find in what temper you are, I am sorry I took the trouble of mentioning the Land... as I do not think you merit the least assistance from

G. WASHINGTON[17]

One did not answer Colonel Washington. He was

a chief. August 2, 1770, the veterans held a meeting
at Fredericksburg and definitely recognized his leadership by selecting him as their representative, in
order to obtain recognition of their rights from England and the Governor of Virginia, and the execu-
tion of an old promise. In February, 1754, at the
beginning of the French and Indian War, Governor
Dinwiddie, following instructions from London, had
promised a gift of two hundred thousand acres of
land to the soldiers and officers who would volunteer
to fight the French.

Since the war, however, there had been only vague
talking of this promise, and the royal proclamation of
1763, closing the West to the Virginians, practically
put an end to the veterans' hopes. They entrusted
Washington with this thankless mission and he set to
work with a will. He insisted about this matter with
Botetourt, entreated Dunmore, and finally won him.
He gathered funds together and spent even more himself. He stirred up public opinion, and finally, in spite
of the disapproval of the English government, which
was always getting more and more restive, he obtained his concession. He hastened to have it surveyed, divided and parcelled out. And all the time
this was going on he had to struggle with the ill-will of
the officials who were difficult to satisfy, and with the
carelessness and impatience of the veterans. Nevertheless, he held the respect of them all, and, what was
even better, he succeeded.

He occupied thus a strategic position of prime importance in Virginian politics, since he not only kept
in touch with his comrades-in-arms, but united them

in a compact group which he controlled, as they knew that without him they would obtain neither the concession, nor a good parcel of land in the concession. Moreover, he managed to break down the artificial barrier which England had set up, and showed them the great route to the West at a time when they were all most anxious to secure lands there, but did not know how to do so. Having been the military leader of the Virginian troops during the years of the French and Indian War, George Washington continued as their political leader for the next ten years. While Virginia orators declaimed about the rights of the colony, he gave the rights definite value.

This important political situation was one outside of the Virginia Parliament where Washington's beginnings were very small. As in all countries governed by a parliament, flowery speeches played the predominant rôle in the Virginia Assembly, and Colonel Washington, who lacked the advantages of a scholarly education, was not able to make fine speeches or debate on natural rights learnedly. A great handicap as, moreover, it was extremely important to talk brilliantly at the House of Burgesses in Virginia because speech-making was often all the Virginians could do. They had in vain imitated in order to supplant the British Parliament. The Ministry remained all powerful, and did not feel obliged to consider their propositions at all.

Washington was very modest in the beginning. The first law to which his signature was affixed treated of a delicate but local matter: 'A bill to preserve the Water for the Use of the Inhabitants of the

Town of Winchester, and the limits thereof, by preventing Hogs from running at large therein.' [18]

From time to time he was entrusted with a military matter. And as it was noted that he conducted his affairs prudently and methodically, and as his social situation and his influence over the veterans became more solid, his colleagues had an increasing respect for him.

He gave an impression of stability. He never failed to have himself reëlected and this at small expense. In 1768, it cost him only twenty-five pounds sterling twelve shillings; in 1771, twenty-six pounds sterling three shillings, and in September, 1769, nothing at all. A man to watch over the ballot box, a ball at the tavern, a generous supply of cakes and rum and a good fiddler, combined with the personal popularity of George Washington, sufficed to assure him of success. For the modest sums he spent he had a respectable majority. In the county of Frederic, which he first represented, he was elected by 505 votes against 400 for George Mason and 294 of Colonel Stephen. At a later date in Fairfax County (where Mount Vernon was located), he received 185 votes, J. West received 142 and was elected with him, while Captain Posey with his 87 votes was defeated.

Washington gave an impression of greatness. Everyone knew that no one could treat him lightly. And his manor house at Mount Vernon conferred special distinction upon him. Admirably situated on the banks of the Potomac, Mount Vernon was at the very boundary of the Southern and Central colonies, not far from Maryland and only a four days' leisurely

journey from Philadelphia, which was then the commercial centre of the English colonies. Mount Vernon,
famous for its hospitality, was the favourite stopping-
place for all distinguished travellers and influential
men on their way from the North to the South. Thus
Washington cemented his close relations with the
Governors of Virginia, of Maryland, and of Pennsylvania, who were pleased to welcome him whenever he
chose to visit them. The great gentlemen of Maryland, the Carrolls, Calverts, and also the powerful merchants of the country, Thomas Ringgold in
particular, as well as the influential personages of
Philadelphia, the Galloways, Allens, Shippens, Penns,
all visited him and were pleased to have him visit
them. The marriage of his stepson, Jacky Custis,
with Miss Calvert strengthened these connections
and gave him a position which was equalled by few
among the great gentlemen of Virginia. He had been
the military leader whom all the colonies admired, and
now he was a gentleman whose prominent social position was the best considered and the most respected
throughout the colonies.

He made his presence felt by being silent, and this
in turn made him much talked about.

A deep seated instinct, which there was no resisting,
compelled the American aristocracy to begin their
struggle for liberation against the British aristocracy.
But the latter, vaguely conscious of danger, constantly shifted its position, avoiding sharp conflicts,
trying to gain time and to baffle the Americans; incapable of acting efficaciously, the English aristocracy
tried to prevent the American aristocracy from acting.

And for ten years, from 1764 to 1774, they succeeded
in doing so. They did not stifle this instinct, but they
successively baffled and disarmed the various revolutionary leaders. The Americans complained of the
lack of currency and wished to print paper money;
they were forbidden to do so, but at the same time
they were promised that all the taxes raised in
America would be spent in America. They rose up
against the Stamp Act, claiming that the British
Government had the right to levy external taxes but
not domestic taxes, since they were not represented in
Parliament. The English revoked the Stamp Act and
agreed to levy only importation taxes and customs
duties.

Thus, by 1774, the English Government had made
all the popular American leaders contradict themselves. Dickinson, the great Pennsylvanian hero of
1765, had protested against the domestic taxes, but
he agreed to the external taxes, and then, finding himself in no position to attack the new measures of the
English Government, he lost the confidence of the
Patriots. John Adams had acted magnificently, but
he was a lawyer, and because he had accepted to
defend the English officers who had fired on the Boston rioters in 1772, he counted himself as good as lost
in the eyes of the Patriots. Franklin had always
preached, wished, and prepared for gradual emanci-
pation of the colonies, but the intermediary measures
he suggested seemed treason in 1774. Suspicion also
fell on him because he was the Deputy Postmaster of
the Royal Mail for America. Hancock and the other
merchants were considered smugglers rather than
patriots.

Washington was the only one without blame or stain. He had been strictly faithful to his own people and to the movement which was sweeping the country. He had not committed himself to any system nor to any untenable theory. At the time of the difficulties about paper money, he had protested like the others and he had made known his dissatisfaction to his London correspondents, not from a theoretical standpoint, but simply as a fact. During the Stamp Act trouble, he had acted in exactly the same way as the Patriots and refused to import any product which was taxed; this he did neither violently nor submissively; he simply wrote to his agents in London, not to send him any food liable to the English tax. He knew very well who was managing matters on the other side of the water. Washington did not make many speeches in the House of Burgesses, but he was one of the most active in the practical politics of the country. Patrick Henry menaced George III with a new Cromwell, but Washington, less old-fashioned, established a solid association of planters in his neighbourhood who systematically refused to import English goods. He was the leading member of this group and held a strategic position. He was one of the first and ablest to undertake the training of 'independent companies' of farmers and townspeople which began to form. They did not hear from him stupid words or extravagant ideas, but they saw him everywhere and knew all he was doing.

Washington did what they all did, and asked no questions. Theories were of no value to him. He found plenty of them in the gazettes and they helped him to this extent that when someone asked him for his ideas, he referred them to Rind's 'Gazette.' If someone wanted to know what were his guiding principles, he referred them to the 'Gazette.' If someone asked him for the fundamental reasons of his actions, he referred them to the 'Gazette.'

He was not the theorist of the Revolution but its born leader. A powerful individual feeling, the reflection of a collective feeling, gave him good reason for being certain of his place. He did not try to define the Revolution; it was his task to guide it.

He had no grudge against the King of whom he always spoke with deference.[19] But when he referred to this conflict, he always mentioned the 'Enemies of America' and said 'them.' He knew that it was a war between the same two antagonists. Less involved than the others, his instinct was more exact and he was better suited to the time because he had submitted himself more simply to the movement which was sweeping on the American people and its aristocracy.

He had none of the moral crises from which Franklin, Dickinson, John Adams, and other revolutionary leaders suffered. Nor had he any of the Messianic enthusiasm which Jefferson sometimes professed. He accepted the Revolution serenely because it was necessary, legitimate, and conservative. Unless it took place the Virginian aristocracy was doomed. He stated as much to his friend Bryan Fairfax:

I am sure I have no new lights to throw upon the subject, or any other arguments to offer in support of my own doctrine, than what you have seen; and could only in general add, that an innate spirit of freedom first told me, that the measures which administration hath for sometime been and are now most violently pursuing, are repugnant to every principle of natural justice; whilst much abler heads than my own hath fully convinced me, that it is not only repugnant to natural right but subversive of the laws and constitution of Great Britain itself, in the establishment of which some of the best blood in the Kingdom hath been spilt.[20]

The revolutionary passion which animated him was conservative and creative. It had grown in him during the years of his hard struggle with himself and of his concentrated effort on the plantation. It had been nourished by Sally Fairfax whom he saw acting in the republican dramas of Addison, and in whom there was the ancient leaven of the English Whigs, and who had kept alive in him the pain which had enriched him.

When the Fairfaxes left Belvoir for England and the country seemed as empty as his heart, when all Mount Vernon, bewildered by the death of Patsy Custis, was desolate as a tomb, George Washington felt a new passion stir within him.

He was certainly the widower of his great love, and the deserted Belvoir symbolized the definite defeat of his dearest dream; the fields and hills, the clouds and the hamlets, the slaves in the fields and the workmen in the villages (to it all he had given the best of himself), all this noble Virginia which remained the core of his heart, filling him with proud joy. In his fields 'the cherry buds were a good deal swell'd, and the white part of them beginning to appear,' when (March 10, 1775) Colonel Washington took a long last look over his lands, orchards, and gardens, and reviewed the Independent Company of Richmond County which had chosen him as their leader and which was preparing under his orders 'to defend their King and their country.'[21]

Then he left for Philadelphia.

CHAPTER IV

THE DICTATORSHIP OF GENERAL
WASHINGTON

GEORGE WASHINGTON, COMMANDER-IN-CHIEF

TOWARD noon on May 9, 1775, when Colonel Washington, in his blue and buff uniform with gold buttons, entered Philadelphia, attended by his servants and slaves in livery, disorder was at its height. The news of the first battle between the Americans and the Redcoats, the battle of Lexington, was known since April 25. The popular imagination was inflamed. Everyone became excited, rushed about and then went on their way, each in his own direction. The Americans all wanted a revolution, but each of them wanted his own particular kind of revolution made to his order and refused to accept that of his neighbour.[1]

They shouted and protested — but they spoke English and felt they were still English; most of them trusted in the English Parliament to settle their difficulties, because they had had the habit of being proud of Parliament; for so many years it had seemed to them to be the chief glory of their time; an admirable lesson offered by the Anglo-Saxons to the despotic and corrupt monarchies. How could one doubt its ultimate wisdom?

They grumbled against the Ministers, but the King retained his popularity. Was he not one of those

Protestant and Hanoverian Whigs who had so ably
led the English against the French and other Papists?
Of course they protested against the decisions of the
Ministry in the name of liberty, but in the name of
'British liberty.'

In Pennsylvania, the Patriots and their famous
leader, Franklin, preached resistance, but they had
been advocating a reorganization of the colony under
the direct control of the King for the last fifteen years
and this complete turn-about spoiled their eloquence.
As a party they feared the revolution more than they
hoped from it. The other group, the partisans of the
Penns, were in a better situation to denounce the
Crown, because they had been opposed to it for ten
years, as having departed from its 'tradition,' and it
was impossible for them to really favour a radical
revolution. In Virginia, the gentlemen, in debt, dissatisfied at seeing the West closed to them by England, irritated by Parliament's insolent attitude, had
by now lost all sympathy for the Government in
London — but they were gentlemen and not revolutionary orators. The merchants in the sea-ports,
knowing that their money was tied up in the trade
between America and England, eagerly desired a reconciliation. Many of the New York traders and a
good number of the New England merchants shared
this desire. In the North, however, the laws forbid-
ding commerce with the French islands and other
various restrictive measures had become so irksome
that the important merchants had found their way to
the radical party and were subsidizing it. In the New
England towns, the merchants relied on the revolu-

tionary committees for support, in order to carry on their smuggling, while the preacher, out of hostility to the Church of England, upheld them by his eloquence. The commonality, for whom England represented a far-away and overbearing aristocracy, a collector of odious taxes, and a detested recruiting officer, followed the movement gladly. The measures of repression, clumsily and feebly enforced by the English authorities, without intimidating them had irritated them. New England was ripe for a revolt. From 1765 to 1790 there was no change in her state of mind.

From month to month the disorder increased. Royal officials were seized, tarred and feathered and then paraded through the streets straddled backwards on donkeys. The sympathizers with England, and with the Cabinet, the advocates of moderation, the lukewarm rich, and the not too generous merchants were treated in the same way. Little local hatreds were often gratified. Various groups denounced each other. The common people, the rabble and adventurers amused themselves enormously, but the rich, the influential and the sober began to be alarmed.

It was necessary that they should find a definite line of action which would achieve and limit the revolution, for otherwise it would fail and be a calamity.

In New England the situation was well in hand; the revolution was to be handled by the town meetings, a traditional institution, a sort of soviet which the Yankees had established ever since their arrival in America and which, under the minister and the lawyers and carefully guided by the merchants' money, gave the power to a strong practical radical group capable of maintaining order. Unfortunately, this institution did not exist in the rest of the country. In Virginia (except in the sea-ports where the merchants were the leaders) the strongly established aristocracy could take their place; the gentlemen controlled the colony and could direct a revolution. But in all the Central and Southern colonies, where social conditions were still fluid, the population thinly scattered, and the classes competing and ill-defined, chaos reigned.

It was useless to hope to find a formula which would unite everyone. Each orator had his own theory to which he clung passionately, and which the others did not think worth anything. The great American leaders, to suit the immediate needs of the cause and by force of circumstances, had, every one of them, sponsored several doctrines in succession, sometimes diametrically opposed, in order to struggle against the 'English encroachments.' Otis, Dickinson, Patrick Henry, Franklin, Samuel and John Adams, all had been prodigiously eloquent and ingenious, and had filled the pamphlets and newspapers until no one knew where they stood. It had to be admitted that the American Revolution was largely provided with political and economic themes, theories, and principles, but had not as yet any doctrine which could be universally accepted and which was capable of uniting together the collective will of the people. Whenever the leaders theorized, they disagreed and were divided.

To the farmers of Connecticut the Revolution was a means of putting the Pope in his place; they burned his effigy in the public squares; for the New

England preachers it was a holy crusade against the Episcopalian Church; for Hancock and the merchants, it meant the freedom of trade; for Franklin, it meant tolerance and liberty; for Samuel Adams, it meant liberty and independence; for Washington, it meant justice and access to the lands of the West; for the children, it meant bonfires in the town squares and processions in the streets. To the impartial observer, the revolution was confused, sound, and inchoate exaltation.

It was action alone that united all these divergent impulses; on the whole, the people wished to defend their possessions and were ready to make great sacrifices, not only because of fidelity to their principles, but also because of the sheer intoxication of this delightful new sensation: American patriotism, which increased rapidly throughout all the colonies, when the 'cruelties' inflicted by the English on their continental brothers became known. From Charleston to Nantucket all kind-hearted people felt the same. The feeling was strong and widespread. It still needed a rallying centre, a flag.

When Colonel Washington strode through the streets of Philadelphia his imposing ways, his tall form in his handsome uniform, followed by his splendid attendants, attracted a great deal of notice.[2] He went here, there, and everywhere in the city buying provisions, arms, and munitions for his Virginians; he did not talk, but quietly purchased and paid. He made a profound impression. He was seen everywhere; in the morning and in the afternoon at Congress; in the evening at the Tavern with the merchants, or dining in

society with Judge Allen, with the famous Doctor
Shippen and at the home of Joseph Shippen, the
Secretary of the Provincial Council, with the ostenta-
tious banker, Morris, or with the well-known lawyer,
Dickinson, with Mayor Fisher, the leading Quakers,
or the richest merchants. He was untiring.

One Sunday morning he appeared at Quaker meeting; in the afternoon he attended the service of the
Church of England; on the Sunday following he went
to hear the morning sermon at the Presbyterian
Church, and attended benediction at the Catholic
Church after lunch. He frequented the taverns where
the New England delegates were lodged; as well as
those where the delegates from Carolina dined. And
going everywhere, wherever he went he gave the same
telling impression of force, resolution, and calm.

He could never be quoted. He had never praised
the King, but on the other hand he had never spoken
ill of him. He had never attacked Parliament, but he
had never asked the people to have confidence in it.
He had never advanced a theory, but had followed his
instinct, which was the popular instinct, and he had
been active. Among all these subtle lawyers, preachers, and merchants he was the only one who had the
habit of facing facts without preconceived opinions.
This was extraordinary. The American Revolution
was neither a lawyer's quarrel, nor a merchant's undertaking, nor a preacher's frenzy, nor a demonstra-
tion in philosophy, in spite of all that has been said of
it; it was the maturing of a profound feeling, which
crystallized itself in George Washington.

He realized this, and to all classes, parties, creeds or

colonies he held out his hand silently. If this were politics, one must admit that of all the members of the Continental Congress who were so busy attacking the King and quarrelling amongst themselves in 1775, Washington, although he was in uniform, was the only one to have an exact political sense.

The ablest politicians deceived themselves. They were still looking for possible combinations. Even Franklin despite his wisdom committed this error. He had returned hostilely from England, with an exact and creative scheme ready to lead the Revolution, and to avoid the spilling of blood. He wanted the Patriots to be very firm and active in organizing America, but at the same time he wanted them to present a definite plan of conciliation to England. Franklin relied on his inexhaustible fertility and resourceful genius to make his plan prevail. It would undoubtedly have prevented war, but he could not make himself heard. The assembled delegates had an unconquerable distrust and dislike of any intellectual or administrative formula. They could not accept it. No matter how large and flexible Franklin's project was, it seemed only burdensome to them. They turned spontaneously away from it.

And they turned toward the corner near the door where Colonel Washington was standing silent.

The delegates of New England, especially influenced by John Adams, who was genuinely intuitive, had Washington named Commander-in-Chief of the Continental Army.[3] They knew him and they realized that Virginia, with him at the head of the army, would join them, and that this would have its effect upon the rest of the country. They felt that if the towns of New England and the aristocracy of Virginia joined in a common cause, the rest of America would fall in step, as the southernmost and the central colonies were leaderless and drifting. The delegates, themselves so talkative, so infatuated with theories and political orations, guessed that his silence would be the great resource of their country, that his reserve was their real force.

Washington knew it too. He accepted them and wrote to Mrs. Washington: 'A kind of destiny has thrown me upon this service.' 4

He had a sudden desire to weep, but he mounted his horse instead, and a man on horseback does not weep.

It was thus that George Washington at the age of forty-three became the Commander-in-Chief of the United Colonies of the American Continent, June 15, 1775.

He left immediately to join the army.

It was not without some emotion, for he left behind him his wife, his past, and all his possessions to undertake an ill-defined and perilous career. He had, fortunately, during the last twenty years learned to subdue his feelings and to keep any emotion from becoming an obsession. He went on then during this hot summer of 1775, anxious but firm, and conscious of the importance and difficulty of his mission. His mind was open, his will was tense and his reactions flexible, he was ready to adapt himself to circumstances and be led by his destiny, while always doing all he could to succeed in his appointed task as Commander-in-Chief of the American Army. After so many years of confusedly struggling with himself, he felt a need of combat and movement, he was animated by a desire to fight and to use his energies. 'I shall feel no pain from the toil or the danger of the campaign,' he wrote to his wife, but to his brother he took keen delight in describing in detail the fine army he was to command and how much money Congress was spending on it. He had always wished for a military career and now it was actually offered to him. Notwithstanding his modesty and his disinterestedness he felt a profound joy at the idea that he was finally to realize his hopes. This was his only illusion.

From the very beginning he had to occupy himself with politics.

Congress had chosen him less for his military quali-ties than for his personal prestige, knowing that the men would rally around him. They hoped that mat-ters would be settled without too much fighting. The Loyalists wanted neither war nor revolution; the Whigs wanted a revolution, but no war, for they were very much opposed to the idea of a permanent army.

As Washington travelled through the country, the people ran out to see him and greet him, the munici-palities and provincial assemblies, delivered cordial and respectful speeches in his honour or wished him Godspeed, quick success, and a happy return to ci-vilian life. The New York Assembly worded their appreciation neatly:

Confiding in you, Sir...we have the most flattering hopes of success in the glorious struggle for American liberty, and the fullest assurance, that whenever this im-portant contest shall be decided by that fondest wish of each American soul, an accomodation with our mother country, you will cheerfully resign the important deposit committed into your hands, and reassume the character of our worthiest citizen.

Washington answered with beautiful politeness.

May your every wish be realized in the success of America at this important and interesting period; and be assured, that every exertion of my worthy colleagues and myself will be equally extended to the reëstablishment of peace and harmony between the mother country and the colonies, as to the fatal but necessary operation of War, when we assumed the soldier, we did not lay aside the citizen; and we shall most sincerely rejoice with you in that happy hour, when the establishment of American liberty, upon the most firm and solid foundations, shall enable us to return to our private stations in the bosom of a free, peaceful and happy country.[5]

He had no intention of imposing himself as a military man upon his compatriots; from the beginning he made this clear to everyone; Congress in Philadelphia and the colonies all felt the same antipathy for everything military, and the former expressed its feeling in an indirect but effective manner by limiting the supplies of the army and disposing very slowly of all the questions which dealt with the war: they did not want Washington to have too large an army nor to keep it for too long a time. They proceeded to watch his movements. Far from resisting, Washington encouraged this tendency; he was used to the Virginian oligarchy and found it easier to work in collaboration with others than to feel himself completely responsible for his own decisions. He had received his rank, commission, and command from Congress; if he could teach the country to respect Congress, he would increase the respect due to himself. And he knew by an infallible instinct that the victors of this struggle would be those whose General Staff was the more active and united; the American aristocracy in opposing the English aristocracy, would have to be in itself a closely coördinated body. From the beginning, Washington kept Congress in touch with all his movements and consulted it on all matters requiring decisions.

He could not have been more deferential if he had been a general of the Sultan; his daily correspondence with Congress fills volumes. In writing so extensively he had the feeling that he was accomplishing what was expected of him, for he very well knew he had not been chosen as the best general available (in the eyes of all Americans, the best general in 1775 was the Englishman, Charles Lee, but he could never have been made commander-in-chief, for he had been born in England, and was also too completely a military man; without any political rôle or any ties to bind him to the country). Washington, on the contrary, was especially famous for his defeats, his activity, the political rôle he had played since 1759, and his large fortune. He was the only great American aristocrat known from Boston to Charleston, who had been seen wearing a uniform and spending his money liberally. Congress counted on him to do all that it was necessary to do and nothing more.

Washington found that the New Englanders also had distrust of military men.[6] The men of the Continental Army had fought well; but they had no in-

tention of being considered soldiers. They were fond
of their chief, Artemas Ward, who was a good man; he
had been a student at Harvard, a country store-
keeper, somewhat later a judge, a politician, and
finally a general. They preferred him to anyone else,
but they welcomed Washington friendlily, for they
realized they needed the help of the Virginians to get
the better of the English. Their reception of him
was not enthusiastic; it was polite, deferential, and
cordial. The Yankees made a point of giving the
ceremony an air of real dignity. To achieve this all the
troops were drawn up in battle array, no attention
being paid to the different uniforms or motley cos-
tumes. When the General arrived to take over the
command, he was preceded by 'one and twenty
drummers all especially drilled respecting their duty
and as many fifers beating and playing around the
parade.'[7] The General, mounted on a powerful black
horse advanced among them and they all together then
sang a hymn. When this was over, they went home;
Washington had a glass of Madeira with Ward, and
the men drank a little rum in his honour.

Very few of them took the trouble of noting in their
diaries any account of the ceremony in which they
had just taken part. Some of them merely wrote on
this date, July 3, 1775, 'Nothing new,' although it was
on that day that General Washington had assumed
the command of the American troops.

Washington was too wise to take offence at their attitude: beside, he found the reception suitable, and he
was delighted by the novel aspect of New England,
fresh and green in the midst of summer. He was not

used to seeing so much grass in July, and it pleased his farmer's heart, and he felt as a soldier it was a presage of the laurels he counted on gathering. The negligent ways of the army did not worry him, for he was going to establish a new discipline and infuse life into his troops; work and responsibility attracted him. He immediately began thinking of the uniforms he would have made for his men, the 'muster rolls' he would compile, the provisions he would get together, the discipline he would establish, the manœuvres he would engage in. At Philadelphia they didn't want him to be a commander for too long a time; they hoped to avoid the cost of a prolonged war, and that with his fifteen thousand men he would expel the English victoriously and then return quietly to his plantation to grow tobacco. It was a simple, reasonable and economical plan. He meant to follow it.

Unfortunately, Washington did not suit the men of New England.[8] The old generals were not at all satisfied with the appointments and promotions made, to be sure, at random by Congress in Philadelphia, and they were not in very good humour. They knew their ground and their troops, and realizing that any attack would be costly and would imperil the existence of the whole army, they did not want to do any attacking. The soldiers were all good men, interested in the war, passionate for liberty and ready to shed their blood for their country; but they were too near their homes not to return now and again to the farm to see how the family was getting along, to find out if the cow had calved — or to change their shirts. In camp, they did their work competently enough, without, however, showing much respect for their officers, whom they treated as equals. One day Washington saw a soldier being shaved by an officer; this upset him very much, it was abhorrent to a Virginian. He also had to become accustomed to their long and noisy drinking bouts which were held on every possible occasion, in season and out. If the weather were too cold, they had to drink, of course, but it was the same when it was too hot; and on pay-day the camp was far too gay. When the English artillery bombarded them and a cannon ball fell within range, the first man to pick it up and to throw it back was entitled to a round of drinks offered by his officer. The men abused this custom. But it did not hinder them from being pious, singing hymns, calling Gage a 'crocodile,' and 'a Second Pharaoh,' and invoking the 'God of Israel.' Young and old, poor and rich, they were all alike; the Harvard students who spent their summers fighting, but who returned hurriedly to their studies at college in the autumn, showed the same instincts as the farmers of Roxbury and Medford, who were always ready, even when on duty in the trenches, to lay down their muskets and hasten home to milk their cows.

Washington wanted to organize their discipline, but by the end of a month he had his troops almost in a state of rebellion.

Washington wanted to train the Yankee officers. His friend and adviser, Joseph Reed, in Philadelphia, had to write to him to be careful.

Washington proposed to his staff that they attack Boston by force, in row-boats, then later on when winter had come, to make an assault, taking advantage of the ice; his staff listened to him politely, but refused without hesitating.

Washington planned a big offensive campaign; he sent to Canada an expeditionary force with precise instructions; it began by being brilliantly successful, but, being poorly supported by Congress and the New England colonies, the expedition failed, and ended piteously, in spite of the heroism of Arnold.[9]

Washington wanted at least to form a solid army, but it dissolved in his hands; he had no ammunition with which to bombard the English, no tents to cover his men, no food to sustain them, no uniforms to clothe them, no money to pay them. He did not even know how his army was constituted, for he could not obtain correct lists from his officers. The troops of the various colonies were jealous of each other. It was impossible to succeed in unifying the regiments, to establish coöperation between them, or to assure any permanency in the corps of the army. It was a phantom army with powderless cannon, guarding the shadow of a blockade.

But the British army on the other side of the trenches was also a phantom army, obsessed by incontrollable fear, lacking wood, meat, vegetables, reenforcements, information, morale, and an energetic leader as well. In the meanwhile, Washington at general headquarters trembled, very certain that in case of a British attack his troops would disband. Gage, and later Howe[10] was trembling in Boston, fearing that a spirited attack by the Americans would annihilate his army. Both were right, but as neither army was in a state to fight, their fears were useless.

The British, terrified by the rigorous winter, the vastness of the continent they had to conquer, the strength of the American entrenchments, huddled closer and closer together in Boston, which they were preparing to evacuate. The Americans, terrified by the impregnable positions of the British around Boston, by the big British cannon, the excellent British discipline, the innumerable shining ships off the coast, cowered in their trenches, shivering in the blasts of the bitter North.

Thus the winter passed. When spring came, Howe left Boston, with his troops and baggage, and as many Loyalists as he could take along. Washington entered the city, as proud of having accomplished his mission as he was disappointed at having been only a policeman when he had counted upon being a general.

He did not understand very well what had happened, nor why it had happened, but he had finished his apprenticeship of the Yankee character; he had a more complete conception of what 'America' was and he knew New England, that curious land where the grass was green throughout the summer, where the soldiers were ready to fight and die, but refused to be sentinels, and alternately drank rum and praised God.

Heaven had granted him success, but not victory. His only activity in camp had been politics and organization. All his military efforts had ended in disappointment. In leaving Boston for New York he was at last to have a real war.[11]

New York, it was believed, would be chosen by the British as their next objective. Located in the centre of the colonies admirably situated and easily attacked by sea and offering an excellent base for a fleet, New York would necessarily attract them — especially since it was filled with Tories. Once established on the Hudson, the British could intercept communications between the South and the North, menace Philadelphia, harass New England and Virginia, control all coastal navigation and organize the political rally to England. Washington thought that the loss of New York would mean the end of the Revolution.

They were of the same opinion in Philadelphia, and Congress ordered him to save New York; unfortunately, this was not easy to do.

The American navy was composed of small privateers and schooners; the army, in spite of all Washington's efforts, remained a crowd of incongruous militia, always in a hurry to return to their homes, and of regular soldiers engaged for very short terms. Moreover, New York was teeming with spies; Governor Tryon, who was fleeing, was a notorious Tory, as was also the Mayor of New York, David Matthews; the high society of the city, the merchants, lawyers, and Anglican clergy did not like Congress; the people themselves, sailors, farmers of Long Island and Haarlem, were very lukewarm to the 'rebel' cause. The devotion of the Committee of Public Safety and other patriotic organizations to it was feeble. All sorts of intrigues, impossible to control, were hatched on the docks, in smoky taverns, or in the isolated inns in the countryside.

However, they would all have to be steadfast if the Americans wanted to hold New York and preserve their liberty, and Washington, knowing the danger of losing both, repeatedly asked for help from Congress, from the neighbouring colonies and from the Patriots of the region. In May, he even went to Philadelphia to prepare his campaign in agreement with Congress and to obtain from it the means to do battle.

Washington came to Philadelphia in a very different frame of mind than he had been in June 1775. His long association with the Yankee revolutionaries had opened his eyes to the real character of the Revolution. He was no longer content to criticize the Ministry in London and demand justice for America. He wanted independence, and he attacked the King. He had learned long ago in Virginia that there was an American aristocracy, distinct from the British aristocracy, and now his experience in the army, the contact with his troops and with the Patriots of Massachusetts, had made him realize that there was an American people distinct from the British people. In camp outside Boston, he had come to realize that there was an 'American nation.'

He had lost his respect and affection for the King. Until April, 1776, Washington claimed he was fighting the 'ministerial troops,' but after this date he fought against 'the King's soldiers.' He had read the King's speech at the opening of Parliament (November, 1775), in which George III·had violently taken side with his Parliament against his American subjects. Washington had always considered that only the King could reconcile the two countries and serve as arbiter, but now the King was changed, and, instead of being a judge, had become an advocate; he had taken the part of the British aristocracy against the American aristocracy, and so there was no longer any hope in him, and the only thing to do was to help the Revolution on its way.

Washington turned against George III the more violently because George III had been his last hope. It was certain that without a clear rallying cry the war could not go on. A political system would have to be organized if the army and resources were kept up, and to organize such a system, a definite program was necessary. Congress, which could not furnish him with an army and ammunition, could give him at least a political weapon which would enable him to keep his army together and to secure ammunition.

The Declaration of Independence was much less a proclamation than it was just a weapon of war. Under the leadership of the noble and popular Lord Howe, and his brother, Sir William Howe, the British navy was approaching New York, thirty battleships and four hundred convoys laden with thirty-two thousand soldiers, ten thousand sailors, twelve hundred cannon, minted gold and promises of pardon. All the Tories, from Philadelphia to New York, in spite of the persecutions they had suffered, plucked up courage; in Philadelphia, the majority of Congress hesitated; in New York, Washington had, with much trouble, gathered together a motley army of twenty thousand men, but he could hardly rely upon it; a conspiracy, which included members of Washington's bodyguard, had threatened his life. When the warships of the British navy cast anchor in the Hudson, just opposite the city, the end of the war seemed clearly in sight.

It was in haste then that the radical members of Congress, the Northern Yankees and the aristocratic philosophers of Virginia, supported by Franklin and the Committee of Public Safety of Philadelphia, which had just forcibly taken over the control of that city, aroused by Washington's courage and need, wrote, amended, and published the Declaration of Independence. This violent and passionate document, intentionally incomplete, unjust in its logic, heroic in its daring, and prophetic in its solemnity, destroyed all possibility of retreating. It established an American nation, concrete and definite, opposed to Howe.

All the country, the towns, congress, and the army were in confusion, but the writers of the Declaration had thrown a clear and striking idea into the midst of an excitable people. It crystallized their thoughts. All other solutions now seemed idle, and Sir William Howe,[10] who had come to make war at the same time that he was seeking an understanding, to pacify the people by intimidating them, and to reorganize the country without a definite plan of action, seemed as uselss and futile as a driveling old woman. Not that he was stupid; he was lacking in neither skill, nor courage, nor sympathy for the Americans; but he represented a majority in Parliament which was blind and which had lost all its political sense. He had been instructed to make war on the Americans but without injuring them, to bring them back without yielding to them, and to buy their leaders without giving them what they wanted. He found himself opposed by the courageous few, who had been united by danger and by a watchword which was sweeping the country.

The political sense of Franklin, of Adams, and of Washington saved the American nation.

The situation was strange. Howe and Washington were face to face and were ready; Howe had an excellent army, but no political strength; Washington had an unreliable army but he was armed with an admirable political weapon. Howe was certain of winning the war, but it would be almost impossible for him to organize the country for peace; Washington had every possibility of carrying his country with him — and of being beaten.

To Howe's keen regret, he was made to fight. Both Howe and his family had been popular in America; he was a Whig politician, what he hoped to become was the pacifier and proconsul of America, not its conqueror. He did not think very highly of the Tories who were his allies; his heart went out to Franklin and the other Patriots. And so he tried, by every means possible to bring about a reconciliation, but Congress refused. He resigned himself to beginning an offensive; but he clearly saw that every blow aimed at his enemy strengthened its army, and stimulated the national anti-English feeling in a country, which had been hesitant. He tried to keep the war from being destructive. He wished to avoid any pillage on the part of his troops, or that any towns should be set on fire by his cannon; he was careful to exchange prisoners as soon as it was possible to do so and to induce those whom he could win to aid the British cause (as was the case with Sullivan and Charles Lee); he returned personal letters addressed to Washington which had been captured or which his spies had se-

cured; he slowed up his operations so as to give the
Americans time to reflect. In a word, he acted as a
perfect man of the world and a conciliatory politician.
He was not a bad general; whenever he set out to
fight, he was victorious. In spite of Washington,
Howe disembarked; he beat the American troops
at Long Island and captured three generals, three
colonels, four lieutenant colonels, sixty-four officers
and ten hundred and six soldiers. He took New York,
sent his ships down the Hudson and seized the American forts which protected this river. He landed in
New Jersey, he obliged Washington to retreat hastily
over the Delaware, in three and a half months he had
reëstablished the King's power over the whole of the
Central colonies (August 25 to December 10, 1776).
Howe not only succeeded in forcing Washington to
retreat, but took from him men, officers, generals,
cannon, and large stores of provisions, as well as destroying almost all his reserves and bases; all this
damaged Washington's prestige and authority, to say
nothing of blasting his hopes. It was a well-conducted
campaign.

Washington had predicted that if New York were
lost, the American cause was lost.[11] In December,
New York was occupied by the British, and the real
war for which he had longed, ended in disaster.
Washington had lost everything but his unconquerable tenacity.

With an army of militia and recruits, which were
changed every six months, it was impossible to
struggle against the finest army of regulars in the
world. Every pitched battle was lost before it was

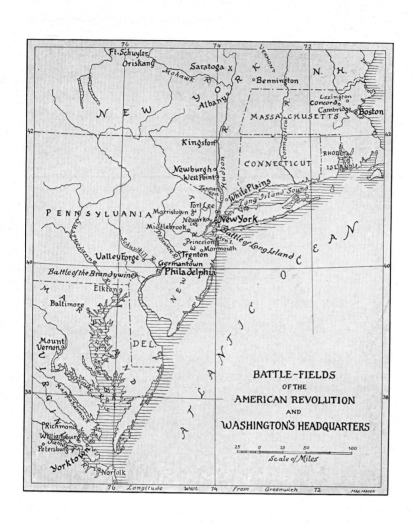

BATTLE-FIELDS
OF THE
AMERICAN REVOLUTION
AND
WASHINGTON'S HEADQUARTERS

Scale of Miles

fought. Washington had no illusions on this subject
and wrote about it in his letters with a violence which
sometimes bordered on frenzy. Any genius less great
than his would have abandoned the struggle without
waiting any longer. But he was used to hoping
against hope, his will never yielded, and his perfectly
lucid mind showed him not only the reasons for his defeats but also the elements of a possible victory.
Poorly trained soldiers and insufficient ammunition
put him at the mercy of an enemy taking the offensive,
but the enormous extent of the country he knew so
well, the rapidly changing conditions, the climate to
which the English were not accustomed, politics in
which Howe lost his way and which Washington understood so clearly, gave him once more a real superiority.

The farther the British advanced, the more difficult
it was for them to solve the political problem. Howe
had not foreseen the possibility of the Declaration of
Independence and had no alternative solution to offer.
Moreover, he could not possibly have had one, for he
was always forced to wait for the instructions from
London — which never came. Americans who were
found within the British lines were forced to swear an
oath of loyalty to the King, and by this means Howe
managed to win individuals to his side, but he was
unable to establish a solid body of adherents. The
farther Howe moved from the coast, his warships and
bases, the more he felt he was lost. His military successes served only to bring out his political helpless-
ness, and to show how very precarious the British
domination really was. On the American side, the

men lived poorly and sadly, but they lived; on the English side, the soldiers camped comfortably and gaily, but they were only camping. The offensive which had been so well conducted was sterile.

Washington's retreat, on the contrary, was perfect in its wisdom. The jealous and suspicious Congress at first made a sour face at Washington's setbacks, but as the enemy gained ground, and the position of Commander-in-Chief became less and less desirable, Congress more and more wanted that Washington should hold it. No matter how desperate his situation, Washington never lost his head; he constantly kept in touch with Congress by means of almost daily correspondence, and did not neglect his connections with civilians. He was pitiless by conviction and in principle to the Tories, but his generosity to the Patriots knew no bounds. Even when his money chest was empty, he always found means to pay his spies. Even when the enemy pursued closely at his heels, he always found time to write innumerable letters to the State Governors, to notables of Congress and Virginia, to his friends in the North and in the South. Even at moments of the greatest distress when he was being cruelly attacked on every side by the Americans, he never turned against his detractors to avenge himself. And so on December 20, the situation in Philadelphia seeming hopeless, Congress made him a sort of military dictator, allowing him complete freedom of action in the organization and administration of the army. Thus an understanding and a collaboration between the two essential institutions of the national American life were solidly established. It was also fortunate for the United States, that Washington's great rival, Charles Lee, was captured by the English (December, 1776). Lee thus lost most of his prestige and all possibility of supplanting his leader. The leadership of the army was now undivided and the army was more manageable. The soldiers commenced to appreciate the value of their general, and after he had led them through two victorious skirmishes (Trenton, December 26, nine hundred prisoners; Princeton, January 4, four hundred prisoners), they were really 'his' soldiers. These fights were only small successes, but they galvanized the troops, impressed the civilians, and intimidated Howe. Though the latter had won a series of pitched battles, had captured New York, the best Harbor in America, and a chain of forts, he had really accomplished nothing. Washington, by leading two surprise attacks, had electrified the country.

He made the most of his advantages; during the winter and spring, when military operations were suspended, he kept up an enormous correspondence with Congress, the State Governors, with Franklin in France, with influential men in various parts of the country, and with his officers, trying to maintain their interest in the army and to secure reënforcements.

He failed in a number of cases; he could not prevent Congress from making untimely nominations and promotions and discontenting the best of his general officers; he could not influence Congress to pass the necessary laws for recruiting and organizing an army; he was unable to quiet their suspicions and their bitterness concerning himself; he could not appease the jealousy which divided the Northern and Southern troops; but by his activity, by being constantly present where he was needed, by the habit he had of never neglecting practical details — the color of uniforms, the pay of chaplains, the swords of prisoner officers — by seeing everything just as it was, he kept a sane, clear vision for all the Americans, and made a strong bond between the various States, and between the civilians and the army. Congress and Washington, united in spite of their disagreements, were the soul of the nation, whereas Howe was the leader of a conquering army, thousands of miles away from its King and Government.

In the spring Washington gathered the fruits of his labour. His army was in a deplorable state, his provisions low, his generals embittered and nervous, but they decided to stay with him to the end, they knew what their goal was, and, grumbling all the while, they wanted to win it. They had a definite plan of action. Howe with all his fine army, abundant stores, ample credits, which the Crown allowed him, felt more perplexed than ever. The connection between him and London was a fiction, while his relations with the armies of Canada (Burgoyne and Carleton) were practically non-existent. Lord George Germain, the Secretary of State for the Colonies, an imperious and careless leader, had no plans; having complete confidence in Howe, he gracefully accepted the general's plans for the occupation of Philadelphia; but he also approved the plan of General Burgoyne, the brilliant favourite of London, who wanted to cut the colonies in two by taking his army down the

Hudson from Canada. Lord George Germain liked both these ideas without noticing that they opposed each other. He pleasantly advised the two generals to come to some agreement over their diverging plans. Howe, courteous gentleman that he was, promised to do so, adding at the same time he would not change his plans one iota. Burgoyne started off on his great adventure counting on the coöperation of Howe who had not promised him anything and who was not his subordinate. And, under the placid eye of the British Minister of War, a British army was coming down the Hudson from Canada to New York to join another British army, which had, in the mean time, already left for the South.[12]

The American generals found the plan very disconcerting. It would also seem to have disconcerted Destiny, which until now had seemed ready to give the victory to the British. At least it upset calculations. The British, with their generals, their troops, their munitions, and provisions, had only to choose an objective, for they were sure of reaching it; no American army could stand up against them in a pitched battle. Half of the country was dissatisfied with Congress and was only waiting for a sign to revolt against the new Government in favour of the old. The British, nevertheless, had to prove that they were the stronger, and had to offer a solution of the political problem. But instead of choosing one objective, Howe and Burgoyne chose two; Howe wanted to intimidate the Americans by occupying their capital, where he hoped to be able to make peace with Congress; Burgoyne wanted to encircle and isolate New

England, the cradle of the Revolution. Both of these plans were good, and had they been followed singly, were certain of success; followed simultaneously, there was the serious danger of dispersing the British forces over an immense territory and transforming a war against the American army into a war against space. This would give the Americans a chance. Moreover, neither Howe nor Burgoyne knew how to establish contact between their soldiers and the people. They had spies, satellites, even partisans, but no real friends. They allowed the Loyalist party to weaken and to stagnate. They took none of the advantages they could have obtained from the numerous persons of note who were on their side. If their imagination was fertile on the subject of military plans, it was sterile concerning politics.

In the midst of all this, Washington was disconcerted, worried, and calm. When he saw Howe leave with all his army, he rightly thought that he had gone to join Burgoyne, and he feared once more that the future of America was compromised. When he heard that the fleet was sailing to the North, he thought a bold offensive on Boston was being planned; when he was told that the fleet had headed for the South, he thought that Charleston would be attacked. Then, when he learned that the fleet had been seen in the Chesapeake, he realized, without understanding why, that Philadelphia was the objective of the British. He prepared to defend the city.

Philadelphia was attacked and taken without any difficulty. Howe even succeeded in beating Washington and routing his army twice, first on the Brandy-

wine where the victory was decisive, then at German-
town where the battle was more evenly fought. The
American recruits and militia could not stand up
against the British veterans and trained Hessians in
an open fight. Washington knew it. He took his defeat patiently. He spent his time harassing the British and keeping his army together. Washington was
no longer the young colonel of former days, who was
fond of hearing the bullets whistle by and whose
supreme joy was to conquer. He realized now how
vain mere victories were, and how valuable defeats
could be when proper use was made of them.

The success of his colleague, Gates, who, having
been aided by space and the climate, had forced
Burgoyne to capitulate at Saratoga, neutralized the
success of Howe, who occupied Philadelphia in
September, 1777. Moreover, Howe's political inactivity, now that he held the capital, made a deplorable impression. It was clear to everyone that he had
nothing to suggest, nothing to propose, nothing to do.
The Loyalists were distressed, the lukewarm partisans
were cynical, the Patriots clenched their teeth, and
across the sea, the French followed the revolutionary
events eagerly. It was the climax of the conflict.
Washington felt it and did what was needed.

He temporized. By keeping his army together and
remaining faithful to the unmanageable Congress, he
had ensured a political victory without a military
triumph.

General Washington Practises the Art of Waiting

From this time on, the American Revolution was as good as ended. The King of England held New York and Philadelphia (winter, 1777–78), but with neither any American Government or any American life in these two cities, formerly so rich and powerful. Congress, wandering from place to place, was the American Government. In only the towns and open country which had escaped the British occupation was there any American life. Thanks to the increased commerce with France and the neutral countries, the harbors had once more become active.

The war continued. Nevertheless, it would have to end. The British generals, dull-minded and obedient to their orders, had not yet realized that everything was lost. They could rightly say that this did not concern them. As military men they felt and knew that America could be easily conquered. This view of the situation was militarily correct, but of what use was it to conquer if they could not impose their will on the defeated? For four years the American armies were continuously beaten as the following list proves: orderly and successful retreat of the British army under Sir Henry Clinton from Philadelphia to New York, in spite of Washington's attack at Monmouth (June 28, 1777), which had no result; repulse of the French and Americans at Newport in August, 1778; capture of Savannah and the whole of Georgia by the British (winter, 1778–79); British occupation of the larger part of South Carolina (winter, 1778–79); destruction of Norfolk and Portsmouth in Virginia by the British fleet (May, 1779); British raids in Connecticut; Loyalist and Indian raids in Pennsylvania and in New York; repulse of the French and Americans before Savannah (October 9, 1779); capture of Charleston by the British; capitulation of General Lincoln with six thousand men (May, 1780); occupation of South Carolina by the British; British cavalry raids in the Carolinas; success of Tarleton at Waxhaw; brilliant victory of Lord Rawdon over Gates at Camden, South Carolina (August 16, 1780); victory of Cornwallis over Greene at Guilford Court House (March 15, 1781); Rawdon's victory over Greene at Camden (March 25, 1781;) successful expedition of Arnold in Virginia; Tarleton's bold raids (January-May, 1781); Cornwallis's pursuit of La Fayette across Virginia (summer, 1781); with all these victories the British made no political advance.

Sir Henry Clinton, Commander-in-Chief from the summer of 1778 until the end of hostilities, realized the difficulties of the American war: he understood that the great enemy was distance; he therefore never engaged his army in the interior of the country; he was satisfied in merely sending out detachments which harassed the enemy and beat them by surprise. Well supplied from the sea, which they never left far behind them, these troops ran few risks, for the English had control of the Ocean, and they succeeded in disorganizing the economic, social and political life of the rebellious colonies. This plan of Clinton's was not without practicalness and efficiency, but it was not reasonable. England, who relied on the Tories and Loyalists, should have shown herself to America as the defender of law and order; but her soldiers behaved really more like pirates, brigands, and bandits. She temporarily weakened the American Government, but induced the various social and political bodies, which were formerly not in favour of independence, ardently to espouse the American cause.

The results were evident. The South (Georgia, South and North Carolina), where the English dominated, was in chaos; New England and Virginia (until 1781), which had been the two centres of the Revolution, remained the two centres of national resistance; Philadelphia became the capital of America and the place of exchange for all kinds of political traffic; New York and its suburbs was still a centre for the Loyalists, although they were becoming less popular there; they were no longer Loyalists by faith, but by profession; only those who were paid remained Anglo-Americans. The British soldiers had come to America as policemen, but had ended by being thieves, and they had caused a panic in America which was only of benefit to the rebel government.

Wherever the Redcoats appeared, the American people were furious. At the same time, on all sides there was a tendency to consider that the war was over and they were surprised that so many efforts and so much money were still asked of them for a war that was ended. Washington was never able to gather more than fifteen thousand men around him at a time, and he could not count on their stability. Washington compared his militia to Providence whose plans and intentions are inscrutable. He said that in order to keep the men with him: 'We shall be obliged to detach one half of the army to bring back the other,' and concluded (it is said) with: 'The men with me are too few to fight, and not enough to run away with....' [13]

Though vigorous fighters and good soldiers, the Americans did not have the military spirit.

✓ Finally Washington formed an army, but it was 'his army'; he managed to make it, thanks to the devotion of his personal friends and to the aid of foreigners. The disciplining of this army was entrusted to the Prussian Steuben; the Frenchman, du Portail, perfected the engineering corps; the American, Knox, and the Frenchman, du Coudray, were in charge of the artillery (which would have been non-existent had French cannon not been sent regularly); the Frenchman, Armand (Marquis de la Rouérie), trained the cavalry; the Pole, Pulaski, did good work, the three best leaders of men under Washington were Greene and Wayne, Americans, and La Fayette, a Frenchman. Thus, he solidly established his General Staff, but it remained a picked body in the country. There was no enthusiasm for the army; the Pennsylvania farmers near Valley Forge in 1776–77 and those around Morristown in New Jersey, would have had no qualms in letting the soldiers die of hunger, freeze in the cold, faint in the sun, or moulder in the rain. However, they liked the soldiers well enough when they had money to pay for their purchases, and they were proud of them when they were victorious. The rest of the time they did not give them any thought. The army, which Congress always suspected and often bullied, was Washington's own creation and his instrument. It belonged to him body and soul, especially after the dismissal of

Lee (suspected of treason in 1778) and after Gates was beaten by Rawdon in 1780. It had but one leader, but one soul. Thanks to Washington the army lived, kept in touch with the country; it was the only permanent body among a disorganized and doubting people, and it came to be the symbol and the instrument of national unity.

The British generals spread disorder all around them; Congress existed and worked among a tumultuous and unruly mob; Washington alone was the personification and exponent of law and order.

The country was deeply grateful to him, and the people's confidence in him was so great that they thought it unnecessary to help him. They felt that this last effort should be made by France. France's entry into the War had greatly diminished the zeal that the Americans had shown, when they had just commenced to fight. Their military expenditures in 1777–78 of $24,000,000 fell in 1779 to $10,000,000; in 1780 to $3,000,000, and to less than $2,000,000 in 1781, the decisive year. Most Americans thought it absurd to have hostilities continue with the British; as Americans they found it reasonable that the British, according to their tradition, should devote all their time and resources to overcome the 'hereditary enemy.' Indeed, more than one American was surprised and hurt that such was not the case. This idea, which in turn could seem displeasing to a Frenchman, was really so natural that the Minister of the English colonies (Lord George Germain) from 1778, devoted his efforts to defending the British West Indies and to attacking the French West Indies. However, England was too deeply engaged in America to change, and a war on the Continent would have been too costly. France and England did not enter into serious military hostilities in Europe. This was deeply regretted by Congress in Philadelphia, who even made the Minister of France feel their disappointment.

Such a point of view seemed strange to Europeans who were used to seeing magnificent wars and were fond of the brilliant spectacle. These patriots, who were heroic when it came to being killed in a corner of their field, defending their farm, and cows, but who were firmly determined not to pay the cost of the war, nor to lead a military life at camp, surprised their philosophical friends as well as their charming feminine admirers. Franklin tried in vain to explain their attitude to M. Turgot and Madame Helvetius.[14] He preferred to talk about Washington.

Washington at least was sublime and comprehensible. As a gentleman, a good soldier, a general, and an organizer, he appeared from far off as the Hannibal or Frederick the Great of the New World. Those who had caught a glimpse of him, surrounded by his aides-de-camp, followed by his black slaves, guarded by his squadron of young Virginians who were all over five feet four inches in height, could never forget the grandeur and serenity of his face, the sunken mouth and unseeing gaze. They looked up to him as to a God.

No doubt they were right. For four years, with the exception of a few rear-guard or outpost skirmishes, he had had to be satisfied with commanding a passive army in face of an inactive enemy, but Washington had never for a moment lost his patience nor his habit

of activity. He was cruelly and unjustly attacked in
Congress in 1777 and 1778; Conway was appointed
general against his will, and they considered replacing
him by Gates. Washington did not permit himself to
recriminate against Congress and if he put his enemies
in their place it was by his serenity and his stern moderation. He had been untiring in reorganizing his
troops, just as he had done between 1753 and 1759,
and had formed them into an army which as constantly dissolved like sugar in water. Not giving himself a moment's respite, he kept up a political connection with Congress, with the States, with the notables
of various regions, with the financiers, and even with
foreign countries. He had direct connections with
France through Franklin, La Fayette, and the French
Ministers in Philadelphia who had visited him in his
camp. In this way, he secured subsidies, an army and
a navy for America. He also gained for himself, and
this without intentions, a position of moral authority
which made it impossible henceforth for Congress to
remove him. In all these relations he practised the
same exactitude which characterized him in all his
efforts and activities. In former times, he had noted
the days when he ought to plant clover and timothy;
now he noted, with the aid of La Fayette, the exact
rank and social position of each distinguished officer
of the French army, in order to be able to treat them
suitably, according to their rank. Being an aristocrat,
he got along quite naturally with aristocrats. He had
more trouble in understanding Rochambeau and
could not hide his annoyance at the French general's
officious disposition; but the straightforwardness of

the old soldier and his admirable military gifts made Washington appreciate him, and they worked harmoniously together.

From his Headquarters in Morristown, Washington, attended by his young aides-de-camp, overwhelmed all America and Europe with his correspondence, and he kept a close watch around him. At no time did his sensitive attention weaken; whether the British became more active or sank deeper into their apathy, they did not deceive him. He knew that his first duty was to maintain the American army, the essential but weak weapon of a new people, and that some day he would have to prove to the British that the War of Independence was over. He realized he could not succeed in doing this without France. If Washington, supported by the Continent, were really invincible on land, the English, aided by the seas which they controlled, were invincible all along the coast. To triumph over them, Washington would have to secure the mastery of the sea, and for this he needed the aid of the French navy. (Congress had had twelve frigates constructed in 1776, but there was only one left at the end of the war!) He obstinately begged for a French navy, asking for it through Congress, through Franklin, through La Fayette, through Rochambeau, through La Luzerne, and through John Laurens; he begged for it so hard and so long from gods and men that finally they gave it to him.

For four years he had proved himself to be an untiring leader, whose concentrated attention, perfect detachment placed him far above all his contemporaries. It is easy for a man to win a battle or to lose it courageously, but it is much greater and far more difficult to prepare and wait for it without ever losing sight of it, without making a false move or a gesture which would have betrayed impatience. Washington's detachment was not due to indifference, but to an extraordinary effort of will; he was in a constant state of tension as is proved by his few but furious outbursts of indignation, when, as for instance, at the Battle of Monmouth General Lee turned traitor, or when his soldiers deserted him, or when Rochambeau refused to entertain his cherished plan of attacking New York. His anger would blaze violently for a moment, but he would master it immediately and would keep it hidden forever after. When everyone else was excited or sleepy, his head was cool, and he never permitted the inner flame, so alive and burning, of his ardour to flicker.

When meals were over in the General Headquarters, Washington surrounded by his silent aides-de-camp, and himself silent, would sit steadily cracking nuts between his powerful hands, while all looked on with timorous veneration, admiring the contrast between his straining rude muscles and his Olympian gaze, which, unwaveringly fastened itself on space.[15] General Washington was training himself to wait.

THE MILITARY TRIUMPH OF GENERAL WASHINGTON [16]

During the six years General Washington had been making war he had not succeeded in beating the British army; he had had fortunate skirmishes; small engagements in which he had displayed genius; defeats in which he had shown heroism; happy events of which he had taken advantage; but as a general he had never won a battle; he knew this very well, and with all his wisdom, he suffered from it. The only great American victory had been won by the scatter-brained Gates and by the passive resistance of space. In the spring of 1781, Washington was still the general whom Fortune had least favoured. All his heroism, genius, and amazing force of character had been lavished on the feeding, lodging, disciplining, rebuking, warming, cleaning, gathering together, and maintaining of his army, and not allowing them, as they tended to do, **to take** their flight as easily as a flock of sparrows.

He had had all the troubles and anxieties of war without having experience any of its rough delights, for which his violent nature longed, and already they were talking of peace. He knew that everywhere they were tired of fighting, the better classes were uneasy, and the common people were beginning to show a spirit of anarchy. In September, 1780, Washington discovered the treason of General Arnold, one of his very best officers, whose heroism and military qualities had been displayed a hundred times on battlefields, but who had attempted to sell West Point, the most important fort of the United States, to Sir Henry Clinton. In the beginning of January, 1781, the Pennsylvania troops mutinied, demanding the money which was owing to them and which they felt was their due; at the end of January, the New Jersey infantry followed their example, and Washington for a

time feared that the contagion would spread throughout the entire army. The civilians were not worth
much more; the new State of Vermont quarrelled
with Congress and negotiated with the English;
Georgia had a British government; Virginia, cowed by
raids of the British, seemed worn out. The Governor
and the Assembly of Virginia were in flight, the administration of the State was overturned, and its
aristocracy, which had always been so energetic, lost
its head and sent calls for help to Washington and to
Congress. Indeed Virginia was one of the two indispensable pillars of the Union. If Virginia were beaten
by the British, the strength of the rebellion would have
been so broken that the British could have successfully
offered their peace. By keeping in America a state of
disorder, they would have prevented the American
nation from forming.

The campaign of 1781 had to be the decisive one.
There had to be such action as would enable the
Central States and the South to have a civil organization. Washington proceeded with infinite care to win
the confidence and friendship of all those of whom he
had need: his troops, his generals; Rochambeau and
all the French generals; the Count de la Luzerne and
other French diplomats; the members of Congress and
the State Governors who sent him reënforcements,
provisions, and munitions; various notables, in particular the banker, R. Morris, who furnished the ready
money necessary for the campaign; the French ad-
mirals, Barras and Grasse, from whom he obtained
all he could get. His aide-de-camp, John Laurens,
now in France was to bring back vessels, food supplies,

troops, and money. Everything was ready. Washington decided to strike the great blow which would vindicate his long waiting and which would assure the definite establishment of the United States: he prepared to attack Clinton in New York.

Toward the middle of June everything was ready. The French army had arrived, the French navy was expected, and Washington already had engaged in a few preliminary skirmishes, when he had once more to renounce his plan. Sir Henry Clinton had received a reënforcement of three thousand Hessians, and Grasse, upon reflecting, refused to join in such a dangerous operation. A military victory slipped from Washington's grasp.

As usual, he had to turn to his political activities. Virginia, ravaged by Cornwallis, called for aid; Grasse was inclined to sail there with his fleet, for it was not far from his base in the French West Indies, and Rochambeau cherished the idea of a campaign in the South. Washington, chagrined, yielded, loyal to his collaborators and generously patient with his destiny.[17]

On August 14, he abruptly decided to transport the largest part of his army, and all the French army, to join La Fayette, who for the past five months had manœuvred opposite Cornwallis, succeeding in keeping him in check, tiring his troops and confusing him. The British general, reluctantly carrying out the orders of his chief, Clinton, had retreated to the ports of Yorktown and Gloucester at the mouth of the James River (August 5-6); here he leisurely fortified his position and quietly waited for the British navy. But what was coming toward him was not the British Navy.

For once, the only time in all the seven years of fighting, Washington and Fortune were of the same mind. La Fayette and his troops duly watched over Cornwallis at Yorktown. Grasse, who was returning from escorting a large convoy of French merchant vessels from the West Indies, bound for France, found a good wind which brought him quickly into the Chesapeake. He entered on August 30, with a fleet of six frigates and twenty-eight warships, carrying thirty-two hundred soldiers under the command of M. de Saint Simon and nineteen thousand sailors. He had arrived without any trouble, for Rodney, with the great British fleet, thought he was still at large in the Atlantic, protecting the fleet of merchant vessels. Grasse found La Fayette on the spot with his four thousand men. Cornwallis in front of them had just finished establishing himself and his seventy-six hundred men. He was fairly caught in the trap. The French admiral, who was eager to conquer and to return to the West Indies, wanted to attack immediately and capture Yorktown without delay. La Fayette, who knew that Washington was on his way to join them, and who wished to reserve for him this perfect victory, refused Grasse's proposition. Providence and the French, even at the risk of allowing Cornwallis to escape, were polite to Washington.

Washington hurried. By the 19th of August, he had the French army and most of his troops across the Hudson. On August 30, he was in Philadelphia with

Rochambeau, and saluted Congress, which was delighted to see the parade of the French divisions. September 9, he was at Mount Vernon and spent three days there, resting, and showing his estate to Rochambeau. During this time the troops had embarked and were proceeding by sea from the Chesapeake to the James River.

Fate worked for Washington: Graves and the British squadron at New York wanted to attack Barras at Newport. But Barras, by chance, had lifted anchor a few days before Graves was ready and had come to the mouth of the James River without any opposition, his eight warships carrying five thousand sailors, a detachment of soldiers, and an enormous train of artillery. Graves, not being able to meet Barras, turned against Grasse, but his squadron, will power, and intelligence were far inferior to those of the French admiral. From September 5 to September 10, the two fleets bombarded and pursued each other until Graves felt he had done his duty, and not wishing to run any further risks, he left Cornwallis to his unhappy fate and returned to New York for repairs.

Greene, La Fayette, Barras, and Grasse were all by a miracle together and surrounding Cornwallis, while the British squadron was being made ready and Clinton was holding council as was his habit; this he did very well and carefully, but he was very slow. Washington had not hoped for so much luck, when he began his advance, but his untiring patience merited it, and now that Heaven had been kind, he neglected nothing to make the most of it.

With extraordinary dispatch, he had led his troops from New York to Virginia. On September 17, he boarded the flagship of the French admiral to visit Grasse. He secured a landing force from him and a promise of detailed and complete collaboration, provided everything was over by October 15. He also obtained his confidence, an even more precious gift.

Then he rejoined La Fayette before Yorktown. On September 26, all the allied troops had disembarked and had begun their work. Washington was burning with impatience, and always anxious lest the French ships would leave, he wanted to hurry rather than to think of his good fortune.

On September 30, Cornwallis evacuated his advance line of entrenchments which were too exposed, and the allies occupied them immediately.

On the 24th, Clinton had written Cornwallis that he was holding council and that he would embark with five thousand men and come to his aid about the 5th of October. Cornwallis answered him the same evening, expressing his approval and his gratitude.

On October 9, the allies, having set up their cannon, began the bombardment of Yorktown at three o'clock in the afternoon. On the 10th, Cornwallis received a very cordial letter from Clinton telling him that he was holding a council and that he would embark no doubt about October 12 to come and help him. Cornwallis answered with perfect courtesy on the 11th, writing that this was very satisfactory and that moreover he could not hold out much longer.

On October 14, the French and the Americans attacked the advanced earthworks of the British and took them at the point of the bayonet. On the 15th, not having received another letter from Clinton, Cornwallis, always courteous, wrote him not to hurry unduly, as he would certainly arrive too late: 'The safety of this place is so precarious that I cannot recommend that the fleet and army should run great risque in endeavouring to save us.'[18]

On the 16th, he tried to save himself by a sally, which was vigorously met and repulsed. During the night he embarked one of his divisions on barges intending to cross the river and slip off to the North. He might have succeeded had not a terrible storm arisen making the movement impossible. He was forced to lead his troops back to Yorktown, and on the 17th he wrote to Washington: 'Sir, I propose a cessation of hostility for 24 hours... to settle terms for the surrender of the posts at York and Gloucester.'

All night long and all morning the bombardment had been furious. The British, in their demolished entrenchment were lacking food and medicines, their ammunition supply was visibly diminishing, and they felt that the end was near. At ten o'clock in the morning one of their drummers mounted an entrenchment bearing a white flag, and began to 'beat a parley.' A wave of joy swept over the American lines, where the soldiers had already begun to talk confusedly and eagerly about peace.

Washington received the tenders of Cornwallis with reserve and discussed them coldly. He was wary of fortune to the end. He granted the British no unnecessary delay, and conceded no advantage that he could refuse. Coldly and calmly without emotion, he dictated a severe and humiliating capitulation (October 19, 1781).

At the very moment when Cornwallis yielded, Clinton, who had stopped writing, had left with Graves's warships (once more in good condition), but they did not arrive in time to see the surrender which took place that day at three o'clock in the afternoon. The British troops, with unsheathed swords and flags furled, marched slowly to an English tune (The World upside down) between the French and American troops ranged in line; they gave up their weapons, and then, disarmed, returned to the town, where Cornwallis had been detained by a well-timed indisposition.

The British had lost 353 men (killed and wounded); the French 186; the Americans 88. Some 32,000 Frenchmen (23,000 sailors, 9000 soldiers), 7000 Americans, and 7600 Britishers had been engaged in the siege.

Washington had finally succeeded in gaining the great victory which assured his glory as a general, but it was not a pitched battle. Yorktown was a siege, as perfectly handled as if it had been a game of chess. Once the soldiers had prepared for the battle, they scarcely had to fight: it was not owing to their bayonets that they had triumphed, but to the sturdy soles of their boots. Destiny had wished to reward Washington politely for having spent so many years in training and organizing his army, in establishing inter-allied coöperation, and harmonizing all the various branches of his services. Yorktown was the triumph of a bold and perfect conception which had surmounted the most difficult conditions and had resulted in the most important military victory of the Revolution with scarcely any bloodshed.

It was the last battle of the War for Independence.

THE MORAL TRIUMPH OF GENERAL WASHINGTON

From one end of the universe to the other, the American victory aroused enthusiasm, for it was as important as it was picturesque. To have gathered two fleets from over the sea and four armies over a continent, at a certain place at a certain time and to have obtained a decisive success with little loss was an achievement which Cæsar or Hannibal in all their glory had never attained. This perfect victory was all the more striking since it followed a long series of defeats, and because the British General who had been trapped was the most brilliant and insolent and formidable ever seen in the New World. America exulted, and in Europe, where for four years it had been customary to believe the American soldiers to be indifferent and the generals to be inexperienced, the victory was the most unexpected one of the century. Washington was universally admired.

He might be modest, but he knew he merited praise; it was due to insistence that he had obtained a French army and fleet; to his skill, that he had established coöperation with them; to his energy, that he had, now tactfully, now rashly, maintained order in his army; to his conciliatory persistence that he had obtained reënforcements and provisions from the Governors and Assemblies; to his personal influence that he had secured the necessary funds from Morris,

the Secretary of the Treasury, as well as barges and
other indispensable resources from rich and notable
people; to his untiring and insistent deference that he
had wakened Congress out of its lethargy. All this
had been done by him and by him alone.

The country vaguely realized this; the troops
realized it clearly. Courageously but without ostentation, Washington had always set an example to his
soldiers and was always present among them, even
at the worst moments of the Revolution, at Valley
Forge (1777–78), when the half-naked American army
seemed more like a horde of sick animals, shivering
from cold and hunger, than a band of men. Washington had always interceded for them with Congress and
the local Assemblies, to obtain food, shelter, and
clothing. Towards the end of July, 1781, when the
Connecticut troops, dissatisfied with their Assembly
(which did not heed their complaints), were about to
disband, Washington stepped in and kept them together.

Other generals had been brilliant, bold, had known
how to organize attacks cleverly, had led their troops
to death with dash and spirit; they were admired; but
the soldier of all times and of every country thinks
more of his mess and shelter than of glory and death,
and the American soldiers were more attached to
Washington than to Gates, Greene, Wayne, or La
Fayette. He at least looked after their rations, lodg-
ings, and uniforms every day, twelve hours a day.
Washington was their real leader, both in war and
peace.

What did they know of Congress? Congress refused

the bounties for enlistments which the soldiers wanted; refused to pay retired officers half-pay; refused to give the generals the consideration they thought their due; talked indefinitely about it without ever succeeding in finding money, not even managing to keep up the standard of American paper money; could not succeed in establishing good will between the colonies — Vermont was still quarrelling with New England, Pennsylvania with New Jersey, while the North was sharply antagonistic to the South. The most distinguished members of Congress had left it: Franklin, Adams, the Lees, and Jay were in Europe; Henry Laurens was in the Tower of London; Jefferson was occupied with local politics in Virginia, Hancock in Massachusetts; a younger generation unknown to the people filled Congress, and now and again, in an access of fervour, would forbid dancing, vote a day of fasting and humiliation, or denounce the army because of its profane language! Some people thought that Congress had not asked enough from France; others thought it treated the French too servilely; it was badly considered everywhere, but above all in the army, where the soldiers were bitter about its innumerable promises, committees, commissions, speeches, and its short memory. Poorly fed, poorly paid, poorly lodged, such was the state of this victorious army, which was conscious of having saved its country and of having assured its future.

The troops were tired and discontented. Even the peace which was approaching did not please the soldiers. They realized that the States would be glad to disband them as soon as possible, without paying or thanking them. The men gathered in secret and discussed these things heatedly. The officers at their mess took a decided tone. The generals at their tables were meditative. Washington seemed deaf and dumb.

It was then that one of the oldest, wisest, and most dignified of all the colonels (Lewis Nicola) wrote him proposing a *coup d'état*, and if, Washington wished it, a crown (April, 1782).

Washington answered:

Be assured, Sir, no occurrence in the course of the war has given me more painful sensations, than your information of there being such ideas existing in the army, as you have expressed, and I must view with abhorrence and reprehend with severity... Let me conjure you, then, if you have any regard for your Country, concern for yourself or posterity, or respect for me, to banish these thoughts from your mind, and never communicate, as from yourself or any one else, a sentiment of like nature.[19]

Then, after having his letter countersigned by two aides-de-camp, he sent it to Nicola. And he remained silent.

The others kept on talking. They all talked. Not only the old officers now, whom he had rebuked, but all the young, ambitious, cunning, bold men who wanted glory, gold, or a revolution. A plot was organized. The ringleaders of the plot were two brilliant politicians, Alexander Hamilton, a former aide-de-camp of Washington, and Gouverneur Morris, the assistant to the Secretary of the Treasury, Robert Morris, who must have known about the plan. These two young men did not think much of the government to which they belonged; they wanted to have a strong government established, and to them this meant a monarchy. Knowing the army was in a state of exasperation, they wanted to take advantage of this situation. The two young men made a proposal to Washington in such a discreet way that he could understand if he wanted to understand, comment on it if he wished to, or ignore it — just as he preferred.

In the army, both the officers and the soldiers continued meeting in secret; the officers were especially disturbed; they insisted on their half-pay and railed against Congress. General Greene in the South, one of Washington's most brilliant lieutenants, was quite as nervous as they. General Knox, who was with Washington, held himself in readiness to follow any bold plan. And Gates, no longer in disgrace, but second to the Commander-in-Chief, would only be too glad to lead the troops should Washington refuse.

On February 7, 1783, Hamilton wrote to Washington from Philadelphia that things were going on badly at Congress, that funds would shortly be lacking and that the country would soon be faced with a grave crisis:

If the war continues, it would seem that the army must, in June, subsist itself, *to defend the country.* If peace should take place, it *will* subsist itself, *to procure justice to itself.*

And he advised him not to discourage the army; on the contrary, to take their part with moderation and guide them and to keep his place as leader so as to impose on the States a political reorganization which Congress was too foolish to understand, too weak to demand, too discredited to obtain. A menace was added to this suave suggestion:

An idea is propagated in the army that delicacy, carried
to an extreme, prevents your espousing its interests with
sufficient warmth. The falsehood of this opinion no one
can be better acquainted with than myself, but it is not the
less mischievous for being false.[20]

On March 4, Washington answered:

I have often thought, but suppose I thought wrong, as it
did not accord with the practice of Congress, that the public interest might be benefited if the Commander in Chief of
the army were let more into the political and pecuniary
state of our affairs than he is....

Thus he showed him that he was rather in sympathy with his idea of establishing a strong central
government. But he added that if the army wanted
to secure justice for itself...

...it would at this day be productive of civil commotions
and end in blood. Unhappy situation this! God forbid we
should be involved in it. The predicament, in which I
stand as a citizen and soldier, is as critical and delicate as
can well be conceived. It has been the subject of many
contemplative hours.... Be these things as they may, I
shall pursue the same steady line of conduct, which has
governed me hitherto.

No revolution, no monarchy, no militarism.
Washington further declared that he would intercede
for the army, that he would ask again in Congress that
justice be given to the soldiers, and he concluded by
suggesting that the members of Congress obtain the
means from their respective States for establishing
a strong military force. It was necessary to have a
change of direction in government, but it had to be
civil, not military.

On March 10, a printed speech was circulated among the officers which boldly and cleverly invited them to unite and demand their rights from Congress and the country. The officers were to hold a meeting on the morrow. The wording of this pamphlet indicated it had been written in Philadelphia, while its immediate success gave rise to many fears. Gates studying the features of the men around him thought that he would win.

He was not right. Washington knew his men and knew that he would hold them. As soon as he read this manifesto and its anonymous convocation, he wrote and circulated a concise statement ordering the officers to meet on Saturday the 15th at noon under the chairmanship of Gates. Thus he gained time, during which the excitement would partly calm down and he gave the conspirators the hope of his support and seemed to be putting Gates at the head of the movement. As a matter of fact, Gates, being obliged to preside, could not talk or influence the men as he would have done had he been with the other officers.

Washington did this himself. At the hour and place mentioned, he came to the meeting to read a report in which he spoke to the men of their common glory, of their services, of all they had suffered, of all that they had defended and would defend again, and all that they represented for America and the world. He promised to plead their cause with Congress and only asked for their confidence, begging them to act in such a manner that posterity could say: 'Had this day been wanting, the world had never seen the last stage of perfection to which human nature is capable of attaining.'[21]

Then he disappeared, leaving the officers deeply moved. Knox and Putnam had no trouble in having passed a unanimous vote of confidence in the Commander-in-Chief and Congress. As a final measure, Gates was entrusted with the pleasant duty of carrying a report of this meeting to Washington.

Washington had refused the crown a second time.

Few decisions in history have been more important. But just because it helped to develop a republic is no reason to consider it a perfect expression of a democratic mind.

Washington was an aristocrat. At the same time that he did all this so nobly, he accepted an invitation to preside at the organization of the Society of the Cincinnati, although it had roused the indignation of all the democrats of Europe and America. It was, of course, in the beginning, an hereditary association of Veterans of the War of Independence, a kind of military order and charitable institution at the same time. They would necessarily be important politically and have a great deal of influence. Washington was its first president, but Franklin thought this society was the most serious menace to the republican and democratic spirit of the New World.[22]

Washington did not agree. He respected the monarchies of Europe. Before the American Assemblies and the British Parliament had begun their quarrels, he had been a faithful subject of the King of England. He was a sincere admirer of the King of France, and he rejoiced in the fact that France, a hierarchic nation, with a solid social system, was closely connected with America. He found this to be a great advantage. He had practical ideas about the masses just as he had about Congress. He had no naïve belief in the right of the majority. At the beginning of the Revolution he had not hesitated in following the minority which was far in advance of the majority; he thought it was quite right that the Committees of Public Safety obliged the people to be patriotic and he persecuted the Tories without respite (winter, 1776–77, and all through the war). He was advanced politically. He knew that Congress did not represent the direct voice of the people and he knew that people are often deceived and majorities wrong.

Washington was an aristocrat; he saw clearly that in America a leader once crowned king by his troops was dedicated to demagogy and disorder. Morris and Hamilton, less clairvoyant in politics than he, did not yet perceive what he already knew: that a national aristocracy was being formed gradually in Congress and around Congress, and that he, an aristocrat of Virginia, did inevitably belong to the nation which was being created by these leaders.

Fate had given him a victory, but it had not been his destiny to be a warrior. He now refused Fate's offer of a military dictatorship and turned to the people, to his troops which he disbanded (June, 1783), and to the State Governors, begging them to unite, to give themselves a strong central government, to pay their debts (thus automatically enriching the rich), and to maintain a solid and permanent army.

As a soldier, he had been the civil dictator of the United States for eight years; the one man on whom the Government depended, the one who alone kept everything moving together, the one who silently knew how to establish order and accomplish things, while Congress merely discussed, voted, and waited.

He had conquered; the United States existed, and the supreme joy he felt was not free of surprise so great that it could only be equalled by the fatigue which overwhelmed him.

He was so weary and so happy that his mind was a blank. He vaguely contemplated this enormous country he had created, this nation he had been the first to know; and for which he had risked his honour, fortune, and life; it was still unformed, but Washington even then clearly foresaw its future power and grandeur.

Chapter V

GEORGE WASHINGTON, THE FATHER OF HIS COUNTRY

In the Shade of the Laurels

WHEN he had disbanded his troops, given his last words of advice to his country, and his greetings to Congress, General Washington dreamed of nothing but of returning to his account books, growing old in his retreat, and dying with dignity. Without waiting for anything further to happen, he returned to Mount Vernon, deserted far too long, to the home which was his own, almost his very self, and to the heart of the Virginia aristocracy which had made him and moulded his life, he established himself there, for the last time as he thought. He wanted to spend the remainder of his days 'in cultivating the affections of good men, and in the practice of domestic virtues.'

He did not refuse the last touch of warmth that life could give, and the glory which had followed him down to his retreat had an exquisite flavour. Tokens of admiration were showered upon him; he was the idol of the people, and the great men of the world paid their respects to him. Books, sent from the four corners of the universe, piled up in his library; but more than anything else, gifts for his garden were sent to him, and these touched him and transformed Mount Vernon into a botanical garden and a variegated managery.

Colonel Jenifer sent him apple trees from Maryland; Governor Clinton sent lime trees and ivy from New York; Henry Lee, horse chestnut trees from Virginia; the Chevalier de La Luzerne sent grapevines from France; General Lincoln, pines and firs from New England; Samuel Vaughan offered him rum from Jamaica; La Fayette, always lavish, sent him golden pheasants and partridges to brighten his fields, donkeys for his stables, hounds for coursing (and a pretty little Masonic apron to wear at the fraternal ceremonies); his brother, John, gave him a swan and wild geese; Gouverneur Morris, Chinese geese and Chinese pigs; Mr. Ogle gave him deer to adorn his woods, Count Williamson foxhounds. Even the noble and proud King of Spain knew his tastes and sent him, under the guard of one Pedro Tellez, the most vigorous and magnificent jackass of all Spain.[1]

Thus Washington was overwhelmed with gifts and honours.

He wanted a peaceful existence, he wanted silence and obscurity; he wanted to live upon his memories. He liked to gallop in the morning as far as the ruins of Belvoir which were already disappearing under their green cloak. In the afternoon, he delighted in taking long rides across the fields, dreaming of the wonderful conversations he had had with Sally, or of exciting battles he had led, and watching his people at their work, meek, obedient, and happy. He rose at sunrise and retired about nine o'clock. The only important event of the day was the dinner, about two o'clock in the afternoon, when he welcomed all the guests who

GEORGE WASHINGTON
Painted and engraved by Edward Savage

had stopped over on their travels to greet him: Americans, Frenchmen, Italians, Germans, Dutchmen: La Fayette, Le Marquis de Chappedelaine, Brissot de Warville, Houdon, M. le Comte Castiglioni, Robert Morris, M. Battaile Muse, Francis Van Der Kemp, Mazzei, Peale, Noah Webster — all came to share his silence, to venerate his glory.

As a matter of fact, silence had not returned to him. His life had been too tumultuous and the fever of ten long years had stayed in his blood. When he awoke in the morning, he awoke with the start of the strenuous days that were gone. He no longer wrote in his diary the peaceful, monotonous sentence, 'Alone all day at home,' for his days were full of activity and his duties multiplied. He galloped almost every day around his whole plantation visiting all his farms. In winter, he was in a hurry to kill his hogs to salt them, cut ice in the Potomac and store it in his cellar, to have the ground graded and fields planted; in the springtime, he grafted his fruit trees, fished in the river with his net; the sowings of spring and fall, spring and summer plantings, the summer and autumn harvests, the haymaking in summer, the labours at the end of the season, allowed him scarcely any time to enlarge his house, to build barns and sheds, and to go in October to the races in Alexandria.

After so many months of seeing war and devastation, he took to planting with passion. He planted lilacs by the garden wall, orange trees near the door, dogwood trees and sassafras near the sheds; he filled his vegetable garden with walnut, pear, apricot,

orange, and cherry trees, Cherokee plums and Spanish chestnuts; around the house he planted syringa,
wild thorn, rowan-trees, filbert and crab-apple trees;
along the garden alleys, he planted poplars, maples,
ash, brambles, willows, lindens, all kinds of chestnut
trees, walnut trees, catalpas, magnolias, alder trees,
yew trees; he bordered his flower-beds with holly, and
on the lawns and in the 'wilderness,' he set up cedars,
papaw trees, sassafras, honey locusts, mulberry trees,
black gum trees, and Canadian firs.[2]

He planted, but when summer came, the pines were
yellow, the ivy seemed dead, the crab and ash trees
had not even budded, the chestnut trees and lindens
were drooping, the green oak and the firs were little
more than sticks; the garden looked dusty and sickly.
Only the laurels had kept bright and green.

He was a great lord, the richest in America it was
said; in the stables of his principal estate (in 1786), he
had 130 horses, 336 cows, oxen, heifers, calves, and
steers; 283 sheep, and more hogs than he could count;
he had 216 Negroes, not counting his white servants
nor day labourers he hired nor all the people on his
other properties in the cities or in the distant West.

He was constantly enlarging his estate; in 1784, he
again bought six thousand acres on the Mohawk and
his possessions in the West became more and more
valuable. He attended to all the details of his affairs
himself cautiously and carefully; he laid the foundations for much greater wealth in the future. He wanted
to owe nothing to a grateful country; the grants of
lands, which it was intimated they wished to make to

him, he rejected majestically and with humility. He wanted only his inheritance and what he himself could add to it. But he neglected nothing that could add to his fortune; everyone that invented anything came to see him and he always listened to them with interest. He invested heavily in an adventurous undertaking, the navigation of the Potomac. This was one of his most cherished ideas, for it was a triple speculation; if it succeeded, it would enrich the investors; it would add to the wealth of those who had bought lands in the West because of the easy access it offered to the Eastern and European markets; finally, it would result in a close coöperation between the States, all of them being interested in the commerce of the West and obliged to work together in order to benefit by it. Washington made every effort to induce the capitalists and the governments of Virginia and Maryland to join him; and at first he was successful; but these were not enough to make his dream possible; the States of Pennsylvania, Delaware, New Jersey, New York, and the Carolinas had to join as well. After taking a great deal of pains and making a great effort, he did not succeed as the Annapolis Convention ended in failure. It was in vain that he had visited the Potomac, examining all the shores carefully, in vain that he had attended all the stockholders' meetings, written to influential politicians and pushed the affair in every way he could, the States could not come to an understanding, and Congress did not know how to force them to it.

He was not less active but just as unfortunate in an

enterprise which was of prime interest to him: the colonization of the West. One of his principal grievances against England before the Revolution was the attitude of the British Government in respect to all the territory in the interior of America, which she would never authorize the Americans to occupy. Washington did all he could to induce Congress to take a firm and energetic stand in this matter. He was eager to acquire vast lands for himself and for his country; he loved the West and he saw there an absolute security for the future grandeur of America and the ultimate union of the States. He tried to make all his friends and all the big politicians realize this: he himself never lost sight of it, and if it were so difficult for him to believe that peace was really permanent, if he continued to have so great an animus against England, it was much less because of all the Americans killed in battle than on account of her attitude in refusing to evacuate the fortified posts in the West in spite of the promises made in the treaty of peace. This was Washington's obsession. In September, 1784, he made a trip to his Ohio lands. He wanted to see how they were, and to get rid of the squatters who, without his permission, and not paying him a cent of rent, had settled on his lands. He travelled uneventfully as far as the Youghiogheny River, where he inspected his holdings, there he found the intruders, had an altercation with them and ended up by agreeing with them that there was no possibility of their coming to terms. He would have liked to have pushed on farther West in order to see his lands on the Great Kanawha, but he was not able to do so, as the Indians were menacing; and he therefore found it impossible for him to defend his possessions from 'Land Jobbers and Speculators... who I had been informed regardless of my legal and equitable rights, patents, &ca.; had enclosed them within other Surveys and were offering them for Sale at Philadelphia and in Europe.'[3] He comforted himself, however:

I say notwithstanding this disappointment I am well pleased with my journey, as it has been the means of my obtaining a knowledge of facts — coming at the temper and disposition of the Western Inhabitants — and making reflections thereon, which, otherwise, must have been as wild, incoherent, or perhaps as foreign from the truth, as the inconsistency of the reports which I had received even from those to whom most credit seemed due, generally were.[4]

Back again at Mount Vernon he dreamed.
Life seemed very complicated to him. The more he knew it, the more did he tend to be prudent. This was only natural, as he now realized all that was lacking in him. After having associated with the brilliant young men, who had served under him as aides-de-camp, and the illustrious gentlemen of Europe, who had been his comrades-in-arms, he was conscious how inadequate his education had been. He felt this deficiency even more when he sat down to read the books which had been recommended to him and which he forced himself to read conscientiously — Raynal's 'History of the West Indies,' for example. He became fearful faced by the enormous quantity of ideas and facts which he might undoubtedly learn, perhaps realize, but which he would never be able to express,

or explain. Meditative, he retired within himself as much as he could.

His home — always filled with his family, neighbours, friends, foreigners, and distinguished personages from everywhere — was no longer a refuge for him. He had to nurse Martha, who was ailing; to visit his old mother and his sister, Mrs. Lewis, at Fredericksburg, where they were lingering on in failing health; to weep for his brother, John Augustin, who had died of a severe attack of gout which had gone to his head; to assist his nephew, Major George Augustine Washington, who suffered excruciatingly from gall-stones; as well as to undertake the care of his nephew's wife, Fanny, who gave birth to a baby (which died soon after) at Mount Vernon. Bushrod Washington bombarded him with political letters; his two nephews, George Steptoe and Lawrence, whom he had sent to school in Georgetown, ran into debt there because they wanted to be dandies; he changed schools and sent them to the Reverend Doctor William Browne of Alexandria, lodging them at the good widow Dade's, after that at Colonel Samuel Hanson's because the poor women had been quite unable to manage the two rascals, so that he could keep a closer watch on them, which was much needed. The two scamps would stay out all night. Once under the care of Colonel Hanson, they refused to allow themselves to be flogged. When Colonel Hanson whipped Lawrence, George Steptoe whipped the Colonel. Then they fled to Mount Vernon, and the General could only reprimand them, pacify Hanson, and pay their debts.

With such a bothersome family, and the whole uni-

verse declaring itself his family into the bargain, what
could George Washington do?

He looked sadly at his table which was heaped with
unanswered letters; and reflected, down-heartedly,
the long days he had spent at his desk without ever
finishing his task; but, worst of all, were the questions,
the innumerable questions, which irritated his weary
mind and which he could neither forget nor answer.

It was in vain that he went galloping over his fields;
they hummed with the confused murmur of the voices
of the world. It was in vain he had retired to Mount
Vernon; his glory had followed him there and had
borne with it troubles of all the world.

George Washington, Dictator in Spite of Himself [5]

Of all the problems that worried him, the one that
lay the heaviest upon him and irritated him the most
persistently was the question of politics. He had been
forced during the Revolution to act the part of a great
leader and a benevolent dictator, there was no escape.
It was the only way in which he could fulfill his task as
Commander-in-Chief and he accomplished this task
with as much skill as loathing. The political instinct
which was his made him a man of infallible judgment
and who had the greatest hesitation in engaging himself in a political career of which he so well knew the
difficulties and the dangers. He was used to living
in his Virginian environment, where he talked with
everybody, rich and poor, and he was very sensitive to
every slight change in public opinion, as are sometimes
violent and nervous people who are habitually silent.

He would not have been able to explain this himself any more than could the others with whom he talked, but the fact was that he always shared the popular feeling of the people of the region in which he was living, and he always realized what were the interests at stake. He led men, not because he had a bold and original mind, not because he had the gift of words, not because of his ideas, not because he was capable of conceiving large plans, but because he carried in himself the same real needs as those who surrounded him and translated them into action more quickly and more energetically than the others.

He had, in 1774, joined his neighbours, his fellow-planters, and they had carried America along with them. In spite of the exhausting vicissitudes of the war, in spite of all its vexation and defeats, he had felt a deep contentment in his activities, and he never doubted their possibilities nor their results. His instincts never betrayed him.

In 1784 it was no longer a matter of fighting well defined enemies. He had to choose. America uncertain and doubtful was waiting, Virginia wavered. They had rebelled against the English Parliament, then they had declared a Revolution against the King of England, finally they had warred against the English nation, all this naturally had upset everybody. There had been so much blood spilled, so much suffering and hope, such frenzy that everybody had lost their heads. Some had fought the revolution in order to be their own masters, others so that they might not have any master, some to destroy the British Empire, others to found an American one. The rich so that the English could not tax them, the poor in order to be able to earn their living more easily. It was a maelstrom of hopes, desires, contradictory interests, which fought with each other in the dark and nobody any longer knew anything.

Washington suffered from it more than any other person, because he was more susceptible to it than anybody else. It was in him as it was around him. As an aristocratic republican of Virginia he had warred against an arrogant Parliament and a stupid King; he now wanted neither one nor the other, but he believed in a strong central government because he had a sense of taste for authority. However, he had honestly accepted the phraseology which had been so popular for ten years and had been so useful as a legal basis for revolt. His philosophical readings and the revolutionary atmosphere in which he lived had their influence on his politics and had made words sound differently. He used democratic phrases. He had struggled against the centralization and the unenlightened despotism which the English had imposed on America; he did not wish to see them imposed again; but he had kept his sense of realism, the American anarchy and the rivalries between the States filled him with horror. He had believed in the rights and in the wisdom of the people, he had fought for them without weakening, and had publicly recognized the people as supreme in authority, but he knew that as masters, they were lazy, unfaithful, and forgetful, very little aware of their real interests.

When he left the army, he presented to the American people the liberty he had conquered for them (and

too often without them), he gave them solemn and
sage advice. Without referring to any of the burning
questions of the day, he had preferred to limit his address to topics on which they could all agree. He advised them to establish a strong government, and to
safeguard their interests honestly; he told them to
organize themselves in a practical, vigorous and moral
way. They all listened to him, some even wept, but
most of them understood nothing and others thought
that he would have better left it all unsaid.

In the existing disorder he wished to protect the
kernel of an organization which would later serve as
the social foundation of the new country. He had
helped to found the Society of the Cincinnati which
united all the veterans of the War of Independence.[6]
These poor fellows, who had been so badly treated by
their country for ten years, who had fought often without shoes or socks, sometimes without shirts, and almost always without a hot meal or powder for their
guns, and who at the end of the war had been paid in
depreciated currency, felt that they had at least the
right to form a mutual benefit association. Unfortunately, the civilians were outraged by it. Washington took part in the dispute, and in vain advised
moderation to the civilians and patience to the Cincinnati; it was in vain that he removed everything
that gave an aristocratic appearance to the Society,
such as the clause making hereditary the title of
Cincinnatus), still outraged the citizens continued
their campaign, even Jefferson and Franklin joining in
the outcry, while Mirabeau in Europe made a great
fuss over the matter. Washington was discouraged

and bewildered, and, while he did not want to abandon his comrades-in-arms, he did not feel he could stem the torrent either, and he regretfully decided to be ill the next time the Cincinnati met. He had to put up with it.

Washington had counted on commerce and the expansion in the West to bring about a close collaboration between the States. He had launched the Potomac Company, and had sent out colonists to the West. He had persistently harassed Congress. But what did he see? Congress becoming weaker and weaker, and, being despised, it could not possibly organize commercial relations between the States nor give a fixed status to the West. Moreover, it could not force England to give up the Mississippi forts as she had promised.

Wedged in between the Spaniards, who jealously kept the river closed to them, and the British, who watched on them narrowly and closed the plains to them; harassed by the Indians, who continued to massacre whenever they could, and exploited by the land speculators, the Western settlers, far from being a great strength to the United States, risked becoming a danger, either by giving themselves up to a foreign enemy or by becoming enemies of law and order within the American boundaries. Washington knew that their anger was rising.

All that he had accomplished was useless. All the ideas he had developed so zealously, the prudent and balanced words of advice he had given himself so much trouble to formulate, were in vain.

They had even done him harm. He decided to say

nothing and to wait. He laughed when he heard that
Franklin, now eighty years old, had, upon his return
from Europe, taken up the reins of the Pennsylvanian
government. Washington, faithful to his aristocratic
training, did not allow himself to become the toy of
parties; he hoped for a pure republic united and peace-
fully governed by the best people, just as Virginia had
been governed since his childhood. If things were
other than this, he could only stand aside. He did
stand aside. He abided by his decision, and with more
austerity than any one around him, his neighbours, his
friends, his advisers, and his recent companions, who
all wavered. He was in 1785 firm about nothing but
standing aloof.

Others had decided to have him as their leader,
even if they had to impose the honour upon him. During the years 1785, 1786, 1787, 1788, the group of
young aristocratic Patriots, John Jay, Alexander
Hamilton, Robert Morris, Gouverneur Morris, and
Madison, gave him no rest. He had kept up a close
intimacy with the Morrises — they visited each other
at Philadelphia and Mount Vernon, exchanging compliments, ideas, and feelings. Mount Vernon had
become one of the most important centres of society
in the United States, and there Washington received
the almost daily visits of this brilliant youthful group
which did not want to be deprived of the fruits of
their victory by an hysterical democracy. Madison
was often seen there, Hamilton frequently sent mes-
sages, Gouverneur Morris visited. Jay, the Secretary
of Foreign Affairs of Congress, kept in close touch
with him. The refusal of the Virginia Assembly to

vote a premium for Thomas Paine the great revolutionary pamphleteer, who was in dire need, in spite of the request of Washington and the efforts of Madison, was very significant for him.

Peace having been restored, fortunes were once more beginning to be made, and social positions were reëstablished, a good many of the lukewarm were again prominent citizens; even the Tories returned to their homes. The merchants of the large cities resumed their commerce with England, the West Indies, and Europe, and were rapidly getting rich, and speculations in land were booming. Philadelphia, the Athens of the West, was splendidly luxurious. Boston, New York, and Charleston had their post-war aristocrats, who were happy with what they had acquired, anxious to protect it, and desirous of increasing it. They were troubled by the radical harangues they heard in the inns, upset by street rumours, and discouraged and disgusted by the feeble speeches made in Congress. These tried to unite and rally Congress to their side, the Congress which was so disconcerted over the moral and social disorders of the country. They won over the Cincinnati, who had not fought ten years to see it all fail now. They carried with them the rich farmers — everyone, in short, who owned anything. Their leaders were brilliant and young: Jay, G. Morris, Hamilton, Robert Morris, Bingham, etc. But they were without the Leader. Jefferson was in Europe, and, besides, he was not generally accepted. Adams was in London and his too violent character was too well known. The aged Franklin was too compromised by his subversive and deistical ideas with a tendency to anarchy. Besides, his popularity was undermined. The only great leader whose place was undisputable was Washington. The newly formed governing classes had need of him.

He had kept himself carefully out of the public eye for five years. He was appalled at the thought of America becoming a monarchy. He had never lived close to a great monarchy, the idea of it repelled him, his nature forceful but confused needing the support of equals. He had been upheld by the Virginian aristocrats all his life. The murmurs which constantly reached him: 'We need a leader,' and 'Only you can save us,' unnerved him and drove him almost to desperation.

However, the revolt, in Massachusetts, of the dissatisfied debtors and the small fry, eager for trouble (Winter 1786–87) nearly destroyed his confidence in the country while it alarmed the entire nation. It seemed to many the prelude of the final dissolution to which the United States was destined. Washington, always cautious, hesitated to say anything about it, but this was due only to an excess of prudence; he really expected the worst to happen.

This panic brought the conservative elements together. They had at last found their watchword. A positive program would have alarmed the country and put a huge majority against them; a negative program: 'no more anarchy,' could not but please the 'rich and well born,' and rally the rest of the people to their side. It was decided to hold a meeting of the principal people chosen by the State Assemblies. Washington was interested but thought and said that it would be a failure. He bided his time, preferring to wait. The vexations and rebuffs he had suffered for the last five years were too fresh in his memory. He decided that he would not go, even if the Virginia Assembly wanted to send him to Philadelphia.

He was calculating without the efforts of Morris, Hamilton, Knox, and Jay. All of those, who five years before had tried to push him, now urged him again. They found others to help them. They were such a noisy crowd around him that in the last moment he yielded.

He left for Philadelphia, but much against his will.

As he entered the city, all the church bells rang. He dined with Franklin that evening. During the course of the week, Bingham, the most brilliant financier of the New World, gave a great dinner in his honour. He was invited from house to house. He was the hero, the King. The delegates elected him President of the Convention. He presided silently, dignified, and majestic. His presence imposed peace, his silence inspired a wise restraint, and his attitude gave weight to their proceedings. As President, he could take no part in their deliberations and this was also his desire. As a relaxation he often went fishing and he talked with the farmers of the vicinity about their farming. In the Convention while he watched, they did not succeed in creating a monarchy, but they did form a stable dictatorship controlled by a president whose powers, though limited, gave him great authority. The Congress was conceived as an aristocratic body, the members to be in all probability elected among the rich and well born and over them was to rule a President whose executive powers were restricted but effective. He had under his control war, navy, finances and the appointment to all federal offices, including judges. From his presiding chair Washington followed it all. He watched the defeat of Franklin and his fellow-democrats with their ideas of a weak plural executive, and others of their cherished doctrines. He saw the hesitant members gradually being influenced to action. Without taking sides and always looking steadily, he saw the tide mount. The final vote was unanimous (May–September, 1787).

During the Convention, Washington had dined a good deal in society and had visited churches of all denominations, Catholic, Anglican, Presbyterian, etc. He had gone fishing for long periods at a time. He had pondered. He had however not come to any conclusion. He returned to Mount Vernon in a thoughtful, meditative mood. He was still dubious of the success of the Convention, and wrote to La Fayette:

It is the result of four months' deliberation. It is now a child of fortune to be fostered by some and buffeted by others. What will be the general opinion, or the reception of it, is not for me to decide; nor shall I say anything for or against it. If it be good, I suppose it will work its way, if bad, it will recoil on the framers.[7]

He took no part. He had not been able from Mount Vernon to observe the extent of the change in social conditions which was going on in the rest of the country. He had not felt the power of this new and dominant oligarchy. In rural Virginia, the land of an old aristocracy, this movement was very ill-defined.

These Virginians did not take kindly to the idea that they were to give up any part of their traditional authority. During the violent campaign for the new constitution throughout the country, General Washington, prudent and meditative, remained at home. He encouraged the champions of Federalism at a distance, he gave them advice and the benefit of his opinions, but he stayed at Mount Vernon to watch his servants scrape the carrots and weed 'pumpions' (pumpkins).

However, the States, one after the other, ratified the new Constitution. The day came when a committee of Maryland Federalists arrived at Mount Vernon and presented to General Washington with great pomp and ceremony the good ship Federalist, a charming miniature ship, six feet long with masts and rigging complete. They anchored it in the Potomac just under the windows of Mount Vernon. A few weeks later, on July 24, a storm, with pleasant irony, buffeted it until it sank with all hands and cargo aboard, while breathless couriers brought the news that the Federalists had been victorious throughout the country.

The General no longer hesitated. He accepted the call of the country as being the voice of destiny. He plucked up his courage and added his all-powerful note to the chorus which was demanding union and national strength. He gave the signal, the people were all waiting for it and they chose him as the first President of the United States of America.

Then, with fear and trembling with a deadly anxiety such as he had never known before, he prepared to go and to accept at the hands of his imperious friends the dictatorship he had refused for seven years.

Before going, he noted in his diary:

April 16 — About ten o'clock I bade adieu to Mount Vernon, to private life, and to domestic felicity, and with a mind oppressed with more anxious and painful sensations than I have words to express, set out for New York in company with Mr. Thompson and Colo. Humphreys, with the best disposition to render service to my country in obedience to its calls, but with less hope of answering its expectations.[8]

George Washington, President

On April 30, 1789, the day of his inauguration, General Washington was ashy-pale. The first time he spoke to the Senate, his hands trembled so violently he could scarcely find his spectacles. His friends were aware of the terror he felt and the critics noted it as well. Despite the encouragement of his faithful friends, despite the complimentary address of the city councils and the ovations of the crowds, the first President of the United States did not have confidence either in himself, or in the people, or in Destiny.[9]

The group which had put him into power against his wishes wanted, just as he did, a strong central government for the country. Both he and his adherents had faith in facts rather than in theories; they flattered themselves that in order to insure national unity they only needed to emphasize material interests and develop a sense of the common need. In this way they counted on winning the aid of the better classes and the approval of the masses. But there their community of views ended; Gouverneur Morris and Hamilton had a hankering for a monarchy, John Adams and Jay preferred an aristocratic republic, a régime that Washington would doubtless have chosen had he had a political system, but he attached more importance to the way of governing than to the type of government. As long as the people were contented, and all the ablest solidly organized, governed, he was satisfied.

Washington, among his brilliant followers, who were gifted with political imagination and capable of embodying it in ingenious constitutional law, must have seemed dull; but he had two attributes of inestimable value.

He had an instinct for practical politics. Hamilton, by all his genius and aggressive temper, had succeeded in imposing the Constitution on the country, without knowing to what extent his work was precarious. Washington saw it, for he had a clear intuition of crowds and their movements. For him the Constitution would have value only if people lived under it and became accustomed to it.

He had a sense of historical continuity. He was not a gambler like Hamilton, or the two Morrises. He felt that every act accomplished in these critical days would have its effect throughout the ages, and that even the least of their creations and inventions would immediately become precedents. He was conscious in every act of the necessity of not endangering or destroying the future in advance.

He had no elaborated system, and in his papers one cannot find any trace of the path he had decided to follow, but his actions all bear witness to a systematic choice and a consistent method. As soon as he was able, he questioned his callers on the state of public opinion, read the gazettes, and attended to his national and international correspondence. He informed himself of the opinions of the better sort as well as those of the masses. Before nominating men to official positions, he examined them with extreme care in order to be sure that he could count on them. The Constitution allowed him a great deal of latitude, but he wished to profit by it only to the extent of creating an administrative and national aristocracy which the new régime needed. He took infinite care in appointing officials so that they might be selected from the best families from all parts of the country, and from all of the society classes (at least all those above the common people) and from all the professions. He chose men of strong characters as officials in this government which was still very weak. He created a ruling class. At the same time he gave poise to the government. Every action, every thing he undertook he did with the desire of impressing his simplicity and grandeur as a force at once friendly and formidable.

He did not busy himself much with foreign relations. He was thankful that Europe was far off, occupied with its own quarrels and not interested in American affairs. Washington's only interest in Europe was to find out if the fortified posts in the West would be shortly given up to the United States and if Spain would concede it the right to navigate the Mississippi. This was his really great idea, his most constant obsession. He felt that the aristocracy of America should be composed of land-owners, and that the real bond between the States and between all American citizens should be that immense reserve of territory, the West, which was still barred to them by the British forts (although the peace of 1783 had guaranteed their evacuation), and which was still blocked by the Spanish Government's closing the Mississippi to the Americans, in spite of their promises to the contrary. Whoever would open the West for him would be his friend, whoever would keep it closed was his enemy. As for the rest, he did not know foreigners and did not care to know them. He had old and tender friendships in England, young and charming friends in France. He was faithful to them. But it was America and America alone which possessed his heart, his devotion, and his desires.

He dreamed of his country night and day. He worked for America body and soul. He all but killed himself. He had one illness after another. In June–July, 1789, a carbuncle put his life in danger. In January, 1790, his teeth tortured him. In May–June, 1790, he nearly died of an attack of pneumonia which left him weak.

His doctor ordered him to take exercise, and Washington, feeling that his duty was to go on living, docilely obeyed. Almost every day he noted in his diary: 'Exercised on horseback between 5 and 7 in the morning.' [10] or: 'Walked around the battery in the afternoon,' or: 'Exercised with Mrs. Washington and the children, in the coach.' Thus gradually he regained his health, but he was still tired and worn, as his drawn face showed; a solemn expression was now habitual to

him; it concealed the uncertainty of each day, the decline of his strength, and the ardour which was con-
suming him.

He rested only when he travelled. In his childhood
he had so often rambled over the roads of Virginia,
and in his youth he had so gallantly galloped along
the paths and through the forests of the West and
South! It was thus he had learned to unbend and to
know the people whose leader he had now become.
Instinctively he resumed these trips as a relaxation
and also to learn again, to put himself in touch with
his countrymen and to talk to them. They were happy
days. Whenever he could escape from Congress,
Philadelphia, and his monotonous duties, he departed
with delight to explore New England (October 15–
November 13, 1789) or Long Island (July, 1790) or
the South (March–July, 1791).

In his coach, accompanied by his little escort and
his servants, Washington travelled in homely majesty
over the dusty roads of his empire. He seemed to
everyone as the immediate and concrete symbol of the
nation. They zealously paid him every honour they
could and he always accepted politely whatever it
might be. 'Oct. 10, 1789. The inhabitants of this
place [Flushing, Long Island] shewed us what respect
they could, by making the best use of one cannon to
salute.' [11]

Washington asked questions everywhere what
people were thinking and feeling, what the economic
conditions were; he chatted with notables, rich men,
officers, patriots, clergymen. If they were not too far
away from his lodging, he would go to a Catholic

Mass, a Quaker meeting, a Congregational preaching, or an Anglican service. He listened without yawning to many a 'lame sermon.' He visited the factories, work-shops, farms, and fisheries. He was always gracious, but he had no weakness.

In Boston, an old 'friend,' Hancock, the Governor of Massachusetts, was decided to give Washington a reception worthy of them both.[12] The two men had hardly met since 1775, when Washington had been made Commander-in-Chief, a post which Hancock believed ought to have been given to him. He had too large a nature and Washington's career was too brilliant for their friendship to have suffered any change. Hancock, Governor of Massachusetts, was as dignified as Washington, President of the United States. He therefore, with great majesty, invited Washington to alight at his house and sent ahead as an escort to meet him the Lieutenant-Governor, a general, and the troops. With the addition of the Light Horse of Middlesex it made a handsome escort. Then Hancock prepared a superb dinner, for he knew how to manage such matters.

This magnificent programme was unfortunately spoiled by two misunderstandings.

The zeal of the municipal authorities led them into conflict with the State authorities. The municipal council had assembled the Boston children at the entrance of the city, where, dressed in their Sunday best, they waited to receive the President with hymns and flowers. The State authorities wanted to be the first with all their cavalry (mounted sheriffs) to welcome the President of the United States on his entry into their capital. Without any warning, they galloped through the ranks of children at the risk of crushing them. There was a great uproar, indignation, and a long quarrelsome discussion as to which party should give way. The two reception committees orated from coach to coach, exchanging bitter and logical arguments in the midst of a crowd exasperated at standing still so long in the harsh north wind. The dispute went on and on. Washington had mounted his horse to make an imposing entrance; he waited and waited, moving nervously in the saddle, and finally not being able to hold out longer, he decided to enter by a roundabout road; just then the quarrel was settled in favour of the children and Washington was able to make his entry into the city, according to the plan and to be enthusiastically greeted by thousands of citizens, who mingled their hurrahs with sneezes, for many of them had waited so long they had caught cold.

Washington noted with satisfaction the smart uniforms, the flattering pennants, the salute of cannon, and the 'well-dressed ladies.' (He was very sensitive to this compliment.)

However, the complications continued. Hancock had got it into his head that Washington, being on his travels, should first visit him; Washington thought that, as President of the United States, the Governor should wait upon him at his lodging. While Hancock awaited Washington at his house, the General was waiting for Hancock at his lodging. He even refused to dine at Hancock's as he had promised. The longer this situation existed, the more difficult it became, and the two great men, thus condemned to the prison of their rooms, might have found no way out of the difficulty had not Hancock accepted the good advice of some of his friends who persuaded him that as nothing could triumph over Washington's obstinacy he would have to yield. Hancock resigned himself once more. He had an attack of gout and wrote to Washington, telling him so. Washington answered that he ought certainly to take care of himself. The following day, Hancock went to see Washington, but had to be carried to his presence by several lusty fellows, his legs being swathed in bandages. He excused himself for having delayed his visit owing to this unfortunate infirmity, and the President was extremely polite to him and very solicitous about his health. Thus the prestige of the National Government was upheld and that of the local government saved, there were no ill feelings between the two, and the people were satisfied. Moreover, Hancock quickly got over his gout, a recovery which was begrudged him by many Bostonians who were still suffering from their colds.

Everywhere he went, Washington on his travels was received enthusiastically everywhere and there were always the 'well-dressed ladies.' Even the weather favoured the United States. After bad years, the harvests of 1789, 1790, and 1791 were good, the price of wheat went up, business began to recover, the imports from Europe and the West Indies were balanced by the agricultural exports. The farmers did not complain, the merchants were satisfied, the factory owners were very hopeful, and the bankers delighted with the business activity which permitted them to speculate successfully. Washington perceived this state of mind and it encouraged him. He saw a people proud of being governed and satisfied with the first results of his administration. Washington returned to New York with more hope and a lighter heart than he had had for the ten previous years.

He resumed his work. He tried to constitute his cabinet. Since John Adams, a middle-class aristocrat of the North was Vice-President, he chose Jefferson, a philosophical aristocrat of the South, as his Secretary of State; Hamilton, a military aristocrat of New York, as Secretary of the Treasury; Knox, a clever General of the North, as Secretary of War; and Jay, the New York aristocrat who had been more or less of a Prime Minister under the old Congress, as Chief Justice of the Supreme Court of the United States. He sent Gouverneur Morris, a New York aristocrat and an old friend and ally of A. Hamilton, to Europe on the mission of obtaining the liberation of the West. And then, without alienating anyone, he tried to form his cabinet into a coherent whole.

Every Tuesday, from two to three o'clock, Washington received callers. He welcomed all the people who came to his 'levee' in a dignified and polite manner, but without inviting them to sit down, as the room was too small. On Friday evenings, after dinner, Mrs. Washington entertained a limited number of guests, who conversed and drank tea. Once a week, the President gave a dinner. He considered these social functions very important and carefully noted how they were composed, just as he noted the daily change of the barometer.

On October 2, 1789, 'The visitors of Mrs. Washington... were not numerous'; on the 9th, they were 'respectable both of gentlemen and ladies'; on November 20, 'The visitors of Gent'n and ladies to Mrs. Washington were numerous and respectable'; on the 27th, 'not many visitors'; on December 4, 'a great number of visitors'; on the 11th, 'Being rainy and bad, no person except the Vice-President visited Mrs. Washington this evening'; on the 25th, the visitors 'were not numerous, but respectable.' It was the same for the 'levee.' On Tuesday, October 13, 'a good many gentlemen attended'; on November 17, the visitors were 'numerous'; on the 24th, 'a good deal of company'; on December 1, 'A pretty full Levee'; on the 8th, 'a full Levee'; on the 15th, the visitors 'were not very numerous though respectable'; on the 22d, 'A pretty full and respectable Levee,' but on the 29th, 'Being very snowing, not a single person appeared at the Levee.' And so the year ended. But the following one began very well, as on Friday, January 1, he noted, 'The Vice-President, the Governor, the Senators, Members of the House of Representatives in town, foreign public characters, and all the respectable citizens came between the hours of 12 and 3 o'clock, to pay the compliments to the season to me — and in the afternoon a great number of gentlemen and ladies visited Mrs. Washington on the same occasion.' [13]

It was a good beginning. In 1790, when a social system had to be imposed on a young people, used to anarchy for twenty years, too many precautions could not be taken. Had the Washingtons entertained more brilliantly, there would have been cries of 'monarchy'; had their entertainments been any more modest, their soirées would have provoked ridicule. Washington succeeded in satisfying his aristocratic friends without going too far in their direction. This was not easily accomplished, to achieve it he had to give all his attention to the matter.

He therefore dismissed everything that could in any way divert his attention. He received all kinds of suggestions from everywhere, along with compliments and praises, but he refused to consider them. One day a young Frenchman called upon him. He introduced himself as the Chevalier de Chateaubriand, who had come to ask Washington's protection and help in his enterprise of searching for the Northwest Passage beyond the Behring Sea. He was ardent with hope and trembling with emotion. He was bursting with genius as yet unrecognized and he needed money. Chateanbriand never forgot this meeting and described it as follows: [14]

A small house, resembling the neighbouring houses, was the palace of the President of the United States: there were no guards, nor even footmen. I knocked, and a young maid opened the door. I asked her if the general were at home; she answered he was. I replied that I had a letter to give him. The maid asked my name, but, as it was difficult to pronounce in English, she could not remember it. She then said very sweetly, 'Walk in; Sir,' and walked ahead of me through the narrow corridor which serves as a hall in English houses; she showed me to a parlour where she asked me to wait the general....

A few moments later, the general entered; he was very tall and seemed more calm and cold than he seemed noble;

he looked like the engravings I had seen of him. I presented
my letter in silence; he opened it, hastily turning to the signature, he read it out loud, exclaiming 'Colonel Armand!'
That was the name he used in speaking of the Marquis de
la Rouérie, who had signed the letter with this simple title.

We sat down. I explained the purpose of my voyage to
him as well as I could. He answered with French and English monosyllables and listened to me with a kind of surprise; I perceived this and said with some liveliness: 'But
it is not half so hard to discover the Northwest Passage as
it is to create a nation as you have done.' 'Well, well,
young man!' he exclaimed, holding out his hand. He invited me to come and dine with him on the following day
and then the visit was over.

Chateaubriand had been given no more than a
'Well, well.' Washington, the builder of a nation,
concerned himself no longer with adventures which
had stimulated the dreams of his youth. He dis-
trusted them. And when he saw his friends engage
themselves in hazardous enterprises, he feared for
them. La Fayette's letters made him shiver. He did
not understand the fervour of the French revolution-
ists, their resounding enthusiasm astounded him, their
liking for abstract ideas remained a mystery to him.
He had always been wary of general theories and
empty eloquence. Now he was more afraid of them
than ever.

La Fayette sent him a key of the Bastille. Paine, in
inclosing it in a letter, said: 'When he mentioned to
me the present he intended you, my heart leaped with
joy. It is something so truly in character, that no remarks can illustrate it, and is more happily expressive
of his remembrance of his American friends than any

letters can convey. That the principles of America opened the Bastille is not to be doubted, and therefore the key comes to the right place.' [15]

On receiving this present, it did not seem that Washington felt his heart leap with joy. He considered the key curiously, toyed with it a moment, and then put it in his pocket.

To thank La Fayette he sent him a pair of shoe buckles, with this amiable note: 'Not for the value of the thing, my dear Marquis, but as a Memorial, and because they are the manufacture of this city, I send you herewith a pair of shoe buckles.'

The Last Campaign of General Washington

Washington carried the key of the Bastille from Philadelphia to Mount Vernon. He often showed it to visitors there. He would look at it curiously, ever so slightly embarrassed and perplexed. It brought back to him the most difficult of his decisions, the last battle he had had to fight.

The weeks and the months rolled on. The President prudently steered the Ship of State in the midst of dangerous reefs; with the aid of his cabinet and financiers, such as Robert Morris and Bingham, who were his friends, he guided the Senate. The finances of the United States under the genius of Hamilton, began to take shape. He had succeeded in having the Federal Government assume the debts of the States, and he had solidly established the new taxes, credit, and the young Bank of the United States. He had in this way won the capitalists for the Government. It was thanks to his able manipulations and to an opportune compromise that the South and North were hindered from quarrelling with one another; a site for the new capital was chosen at the boundaries of Maryland and Virginia. Government was for the present to remain in Philadelphia. North Carolina and Rhode Island at last submitted to the Federal Government, Kentucky and Vermont were admitted as new States. Commerce and agriculture prospered, and industries began to be organized. The negotiations with Spain and England were continuing. The Indians in the West, though still menacing, were not indulging in any of their worst excesses. Washington began to breathe more easily, and in moments of leisure looked after the management of Mount Vernon and the education of his nephews.

But this troublesome key of the Bastille, gleaming dully on the what-not, brought cruel memories to his mind. Washington had foreseen a conflict that was constantly increasing in his cabinet. Hamilton and Adams wanted to discourage any democratic enthusiasm, any new experiments in democracy, and wished to create an aristocratic empire with a strong, and, if possible, a brilliant nobility. Jefferson, on the contrary, was much interested in all the European revolutions, and was not in the least attracted to the new middle-class aristocracy of finance which his colleagues wanted to transform into a nobility. Washington intended to solidify the actual régime. Jefferson, attracted to him men who advocated bold and radical doctrines. His lively but disingenuous character, his subtle, complicated mind, did not easily harmonize with the direct, brutal, and sometimes cynical intelligence of Hamilton, whom he perhaps envied. He remarked that the President, often tired and always finding it difficult to express himself, relied more and more on this young colonel-lawyer-financier who was so lucid and so eloquent. The conflict between the democratic gentleman of the South and the foundling aristocrat of New York became bitter. Washington remonstrated with them in vain, he tried to induce them to think a little less of themselves and their theories and a little more of their work, their country, and peace. But the situation grew steadily worse. They tried vainly to come to an understanding; they only understood each other well enough to hate each other. And Washington, no matter what his personal difficulties may have been in expressing himself, could not hinder these two from completely expressing themselves.

As long as it remained a dispute between the two men, Washington could tolerate it, but the day came when Washington felt himself caught between two parties.

Washington was so little a democrat that he could not conceive of a republic with distinct parties. For him there were no other differences than the good and the better, rich and poorer, nothing to discuss except who were the best possible men to govern, and let them govern in peace. He thought any other kind of political activity was dangerous. The idea of anyone coming between the ruling aristocrats and the common people was extremely disagreeable to him. The notion of any organization among the voters was absurd. When he accepted the Presidency, one of his chief sources of anxiety had been the prolongation of the opposition between the two parties, the Federalists and the Anti-Federalists, continued. One of his greatest joys in 1789–90 was to be certain that the Anti-Federalists no longer constituted a party or even a coherent group, but were only dissatisfied and isolated individuals.

He was all the more frightened in 1792–93 to see the party spirit rise again, and to realize that a new party was being formed.

Jefferson, left alone, would not have tried to constitute a party. Perhaps he did not wish to. He was neither violent nor combative nor eloquent. Hamilton was too generous to try to destroy a solitary colleague, too clever to make their discussions known. Their quarrel could have been carried on with discretion, and so remain, within bounds.

Unfortunately, just at this time the Government of the United States had to make its first important political decision about foreign affairs.[16] France, their ally, had declared war on England. The entire problem of the future direction of American policy depended upon the decision they would now make. The treaty of alliance, ambiguous and complicated as treaties generally are, did not strictly oblige the United States to take any part in the war — at least if the war was not clearly a defensive one on the part of France, and if it did not extend to the West Indies — and certainly in 1786–89, the Government of Louis XVI had been inclined to accept the neutrality of America. But the treaty, both in text and spirit, obliged the United States to treat France as a favoured nation. The feelings of the American people were in accord with the spirit of the treaty. No one in the United States wanted war, but everyone continued to hate the British, who refused to evacuate the forts in the West or to sign a commercial treaty, and who were always insolent in their dealings with America. Washington felt a sincere gratitude to France and often showed it; he had many friends among the French. Jefferson was intimately connected with France. Hamilton himself had very much liked his French comrades-in-arms.

But Washington wanted to avoid war; he was determined to secure these famous Western outposts by peaceful means, and it was indispensable to reorganize the country solidly before submitting it to new shocks. The Americans could not crusade for France. The French had been induced to make war for the liberty of the United States by the pacifist-philosophical friends of liberty, uniting with the anti-English and warlike conservatives. In America, the philosophers were pacifists and Francophiles, but the conservatives were also pacifists in order to be able to establish their power solidly. There was no incentive to break with England, while everything tended to induce the United States adopting a friendly neutrality towards France. On April 22, 1793, the President published a proclamation of neutrality.

A few days before, a young Frenchman disembarked at Charleston; he was charming, brilliant, cultured, good-hearted, filled with courage and patriotic zeal. His name was Edme Genet and he was the new Min-

ister of the French Republic to the United States.[17]
He dreamed of fame and immediately upon arriving,
he made speeches, inciting the people against the
English; he had several privateers armed to fight
against them, and he travelled from Charleston to
Philadelphia with great ostentation, arousing enthusiasm wherever he went. He thought he would be
a new Franklin. He was mistaken.

Nothing could have annoyed Washington more
than this conduct. Washington wanted peace. He
had proclaimed neutrality and was trying to prevail
upon the public to control their emotions and to calm
their excitement. Genet had come at the wrong time.
Jefferson was instructed to tell him this, which he did.
Genet replied disdainfully. To his mind the Government of the United States did not matter much. Only
the people interested him. He considered Washington
to be an old man, no doubt eminent, but a man who
had seen his day. He thought that the people were
the only sovereign and had only to speak, Washington
would yield. He endeavoured to make the people
speak.

The American people at this time were quite inclined to speak, even to shout if they were urged.
Washington had gathered around him the commercial
and landed aristocracy, the urban middle class and
the big farmers; but he had not yet conciliated the city
population burdened by poor, nervous immigrants,
recently arrived from Ireland, France, Germany, the
West Indies, and all the regions where there was an
economic crisis and political disorder. The Western
settlers, always dissatisfied because they felt they

were poorly supported against the English and the
Spanish, were attracted by the radical conceptions of
democracy and they did not regard the new middle-
class government very favourably.

These 'disaffected' were composed of incongruous
and scattered elements, but they were many and energetic, capable easily of becoming influential if they
found leaders. Genet, in spite of his faults, had a good
idea. He organized these heterogeneous elements by
creating popular societies (called either patriotic or
democratic). These were not really new, similar ones
having existed before and after the Revolution. But
they had fallen into neglect, and Washington, who
sharply disapproved of them, had helped to consign
them into oblivion. Genet had re-formed them with
the aid of the Jacobin French in America, the French
merchants, the German and Irish immigrants, and
the very cultivated philosopher-friends of Franklin.
Washington and the other Federalists had not known
how to attract these cultivated and liberal groups
which Franklin, in former times, had gathered together at the Masonic lodge in Philadelphia and at
the Philosophical Society. Jefferson, who doubtless
could have attracted them and conciliated them with
the new Government, had not taken the trouble to do
so. These doctors, lawyers, educated chemists, Jewish
lawyers, and German grocers, who were not profiting
directly from the new institutions, and to whom
Franklin had bequeathed the cult of philosophical
principles as well as a deep respect for France, worked
might and main to reëstablish these patriotic societies
and give a voice to the obscure, dissatisfied crowds of

immigrants. Genet, the orator, rose against Washington. He spoke insolently and menacingly.

His triumph did not last long. The President had him notified to stop his proceedings, to stop arming privateers in American harbours, and to respect the neutrality of the United States. Genet was intimidated by the cold severity of Washington. His weakness was making promises, and, what was worse, not keeping his promises. Washington, supported by his cabinet, signified to the French Government that he desired the recall of Genet. This suggestion was well taken in France, where the Girondin friends of Genet had just fallen under the attacks of the Montagnards, who would doubtless have found it a pleasure not only to cut off Genet's diplomatic career but also his head.

Disdainful and magnanimous, Washington allowed Genet to take refuge in the United States. He had eliminated him as a dangerous enemy. He had not, however, been able to break up the popular societies and they were a thorn in his flesh. The most annoying thing was that the newspapers were interesting themselves in them, as they were attempting to constitute a party, and Jefferson undoubtedly had some connection with them.

Another in Washington's place would have been intimidated. Washington himself would have been in 1789. But now, Washington neither retreated nor avoided the issue: 1789 had passed. He was no longer hesitant and did not feel himself abandoned with a hesitant Virginian aristocracy and a still weak national aristocracy. A ruling class now existed and had re-elected him unanimously in 1793. He was ready to struggle vigorously for it and had occasion to do so some months later.

During the autumn of 1794, there was a rather serious uprising in the West against the levying and collecting of the excise tax on whiskey; it soon became armed rebellion, and Washington, after having put it down energetically and with little trouble, was able openly to attack the popular societies. He denounced them as being responsible for the disorder and held them up to public scorn. A republican, he took a definite stand against the democracy. He had the 'rich and well born' with him (December, 1794). But he did not succeed in destroying the societies nor in calming the popular discontent. On the contrary, the spirit of the party in opposition crystallized, and as Jefferson had retired to his estate he seemed like a martyr to their cause; the party adopted him, if not as its leader, at least as its patron saint.

A violent press campaign commenced against Washington. It seemed that, by a curious turn of events, all the revolutionary ardour of former days, once directed against England, was now turned against him. Tom Paine, whom Washington had admired very much, and whose writings had greatly helped the revolutionary cause, was the leader of this campaign. He said of Washington (and to Washington): 'As to you, Sir, treacherous in private friendship (for so you have been to me, and that in the day of danger) and a hypocrite in public life, the world will be puzzled to decide, whether you are an apostate or an imposter, whether you have abandoned good principles, or whether you ever had any.' [18]

And the important republican newspaper 'The Aurora,' published a still stronger statement: 'Under the pantomime of a great man, Mr. Washington conceals much negative intrigue.' [19]

Tom Paine in 1797, wanted to humble George Washington exactly as he and Washington together had humbled King George. Washington was indignant at all these vulgar and brutal insults. The Republicans, on the other hand, just as sincerely thought that Washington was a traitor, who, after having guided America through the Revolution, was betraying his country to the rich, to the 'monocrats,' as they were then called, and to the Anglophiles. They saw in him one who was turning his back on beliefs that he had defended apparently from 1774 to 1783.

But George Washington never had accepted these beliefs. He had made use of them when their vitality and vigour served in creating a new nation. In him, doctrines had ever had but strange veiled faces. His instincts were all that were his own. He had followed democratic ideas as long as they were in harmony with his habits of living, with his aristocratic Anglo-Saxon traditions, with the impetus of this free land, but now they had turned against him, against unity, against the land he loved. They were no longer the same in his eyes. He rejected them with horror.

To destroy the germs of schism and to seal the Union forever, Washington decided on a bold move. He had sent John Jay to London promptly and almost secretly in April, 1794. Jay was a persistent, distinguished, and clear-thinking gentleman who cherished an undying hatred for France because of what he believed to have been underhand conduct in 1781–82. He felt a sympathy for England, which was all the deeper because of his protestantism which made him understand the English spirit. He left determined to make possible a reconciliation with the British Government.

For a long time there was no news of him. The winter of 1794–95 was long and hard. The coasts of America were swept by winds and tempests comparable to the violent passions which held sway over the nation. The popular societies and democratic newspapers attacked Washington, while in the rich and luxurious Philadelphia his circle of friends became more and more like a provincial aristocracy and his house like a middle-class court. The exiled nobility of Europe frequented the house of the banker, Bingham, and felt at home there. The fluent and adroit English Minister, George Hammond, made it his general headquarters. All the fashionable world was on his side. Meanwhile, the French Ambassador continued his recriminations, and walked about the town, accompanied by his filthy Jacobins, shabby political friends, and American democrats, wearing the French Revolutionary cockade. The fashionable world turned aside from him. He no longer came to see the President for fear of meeting with French exiles. Were not all the French friends of Washington aristocrats? Rochambeau, La Fayette, Noailles, Chastellux, were all nobles. The French Minister would have lost all contact with the American Government had not a curious and deep intimacy existed between him and the Secretary of State, Randolph, Jefferson's successor.

It was not until March, 1795, that the treaty arrived from London, although Jay had accepted it in December. Washington read it carefully. It was bad, very little in their favour, not even just. However, it offered three advantages: it settled, temporarily at least, the live questions of the moment; it avoided war; and it assured the Western outposts to the Americans. That was sufficient. Washington, although he was not enthusiastic about the treaty, resolved to go on with it. He submitted it to the Senate. At first, the Senate was filled with consternation. They had not expected it to be so unpleasant. But it was either that or war, as George Hammond, who did not leave Philadelphia, and whose house was open to everyone, made them understand. The Senate understood, and ratified the treaty, June 24, 1795, asking for the modification of a detail in order to keep up appearances.[20]

This treaty, which put the American merchant ships at the mercy of the English, which transformed the American neutrality into a neutrality favourable to England, was certainly contrary to the spirit of the treaties of 1778. But Louis XVI and Marie Antoinette had been beheaded, Vergennes was dead, Gérard was dead, La Fayette exiled and detained in an Austrian dungeon, Rochambeau in prison in Paris, La Rouérie was dead, Ségur in prison, Lauzun beheaded, Chastellux dead, La Luzerne dead... only Genet was left.

The American Government honestly felt itself freed of its obligations to France.

The majority of the American people did not think

so. It had come to be vaguely known that the President had the treaty. But Washington, anxious that Congress should deliberate on the treaty in peace, had not wished to communicate the text of the document to anyone. He knew what the public would think of it. However, a week after the treaty had been ratified by the Senate, the republican paper, 'The Aurora,' published the treaty, the text of which had been transmitted to them by a senator of the opposition, Mason. The newspaper was circulated throughout the country, and in a week the people of the United States were boiling with indignation. Farmers, Western colonists, all the Francophile radicals raised an angry stir, the merchants in the seaports pulled a long face, the sailors were furious. There was a general uproar. The grandson of the great Franklin, Benjamin Franklin Bache, editor, although he was only twenty-five years old, of 'The Aurora,' led the attack against Washington, and travelled through all the Eastern cities, organizing meetings in New York, Connecticut, and Boston, to denounce the treaty. The venerable Samuel Adams joined with him. Public fury and patriotic indignation were rampant everywhere.

Washington was surprised, but he was not shaken. The treaty was bad, but it guaranteed the West to America; that was enough. He was all the more firm in his stand because of the campaign directed against him and his work. His friends undertook the defence of the treaty eloquently and skilfully, but with no great results; the rich merchants organized manifestations in favour of it with more success. But none of these efforts would have been of use had not Washington, by his sheer obstinate silence, disconcerted his enemies.

He imposed his will on the people and signed the treaty.

But he would not have won the battle against public opinion had it not been for a master stroke of the British. In March, 1795, the English had seized a despatch from the French Minister, Fauchet, which seriously compromised Randolph, the Secretary of State. Fauchet revealed in terms that were only too clear that Randolph had received money from him, either for his personal use or to give to American politicians. The English Government hastily sent this paper to Hammond, who showed it to his friend Wolcott, the Secretary of the Treasury (July 28, 1795), who in turn showed it to Washington.

The scandal which burst, and which stripped Randolph of his honour if not of his respectability, distracted the people's attention, discredited Fauchet and the French Government, and gave back Washington his power over the public.

By his silence and his high-minded inflexibility he had held his own against the unchained fury of the 'mob.'

He was tired. The noise and excitement had worn him out. He had never liked political quarrels. Now they were odious to him and using up the last hours of his life. The violent attack which the newspapers had launched against him gave him bitter pleasure — too bitter for an old man. It was time to go. His friends insisted in vain, he refused to accept the Presidency a third time.

Had he not done all that there had been for him to do, establish a strong central government, gather and organize around him able men, who would understand, represent and guide their country, win and hold the West as a security and a bond of their union? The other cares he left to his successors.

Before departing, he gave a last and solemn admonition to the country. After having mentioned with humble pride what he had accomplished for his fellow citizens, he begged them to allow time to finish the work, to protect sedulously their unity and the established government, to avoid scrupulously the spirit of parties and party strife, to remain Americans above all else, to be friendly with other nations, but to remain firmly attached to their own, which its vast waters safeguarded so well. He told them that he could leave them since he left them a continent.

The Return to the Land

And now General Washington was through. As he left Philadelphia, the Vice-President, John Adams had, with great difficulty, been elected by the Federalists to succeed him. Washington retired to his estate at Mount Vernon, among his slaves, his family and his neighbours. There he found peace once more. In the winter, the gazettes rarely came, and the state of the roads protected him from visitors. His inner fever had abated. For the first time since 1774, he felt at home. And again on March 16, 1797, he wrote in his diary, as in former times: 'At home all day alone. Wind at East and very Cloudy all day.'   Again he noted the temperature day by day. [21]   Again he opened his hospitable house to travellers passing through the country. But Mount Vernon was no longer invaded, the ambitious no longer sought him. Again he superintended the work of his fields. Washington had need to do so, for he, the richest man of America, was short of money. But he could no longer permit himself long rounds across his farms. He would slowly trot on horseback along the roads — 'an old gentleman riding alone in plain drab clothes, a broad-brimmed white hat, a hickory switch in his hand, and carrying an umbrella with a long staff... attached to his saddle-bow...'

Now and again he went on inspecting the progress of the 'federal city' or he visited Philadelphia, where he received the respectful welcome of the fashionable Federalists and kept in touch with current affairs. He had a final excitement; there was talk of a war with France, and Adams begged him to be the Commander-in-Chief. He accepted on condition that he join the army on the day when they would have to go to war. Besides, he did not think that there would be a war. But, as formerly, he had all the trouble of war; the jealousy of generals and officers, the ill-will of recruits, the negligence of recruiters, the red tape of the government offices. What was the date? — 1753, 1758, 1775, 1782, or 1798? It did not matter; it was always his lot to establish order where others had spread disorder.

He spent long hours in his library arranging his papers; he made up his accounts; he jotted down notes on various political pamphlets and succeeded in justifying himself in his own eyes. He had more trouble in justifying to himself 'Demos' whose vagaries were so annoying. He looked for reasons in his own mind. He, too, needed to express and to debate to clear his thoughts and explain himself. He never found this agreeable, but he had become used to it. Now in his shelter, he meditated on his past. He dreamed.

He was worried by rumours which reached him. The Democratic Party was being organized and strengthened. By a supreme insult of Fate, it dominated Virginia. The Federalists were divided among themselves. Hamilton against Adams, Adams against Hamilton, but Adams chiefly against himself. Anxious to smooth over difficulties, Washington discreetly hinted to Adams that he would be glad to see him. But the proud sage, more proud than wise, did not respond, and Washington was left alone with his lands.

He, in America, wrote to Sally a fading, ageing widow, and she, in England, solitary and impoverished, was always the queen of his thoughts: 'Nothing,' he said, 'has ever been able to eradicate from my mind the recollection of those happy moments, the happiest of my life, which I have enjoyed in your company.'

He was tired, indeed. He noted 'his declination'; he wearily wrote in his diary once more: 'Commenced the survey on 4 Mile Run.' [22] As in the old days, he 'dined at Lord Fairfax's.' He went surveying, stooping over the ground, to which he always returned.

On Thursday, December 12, 1799, Washington went out to visit his farms, but he had scarcely started when the weather became very bad, alternately raining and snowing. He returned at three and dined without changing his clothes. The next day he complained of a sore throat and by evening he had become very hoarse. He did not feel at all well.

Doctors came hurrying to Mount Vernon; his old friend, Doctor Craik, as well as Doctor Brown and Doctor Dick, had him bled. Everyone wept in the house except Washington. On Saturday, December 14, 1799, at ten o'clock in the night, he died. [23]

And suddenly the people of America, who had not paid much attention to the bitter attacks made against him during his lifetime, acclaimed him as the Father of His Country.

He was buried in the ground of Virginia which he had loved so dearly. And the American school-children now make pilgrimages to his tomb on the Potomac. They are told that he was a great Soldier, a great President, a great Sage. They are told that he was good, generous, untiring, disinterested, sublime. And no doubt it is all true.

But the children are not told that he was the last of the great land barons; that because of his love of land he directed the United States to the West; that he made great efforts to keep Americans from dispersing their strength in discussing theories; that with all his energy he had worked to give them a strong central government in order to destroy their tendency to quarrel among themselves; and that he had instructed them to love their country above everything else.

The children are not told that he was the first of the great modern politicians who had an infallible instinct for public opinion and that this made him create a practical aristocracy which the United States needed, while Adams and Hamilton completely failed in realizing their vain dreams of monarchy and nobility, and Jefferson, in his democratic philosophy, was eclipsed by a sterile triumph.

They are not told that had he lived a year longer he would have seen the American people disavow him and all his work by a solemn vote, and that without doubt he would have entered into a tragic conflict with Jefferson. The snow, wind, and rain of Virginia and the doctors at Mount Vernon, in their cruel wisdom, had done well by George Washington.

The children are not told all this. But it does not matter, since he has left them all that he cared for, all that is needed to teach them: the continent of America, the land of Virginia.

THE END

SOURCES AND NOTES

SOURCES

THE sources of information for the life and time of George Washington are innumerable. Under the name of 'Washington,' the card catalogues of the Library of Congress, the Library of Harvard University, the New York Public Library, the Library of the British Museum, the Bibliothèque Nationale give hundreds of titles. To classify them would be a life's work. I am only giving here the principal sources on which I actually based my conclusions, and the references for my quotations.

The most important source, of course, is the large body of the writings of Washington.

I. WRITINGS OF WASHINGTON

The Writings of George Washington, edited by Jared Sparks, 12 volumes, 1837.

The Writings of George Washington, edited by Worthington Chauncey Ford, 14 volumes, 1889–1893.

The Diaries of George Washington, edited, by John C. Fitzpatrick, 4 volumes, 1925.

List of Washington Manuscripts... 1592–1775, edited by John C. Fitzpatrick, 1919.

Calendar of the Correspondence of George Washington, edited by John C. Fitzpatrick, 4 volumes, 1915.

John C. Fitzpatrick: *George Washington: Colonial Traveller*, Indianapolis, 1927. (Contains many very curious and accurate details taken from unpublished Washington papers.)

II. BIOGRAPHIES AND ESSAYS

John Marshall: *Life of Washington*, 5 volumes, 1804. (The first one, giving the traditional point of view.)

Henry Cabot Lodge: *George Washington*, 2 volumes, 1889. (A very fine piece of work.)

Charles Moore: *The Family Life of George Washington*, Boston, 1926. (A most interesting and stimulating group of studies on Washington and his surroundings, filled with new material.)

Rupert Hughes: *George Washington*, 3 volumes, 1926, 1927, 1930. This much-discussed and criticized work is, really, a very fine achievement. Mr. Hughes has studied a great deal of material and has used it with acute curiosity and honesty. Even those who cannot sympathize with his attitude have to acknowledge that his point of view is sincere, his work thorough, and his book exceedingly stimulating.

III. MANUSCRIPT SOURCES

There are still many unpublished documents and data on Washington.

The most interesting are to be found at the Library of Congress in Washington, D.C.; at the Huntington Library (in Pasadena, California); at the Clements Library (Ann Arbor, Michigan); in the Public Record Office (London); and in the Archives of the Ministry of Foreign Affairs in Paris.

NOTES

INTRODUCTION

1. The quotation is taken from *Voyage de M. le Chevalier de Chastellux*, Paris, 1785, I, 119–21.
2. Quotation taken from Chateaubriand: *Mémoires d'Outre tombe*, Edition Biré, I, 360.

CHAPTER I

1. The description of Virginia is based upon *The Planters of Colonial Virginia*, by Thomas Jefferson Wertenbaker, 1922; *The American Colonies*, by Marcus Wilson Jernegan, 1929; *American Colonies*, by Reuben G. Thwaites, New York, 1902; *The Colonial Period*, by Charles M. L. Andrews, New York, 1912; Herbert L. Osgood: *The American Colonies in the Eighteenth Century*, New York, 1924, 4 volumes; Chandler Thames: *Colonial Virginia*, Richmond, 1907; Philip Alexander Bruce: *Social Life in Virginia in the Seventeenth Century*, Lynchburg, 1927; and a careful reading of the southern newspapers of the eighteenth century, more especially the Virginia Gazettes (Rind, Purdie, Dixon, etc.).
2. Quotations from *Virgo Triumphans*, 1650, quoted in Pasquet: *Histoire des Etats Unis*, I, 129.
3. Conditions on board the ships which carried immigrants, see Pasquet, 131–34; Jernegan, 56–58.
4. These figures are taken from Jernegan, 56–58, 86, 87. On the importation of criminals in Virginia, see A. Wyatt Tilby: *The American Colonies*, Boston, 1916, 197. On indenture and indentured servants, see Pasquet, 134–38, Jernegan, 97.
5. On the life of women in Virginia, see Marion Harland: *Some Colonial Homesteads*, New York, 1899. On the social and economical evolution in Virginia between 1620 and 1740, see Wertenbaker, 150–58; Jernegan, 86–100.
6. The figures concerning landholders are taken from Charles Moore, 31; Pasquet, 203; Jernegan, 338; concerning slaveholders, Wertenbaker, 157–58; Jernegan, 358–60.

7. The quotation is taken from A. Wyatt Tilby, 200.
8. On the establishment of the Washingtons in Virginia and their life, Charles Moore, 15–19; Fitzpatrick: *George Washington, Colonial Traveller*, 1–5; Rupert Hughes, I, 1–15, *Writings of Washington* (Ford), XIV, 391–96; *Diaries of Washington*, I, 138, etc.
9. Will of Augustine Washington: *Writings* (Ford), XIV, 410–15.
10. On the Fairfaxes, see Moore, 29–31.
11. On the education of George Washington, see Moore, 28; *Diaries*, I, 2, 12, 22, 36, 136; Fitzpatrick; *Washington, Colonial Traveller*, 4–8, etc.
12. The rules of civility are quoted from *George Washington's Rules of Civility*, edited by Charles Moore, 1920.
13. The quotation is taken from *Writings* (Ford), I, 2.
14. The quotation is taken from *Writings* (Ford), I, 3; the other from *id.*, 5.
15. Washington's earnings, see Fitzpatrick; *Washington, Colonial Traveller*, 17–33.
16. See *Diaries*, I, 16, 17, 21–27.
17. Death of Lawrence and inheritance: *Diaries*, I, 138, II, 2; Paul Leland Haworth: *George Washington, Country Gentleman* (formerly *George Washington, Farmer*), 1–10, etc.

CHAPTER II

1. Quotations and anecdote taken from Bonneville de Marsangy: *Le Chevalier de Vergennes*, I, 37–38, 66–67.
2. Quotation of Voltaire: Voltaire: *Candide*, Edition Morize, Paris, 1913, 170, and letters of Voltaire dated February 29, 1756; March 23, 1757, etc. Quotation of Rouillé: *Ministère des Affaires Etrangères, Correspondance Politique, Angleterre*, vol. 438, folio 282.
3. On the origin of the Seven Years' War, see *id.*, folios 20–30, 386–400, 122–25, etc.; Osgood, IV, 77–80, 222–25, 287–89, etc.
4. On the Lemoyne brothers, see La Roncière: *Une épopée Canadienne*, Paris, 1930. On the mistakes of the maps, and the difficulty of understanding the geography of the Ohio Valley, see *Ministère des Affaires Etrangères, Correspondance Politique, Angleterre*, vol. 438, dispatch from Mirepoix, Jan. 16, 1755, folios 1–20.

5. 'Black Islands,' see *Writings* (Ford), I, 15–16.
6. On the Indian Wars, see Osgood, IV, 265–70. On the Crow warrior, *Writings* (Ford), II, 24.
7. On Dinwiddie, see Osgood, IV, 221–30.
8. On Betsy Fauntleroy, see *Writings* (Ford), I, 9.
9. Quotation from *Diaries*, I, 43.
10. Quotation from *Diaries*, I, 59.
11. Quotations from *Diaries*, I, 61 and 66.
12. Quotation from *Pennsylvania Gazette*, February 5, 1754; *Boston News Letter*, March 7, 1754.
13. On the death of Jumonville, see *Gazette d'Amsterdam*, July 23, 1754; *Writings* (Ford), I, 80–92; *Writings* (Sparks), II, 449–60; Hughes, I, 80–110; *Ministère des Affaires Etrangères*, vol. 437, folio 292, vol. 438, folios 20–25.
14. Quotation from *Writings* (Ford), I, 84.
15. The Campaign of 1754, see Hughes, I, 113–52; *Gazette d'Amsterdam*, September 23, 1754; Thomas: *Jumonville*, pp. i-vi; *Writings* (Ford), I.
16. Quotation from *Ministère des Affaires Etrangères*, vol. 438, folios 21–22.
17. Criticism and praises of Washington, see Thomas: *Jumonville, passim; Writings* (Sparks), II, 465; *Boston News Letter*, September 5, 1754.
18. Quotation from *Writings* (Sparks), II, 465.
19. Quotation from *Writings* (Ford), I, 139.
20. The Braddock expedition, see Hughes, I, 205–69, 531–38; *Writings* (Ford), I, 130–200. On Washington's health at that time, *Writings* (Ford), I, 150–54.
21. The quotation is from *Writings* (Ford), I, 155.
22. The quotation is from *Writings* (Ford), I, 166, 167.
23. Attitude of the French Government: *Ministère des Affaires Etrangères*, vol. 439, folios 317–30.
24. Quotation from *Writings* (Ford), I, 90. See also the Loudoun Papers at the Huntington Library.
25. For Washington's popularity in America and Europe after 1755, see *Almanach of N. Ames*, Boston, 1756 and 1763; *Gazette d'Amsterdam*, October 24, 1755; *Courrier d'Avignon*, November 4 and 11, 1755; *A Short History in Miniatures of the Origin and Progress of the Late War from its Commencement to the Exchange of the Ratification of Peace*, London, 1765 (?), etc.

26. Quotation: *Writings* (Ford), I, 197. The details on the behaviour of the militia taken from *Writings* (Ford), I, 264, 274, 278, 282–83, 291, 303, 331, 350, 374, 427, etc.
27. The details on the Dagworthy-Washington quarrel are taken from *id.*, I, 205–08, 209, 211, 215, 224–27.
28. See Fitzpatrick: *George Washington, Colonial Traveller*, 91–96.
29. The aristocratic attitude of Washington: *Writings* (Ford), I, 181.
30. Quotation: *id.*, I, 331. The dissatisfaction of the Assembly concerning the troops, *id.*, I, 245, 255, 406, and Hughes, I.
31. Quotations: *Writings* (Ford), I, 375, 376.
32. Quotations: *id.*, 315, 350. On the amount of money paid to the soldiers, *id.*, I, 315–17.
33. On deserters, see *id.*, I, 282, 326, 335, 458, 462, 465, 471, 477, 500.
34. Quotations: *id.*, I, 394–458.
35. Quotation: *id.*, I, 477.
36. Quotations: *id.*, 281, 312, 313.
37. Quotations: *id.*, I, 97, 384, 389.
38. Quotations: *id.*, I, 397, 398, 403.
39. Quotation: *id.*, I, 446.
40. Quotation: *id.*, I, 486.
41. Quotation: *id.*, I, 486, 487.
42. Quotation: *id.*, I, 495.
43. Quotations: *id.*, II, 72, 84, 85.
44. Quotations: *id.*, II, 101, 104, 109.

CHAPTER III

1. On the great love affair of Washington, see the very fine pages of John Corbin in his *Unknown Washington*, 1929.
2. Quotation taken from Corbin, 61.
3. On Martha Custis, see Ann H. Wharton: *Martha Washington*, 1897.
4. Quotations: Corbin, 66–68.
5. The life at Mount Vernon and Belvoir, see *Diaries*, I, 109, 123, 140, 141, 246, 247, 262, 284, 291, 300, 307, 328, 346, 361, 377, 387, 453; II, 3, 8, 14, 30, 61, 68, 71, 106, 110, 117, etc.
6. Quotation: Corbin, 67–68.

Washington, was. On the same page,
you speak of Washington's sense of
"historical continuity"; — that also
could be supplemented.

What was Washington's
attitude toward Hamilton and
Jefferson when their rivalry first
became apparent?

I think that you should re-do parts of this paper. Your first two pages should be unified in treatment i.e. you should give a clean account of inherited tendencies, early education and its effect on his later life. As the first pages stand, the reader has an impression of luck, Rules of Conduct surveying a diary, a trip to Barbados all mixed together.

In treating of the western question you should show the importance of French-English rivalry in the Ohio to Washington and the importance of the western expansion question in shaping Washington's attitude toward England. In your last paragraph on page four, you ought to make clear what you mean by "social discipline" of the soldiers, and why the assembly (?) wished peace with the French and Dinwiddie wished war and Washington's relation to this trouble. On page six, explain what you mean by Washington trying "to uphold his aristocracy." On page eight, you should explain clearly what the political situation that stirr

7. Washington's worries, *Writings* (Ford), II, 201, 205. Debts: *id.*, II, 189; *Diaries*, I, 130.
8. Washington and French: *Diaries*, I, 107, 110, 111; Washington and the Oysterman: *id.*, 108, 109; Washington and J. Ballendine: *id.*, 109; Washington and Stephen: *id.*, 118; quotation on the ball: *id.*, 126; Washington and Clifton: *id.*, 135, 137, 140.
9. Washington and Laurie: *id.*, 151; angry letters to his London agents, *Writings*, dated August 10, 1760, and September 28, 1760; Washington and Cocke; *Diaries*, I, 112.
10. Quotation: *Writings* (Ford), II, 472.
11. *Writings* (Ford), II, 404, 408, 446, etc.
12. Quotation: Haworth, 2–3.
13. See *Diaries*, *passim*, vol. II.
14. Washington and land; *Diaries*, I, 119–72, 318, 319, 427–50, etc.; *Writings* (Ford), II, 176, 218–24, 372, 373, 388, 392, 446–50, 461–62; Haworth, 9–36, etc.
15. Quotations: *Writings* (Ford), XI, 341; Haworth, 2, 3.
16. See my *Franklin*, Book III.
17. Quotations: Washington and Askew, *Writings* (Ford), VI, 187; Washington and Posey: *id.*, VI, 226–30; Washington and Dalton: *id.*, VI, 364–66; Washington and Weggener: *id.*, VI, 369–70; Washington and Black: *id.*, VI, 398, 403; Quotation: Washington and Muse: Corbin, 43–44; Washington and the officers of the French and Indian War: *Diaries*, I, 391, II, 9, 37–39, 84; *Writings* (Ford), II, 272–75, 324–28, 339–47, 351–54, 356–62, 366, 371, 386–88, 394–408, 465–69.
18. Quotation: Moore, 73.
19. Washington and the Crown, see Fitzpatrick: *Washington: Colonial Traveller*, 240.
20. Quotation: *Writings* (Ford), II, 434, 435.
21. Quotations: *Diaries* (March 10, 1775); II, 179; *Writings* (Sparks), II, 466.

CHAPTER IV

1. For the conditions in America in 1775–76, see my *Franklin*, Book IV (beginning).
2. Washington in Philadelphia in 1775, see Fitzpatrick: *Washington: Colonial Traveller*, last pages, and *Diaries*, II, 162–68, 195–99.

3. Choice of Washington as Commander-in-Chief, see Corbin, 137, 202, 205; Hughes, II, 234–56. Quotation: *Writings* (Ford), II, 484.

4. Quotations: *id.*, II, 485, 491–92, 500–01.

5. Quotation: *id.*, II, 501–02.

6. On the conditions of the American Army in 1775–76, see the excellent book of Charles Martyn on *Artemas Ward, passim*, and especially, 150–60; *Writings* (Ford), III, *passim*, and especially 28–36, 44–48, 67, 73; Hughes, II, 283, 295, III, 68, 72, etc.

7. Quotation, Charles Martyn, 151–53. On Washington's hopes and plans: *Writings*, (Ford), III, 114, 145, etc.

8. Unrest of the Army; Hughes, II, 283, *Writings* (Ford), III, 90–99, 340–44, *Writings* (Sparks), III, 200. Washington and the offensive, *Writings* (Ford), III, 114, 145, 197, 415, 425–27, etc.

9. Washington and politics: *Writings* (Ford), III, 44, 75, IV, 105–07.

10. Howe. See my *Franklin*, Book III; and the Germain papers at the Clements Library.

11. Washington and New York, *Writings*, (Ford), III, 315; IV, 47–48.

12. Howe and Burgoyne in America. See Germain papers and Clinton papers, Clements Library. On Washington's ideas and intentions, see *Writings* (Ford), V, 502, 514, 518, 519, etc.

13. Quotations: *Writings* (Ford), V, 251; Hughes, II, 295 (Letter of Washington of Jan. 31, 1777); III, 68.

14. On Turgot and America, see my *Franklin*, Book IV.

15. Washington at his headquarters, see Chastellux, I, 110–18.

16. See *Writings* (Ford), IX, 200–314.

17. See *Writings* (Ford), IX 330–97; *Writings* (Sparks), VIII, 528–36; Hughes III, *passim*.

18. Quotation: Hughes III, 672.

19. Quotation: *Writings* (Ford), X, 21, 22.

20. Quotations: *Writings* (Ford), X, 163–66; *Writings* (Sparks), VIII, 388–89.

21. Quotation: *Writings* (Sparks), VIII, 551–66; Washington and the officers: Corbin, 223–52; *Writings* (Ford), X, 165–84.

22. Washington's ideas, see *Writings* (Sparks), VIII, 300, 317,

345, 418–20, IX, 34, 62–64, 119, 156, 173, 188, 198–200, 218, 247, 358, X, 69, 70, 89, 306, etc.

CHAPTER V

1. Gifts made to Washington, visits at Mount Vernon, see *Diaries, passim* (years 1785–86). Quotations, *Writings* (Sparks), IX, 1–2, 166.
2. Washington and his trees, see *Diaries, passim* (years 1785–87).
3. Quotation: *Diaries*, II, 317.
4. Quotation: *Diaries*, II, 317.
5. See the very good description and analysis of the 1785–89 period in Corbin; *The Reaper and his Scythe*, 276–312.
6. Washington and the Cincinnati, *Writings* (Ford), XI, 86, *Writings* (Sparks), XI, 213. See also my *Franklin*, Book III; and my article on 'Franklin et Mirabeau, collaborateurs,' *Revue de Littérature Comparée*, January–March, 1928.
7. Quotation: *Writings* (Sparks), IX, 265. On the ship Federalist see *Diaries*, III, 393.
8. Quotation: *Writings* (Sparks).
9. Washington's fears in 1789, see Corbin, 411–12.
10. Washington's exercises, *Diaries*, IV, 129–43, *passim*.
11. Quotation: *Diaries*, IV, 19 and following.
12. Hancock and Washington, *Diaries*, IV, 31–37.
13. Quotations, see *Diaries*, IV, at the mentioned dates.
14. Quotation: Chateaubriand: *Mémoires d'Outre tombe* (Edition Biré), I, 358.
15. Quotations: *Writings* (Sparks), X, 104, *Writings* (Ford), XI, 498. Washington and the key of the Bastille, Chateaubriand, *id.*, 359–60; Haworth, 277, etc.
16. See my *Revolutionary Spirit*, Chapter IV, 243–329.
17. On Genet, see papers at the Library of Congress; and *Ministère des Affaires Etrangères, Correspondance Politique, Etats Unis*.
18. Washington and Paine: *Writings* (Ford), III, 396; quotation: *Writings* (Ford), XIII, 361.
19. Quotation: B. F. Bache: *Remarks occasioned by the late Conduct of Mr. Washington...* pp. 62–65, Philadelphia, 1797.
20. On the Jay Treaty, see my *Esprit Révolutionnaire*, 242–57; and the excellent book of Mr. Bemis, *The Jay Treaty*. See

also the manuscript sources at the Public Record Office in London; the Library of Congress; and the Ministère des Affaires Etrangères.

21. Quotations: *Diaries*, IV, 255; Haworth, 309.
22. Quotations: *Diaries*, IV, 301; *Writings* (Ford), XIII, 191.
23. *Diaries*, IV, 320.

INDEX

INDEX

Adams, John, defends English officers, 164; moral crises of, 166; uncertain position of, 172; influential in the naming of Washington Commander-in-Chief, 175; political sense of, 189; leaves Congress, 217; in London, 239; prefers aristocratic republic, 245; Vice-President, 252, 257; elected President, 270; and Hamilton, 272, 274

Adams, Samuel, 172, 173, 268

Aix-la-Chapelle, Treaty of (1748), 53

Aliquippa, Queen, 70, 78

Allen, Judge, 174

Alton, J., Washington's groom, 103

Annapolis Convention, 229

Anti-Federalists, and Federalists, 259

Anville, Jean Baptiste B., 55

Appleton, Capt. John, his widow married to John Washington, 22

Argenson, Marquis d', French Minister for Foreign Affairs, 50

Aristocracy, in Europe, 2; in England, 2, 3, 156, 157, 163, 164, 179, 187; an independent, 3; American, 10, 152–57, 163, 164, 166, 179, 187; national, 223, 246

Armand, Col. (Marquis de la Rouérie), 201, 255

Arnold, Benedict, heroism of, 183; in Virginia, 199; his treason, 207

Askew, carpenter, 158

'Aurora, The,' 265, 268

Austrian Succession, War of, 29

Aylett, Ann, marries Augustine Washington (2), 27

Bache, Benjamin Franklin, 268

Ball, Mary, marries Augustine Washington (1), 24, 25

Balladine, John, 141

Barbadoes, 46, 47

Barras, Admiral, in American Revolution, 208, 211

Beaujeu, French chief, in attack on Braddock, 96

'Belvoir,' estate of Fairfaxes, 30, 33, 41, 130, 133, 137, 167, 226

Berkeley, Norborne, Baron of Botetourt, 151, 160

Berkeley, Sir Thomas, Governor of Virginia, 9, 23

Bingham, financier, 239, 241, 256, 266

Bishop, T., Washington's groom, 103

Black, William, 159

Blainville, Céloron de, ordered to reconnoitre Ohio country, 66

Boston, siege of, 183, 184; visited by Washington, 249–51

Boston Massacre, 164

Bouquet, Col., 113; his plan of advance on Fort Duquesne, 122–26

Boutet, French Chargé d'Affaires in London, 85

Braddock, Gen. Edward, his campaign, 91–96, 99, 100

Brandywine, battle of the, 196, 197

Brissot de Warville, 227

Brown, Dr., in attendance on Washington, 273

Browne, Rev. Samuel William, of Alexandria, 232

'Bullskin Plantation,' property of Washington, 45

Burgoyne, John, his plan of campaign, 1777, 194–96; defeated at Saratoga, 197

Butler, Jane, marries Augustine Washington (1), 24

Byrd, Col. William, 17

Byrd, William II, 14, 18

Byrds, the, 13, 22

Calvert, Miss, 163

Evaluation
ecedent as president
govt. an experiment - difficulties & criticisms